# Fluency in L2 Learning and Use

SECOND LANGUAGE ACQUISITION
*Series Editors*: **Professor David Singleton**, *University of Pannonia, Hungary* and Fellow Emeritus, *Trinity College, Dublin, Ireland* and **Associate Professor Simone E. Pfenninger**, *University of Salzburg, Austria*

This series brings together titles dealing with a variety of aspects of language acquisition and processing in situations where a language or languages other than the native language is involved. Second language is thus interpreted in its broadest possible sense. The volumes included in the series all offer in their different ways, on the one hand, exposition and discussion of empirical findings and, on the other, some degree of theoretical reflection. In this latter connection, no particular theoretical stance is privileged in the series; nor is any relevant perspective – sociolinguistic, psycholinguistic, neurolinguistic, etc. – deemed out of place. The intended readership of the series includes final-year undergraduates working on second language acquisition projects, postgraduate students involved in second language acquisition research, and researchers, teachers and policymakers in general whose interests include a second language acquisition component.

All books in this series are externally peer-reviewed.

Full details of all the books in this series and of all our other publications can be found on http://www.multilingual-matters.com, or by writing to Multilingual Matters, St Nicholas House, 31–34 High Street, Bristol BS1 2AW, UK.

SECOND LANGUAGE ACQUISITION: 138

# Fluency in L2 Learning and Use

Edited by
**Pekka Lintunen, Maarit Mutta and Pauliina Peltonen**

MULTILINGUAL MATTERS
Bristol • Blue Ridge Summit

DOI https://doi.org/10.21832/LINTUN6300
**Library of Congress Cataloging in Publication Data**
A catalog record for this book is available from the Library of Congress.
Names: Lintunen, Pekka, editor. | Mutta, Maarit – editor. |
Peltonen, Pauliina – editor.
Title: Fluency in L2 Learning and Use/Edited by Pekka Lintunen, Maarit Mutta and Pauliina Peltonen.
Description: 1st. | Blue Ridge Summit: Multilingual Matters, 2019. | Series: Second Language Acquisition: 138 | Includes bibliographical references and index. | Summary: "This interdisciplinary book brings together a selection of theoretical and empirical approaches to second language (L2) fluency. The volume includes chapters approaching fluency from an SLA perspective and integrates perspectives from related fields, such as psycholinguistics, sign language studies and L2 assessment"— Provided by publisher.
Identifiers: LCCN 2019029662 (print) | LCCN 2019029663 (ebook) | ISBN 9781788926294 (paperback) | ISBN 9781788926300 (hardback) | ISBN 9781788926317 (pdf) | ISBN 9781788926324 (epub) | ISBN 9781788926331 (kindle edition)  Subjects: LCSH: Fluency (Language learning) | Second language acquisition—Study and teaching.
Classification: LCC P53.4115 .F58 2019  (print) | LCC P53.4115 (ebook) | DDC 407.1—dc23 LC record available at https://lccn.loc.gov/2019029662
LC ebook record available at https://lccn.loc.gov/2019029663

**British Library Cataloguing in Publication Data**
A catalogue entry for this book is available from the British Library.

ISBN-13: 978-1-78892-630-0 (hbk)
ISBN-13: 978-1-78892-629-4 (pbk)

**Multilingual Matters**
UK: St Nicholas House, 31–34 High Street, Bristol BS1 2AW, UK.
USA: NBN, Blue Ridge Summit, PA, USA.

Website: www.multilingual-matters.com
Twitter: Multi_Ling_Mat
Facebook: https://www.facebook.com/multilingualmatters
Blog: www.channelviewpublications.wordpress.com

Copyright © 2020 Pekka Lintunen, Maarit Mutta, Pauliina Peltonen and the authors of individual chapters.

All rights reserved. No part of this work may be reproduced in any form or by any means without permission in writing from the publisher.

The policy of Multilingual Matters/Channel View Publications is to use papers that are natural, renewable and recyclable products, made from wood grown in sustainable forests. In the manufacturing process of our books, and to further support our policy, preference is given to printers that have FSC and PEFC Chain of Custody certification. The FSC and/or PEFC logos will appear on those books where full certification has been granted to the printer concerned.

Typeset by Nova Techset Private Limited, Bengaluru and Chennai, India.
Printed and bound in the UK by Short Run Press Ltd.
Printed and bound in the US by NBN.

# Contents

|  | | |
|---|---|---|
|  | Contributors | vii |
|  | Preface | xi |
| 1 | Defining Fluency in L2 Learning and Use<br>*Pekka Lintunen, Maarit Mutta and Pauliina Peltonen* | 1 |
| 2 | What is Fluency? Learner Perceptions of the Concept<br>*Pekka Lintunen and Pauliina Peltonen* | 16 |
| 3 | Cognitive Fluency in L2: What Inaccuracies Can Reveal about Processing and Proficiency<br>*Sanna Olkkonen and Maarit Mutta* | 34 |
| 4 | Fluency in L2 Listening<br>*Joanna Anckar and Outi Veivo* | 49 |
| 5 | L2 Fluency and Writer Profiles<br>*Maarit Mutta* | 63 |
| 6 | Fluency in English as a Lingua Franca Interaction<br>*Niina Hynninen* | 81 |
| 7 | Fluency in Sign Language<br>*Laura Kanto and Ulla-Maija Haapanen* | 96 |
| 8 | Gestures as Fluency-enhancing Resources in L2 Interaction: A Case Study on Multimodal Fluency<br>*Pauliina Peltonen* | 111 |
| 9 | Fluency in Language Assessment<br>*Ari Huhta, Heini Kallio, Sari Ohranen and Riikka Ullakonoja* | 129 |
| 10 | Fluency in Evaluating and Assessing Translations<br>*Leena Salmi* | 146 |
| 11 | The Effects of Songs on L2 Proficiency and Spoken Fluency: A Pedagogical Perspective<br>*Leena Maria Heikkola and Jenni Alisaari* | 166 |

12  Synthesising Approaches to Second Language Fluency:
    Implications and Future Directions                           186
    *Pekka Lintunen, Maarit Mutta and Pauliina Peltonen*

    Index                                                        202

# Contributors

**Jenni Alisaari** (PhD) is a university teacher at the Department of Teacher Education, University of Turku. Her main research interests include linguistically and culturally responsive teaching, advocating multilingualism, language learning, and especially language learning by singing. Recently, her research has also focused on how singing affects written or spoken fluency in second language learning.

**Joanna Anckar** (PhD) currently works as a study counsellor and lecturer at Åbo Akademi University. She has been involved in several national language assessments, such as the Finnish Matriculation Examination and the Finnish National Certificate of Language Proficiency. Her research interests include the assessment of L2 listening comprehension, especially the possibilities of combining learners' verbal protocols to quantitative data in test validation processes.

**Ulla-Maija Haapanen** is an interpreter coordinator at the University of Jyväskylä. Haapanen's main fields as a native bilingual bimodal professional are teaching and interpreting in academic contexts. She is interested in Finnish Sign Language syntax and verbals, especially the behaviour of descriptive verbals in signed expressions. Recently she has focused on the process of forming a scale of evaluation of Finnish Sign Language according to the European Framework of Reference.

**Leena Maria Heikkola** (PhD) is a postdoctoral research fellow at the Center for Multilingualism in Society across the Lifespan (MultiLing), University of Oslo. Heikkola's main research interests are second language acquisition and clinical linguistics. Most of her research focuses on how singing affects second language pronunciation and fluency, how cognitive fatigue affects language in Multiple Sclerosis, and linguistically and culturally responsive teaching.

**Ari Huhta** (PhD) is a Professor of Language Assessment in the Centre for Applied Language Studies, University of Jyväskylä. His research interests include assessments that support learning (e.g. diagnostic and formative assessment), self-assessment and feedback, assessing and rating writing, computer-based assessment, and combining second language acquisition research and language testing perspectives in research.

**Niina Hynninen** (PhD) is a Senior Lecturer in English Studies at the University of Helsinki. Hynninen's main research focus is on English as a lingua franca and language regulation. Her current research is concerned with writing practices of multilingual scholars, and recently, she has developed an interest in fluency and spoken language testing.

**Heini Kallio** is a doctoral candidate at the Department of Digital Humanities, University of Helsinki. Kallio is currently working on her doctoral dissertation on the acoustic-phonetic basis of spoken L2 assessment. Her interest lies in practical implementations of phonetic knowledge, and she has collaborated on projects that study and develop automatic assessment applications for the language learning field.

**Laura Kanto** (PhD) is a postdoctoral researcher at the University of Jyväskylä. Kanto's main research fields are the Finnish Sign Language acquisition of hearing and deaf children and the Finnish Sign Language learning as a second or foreign (L2) language. Recently she has also focused on developing assessment tools for evaluating Finnish Sign Language development.

**Pekka Lintunen** (PhD) is a Senior Lecturer in English Linguistics, University of Turku, and an Adjunct Professor in Applied Linguistics, University of Jyväskylä. Lintunen's main research field is the development of L2 pronunciation. Recently his research has also focused on the fluency and complexity of learner language, learner perceptions and beliefs, and informal language learning.

**Maarit Mutta** (PhD) is a Senior Lecturer in French, University of Turku, and an Adjunct Professor in Foreign Language Learning with a specialisation in second/foreign language (L2) writing at the Centre for Applied Language Studies, University of Jyväskylä. In her research, Mutta has mainly focused on online processes of writing, writing fluency and writer profiles. Recently she has also studied informal language learning.

**Sari Ohranen** is a Project Researcher in The Finnish National Certificate of Language Proficiency (NCLP) and a doctoral student in the Centre for Applied Language Studies (CALS) at the University of Jyväskylä. Ohranen is involved in language assessment and activities for developing the NCLP. In her research, she is interested in raters' use and views of speaking assessment criteria and how these views are reflected in speech proficiency ratings.

**Sanna Olkkonen** (PhD) is a postdoctoral researcher at the School of Languages and Translation Studies, University of Turku. Olkkonen's main research interests are fluency and cognitive processes in second language learning, especially in relation to L2 reading and writing. In her PhD, Olkkonen examined the efficiency of lexical access (speed and accuracy) as a sign of fluency.

**Pauliina Peltonen** is a doctoral candidate at the English Department, University of Turku. Peltonen is currently working on her doctoral dissertation on the interplay between fluency and problem-solving mechanisms. Recently, she has also co-edited publications for the Finnish Association for Applied Linguistics and collaborated on papers focusing on intonation and fluency and pronunciation feedback.

**Leena Salmi** (PhD) is a Senior Lecturer in French, University of Turku, and an Adjunct Professor in Translation Studies, University of Helsinki. Her current research interests include machine translation and post-editing, translation assessment and themes related to the production of legally valid translations. She is also involved in the Finnish examination for certifying translators to translate official documents.

**Riikka Ullakonoja** (PhD) is a postdoctoral researcher at the Department of Language and Communication Studies, University of Jyväskylä. Ullakonoja's main research interest is pronunciation learning and assessment, but she has also studied L2 reading and writing, vocabulary learning and motivation. Furthermore, she is also interested in Russian as a heritage language.

**Outi Veivo** (PhD) is a University Teacher in French at the University of Turku. Veivo has studied the role of orthographic information in the processing of spoken L2 words with different psycholinguistic methods, such as eye-tracking. Her research interests also include fluency in L2 listening, lexical knowledge in L2 and the development of translation competences.

# Preface

The common goal of second and foreign language (L2) learning is to become a fluent user of the target language. As a concept, fluency is commonly applied by learners and teachers, and it is often explicitly listed in formal curricular goals or as a criterion in L2 assessment. Despite being intuitively a familiar concept for language learners and users, its definitions vary to a great extent. Based on the Latin word 'fluentem' – 'to flow', fluency generally refers to ease and effortlessness, but the concept of fluency can be applied in various ways in different contexts. In the first chapter of *Perspectives on Fluency* (edited by Heidi Riggenbach and published by University of Michigan Press in 2000), which brought together research approaching fluency from different angles and in different fields for the first time, Koponen and Riggenbach highlighted that despite the usefulness of fluency as a construct in teaching, assessment and research contexts, its meaning should be specified further. Now almost 20 years after this seminal collection, the notion is still accurate, and more interdisciplinary and multidisciplinary approaches to fluency are needed to bring the different senses of fluency together and to refine the use of the term further. This volume, with its collection of approaches to fluency from different disciplines, shows how much the field has expanded in recent years and opens new avenues for fluency research to focus on in future to better understand this multifaceted phenomenon.

The motivation for this volume stems from our previous L2 fluency research and from the observation that various approaches have been used to investigate the same phenomenon. In addition, even though fluency research has been popular in recent years, we have often observed that many researchers discuss the same theme without explicitly referring to fluency or using concepts from this research field. Therefore, to extend the focus of existing fluency research, we have challenged researchers to reconsider their earlier approaches to fluency-related features in L2 learning and use to produce this comprehensive presentation of the topic.

The volume is of interest for undergraduates working on second language acquisition (SLA) projects (e.g. MA theses), postgraduate students involved in SLA research, and teachers and researchers focusing on the teaching, learning or assessment of L2 fluency or fluent L2 use. These readers will benefit from the empirical findings, theoretical definitions and methodological solutions presented in the volume. L2 teachers, translators and language assessment specialists, among others, will also find this volume useful. Our volume, or its chapters independently, can also be used as supplementary reading material on university-level courses on SLA and other related topics.

We are extremely grateful to all authors, reviewers and our collaborators during this book project. All chapters have been blind reviewed, and the multidisciplinary reviewers' insightful comments have been very helpful. We would like to thank our publisher, Multilingual Matters, for their help and cooperation, and especially Laura Longworth, Florence McClelland, Anna Roderick and Sarah Williams, who have always been encouraging, supportive and flexible.

We would like to thank Miro Laaksonen for his help during technical editing. We thank Damon Tringham for efficient proofreading. Finally, we extend our thanks to the School of Languages and Translation Studies, University of Turku for funding the proofreading stage.

Pekka Lintunen, Maarit Mutta and Pauliina Peltonen

# 1 Defining Fluency in L2 Learning and Use

Pekka Lintunen, Maarit Mutta and Pauliina Peltonen

## Introduction

Second language (L2) fluency or fluent second language use are important concepts for anyone using, teaching or assessing additional languages. It may be that learners want to improve their fluency, teachers need ways to approach and discuss fluency in class, or language assessment specialists want to measure or provide feedback on fluent or disfluent language use. This volume brings together current approaches to fluency from the perspective of second language learning and use, providing an in-depth and multi-faceted examination of a complex phenomenon. Including empirical studies and theoretical new openings on the processing and production of fluency, it contributes to the discussion on how the term 'fluency' is operationalised for different purposes and how fluency can be defined and studied further. As also recent contributions on fluency have shown, including the special issue of *IRAL* on L2 speech fluency in 2016 (edited by C. Wright and P. Tavakoli) and Segalowitz' (2010) monograph *The Cognitive Bases of Second Language Fluency*, fluency is a prevailing research topic among researchers in several fields. However, even though the topic is widely studied and a contemporary theme in the field of second language acquisition (SLA), the findings do not always cross disciplinary boundaries, as the research reports are mostly published in article format in discipline-specific journals. The special issue of *IRAL* is an exception, but its particular focus is L2 speech fluency. The focus of the current volume is broader, as fluency is also approached from the perspectives of L2 writing, listening and reading as well as from other perspectives beyond SLA. Therefore, for the first time since Riggenbach's (2000) seminal volume *Perspectives on Fluency*, this volume brings together fluency research from different fields and offers an extensive look at L2 fluency.

This book can be viewed as a continuation of Riggenbach's (2000) volume, since both have an interdisciplinary approach to fluency. However, since the publication of Riggenbach's volume, data collection and analysis have been significantly affected by technological advancement, contributing to methodological developments in the field. Furthermore, the current volume also introduces new aspects to fluency, including, for instance, chapters from researchers within the field of translation and sign language studies. Riggenbach's volume also has a theoretical emphasis, while the chapters in our volume manifest an interplay between theoretical and empirical perspectives and offer a selection of both theoretically and empirically oriented approaches to fluency.

The strength of the volume is its interdisciplinary approach to fluency: in addition to compiling research from different fields within the same volume, the authors of the individual chapters also approach fluency from non-traditional starting points and go beyond disciplinary boundaries in their contributions. Besides including chapters approaching fluency from an SLA perspective, the volume also integrates perspectives from related fields, such as psycholinguistics, sign language studies and L2 assessment. This adds strength to the collection of perspectives, as, for example, sign language and translation studies are fields in which fluency is still largely under-researched in an explicit manner. In addition, including a chapter on English as a lingua franca (ELF) interaction challenges the concept of the native-speaker norm as a common point of reference in fluency studies. All in all, this book is an important contribution to our current knowledge regarding L2 fluency. By extending the common foci and approaches of fluency studies, this book offers new perspectives that also enable us to critically evaluate existing paradigms and models. This, in turn, creates opportunities for developing more comprehensive frameworks and will hopefully encourage future L2 fluency investigations into this central feature of L2 learning and use.

In this chapter, we first present current frameworks and definitions of L2 fluency to contextualise the approach to L2 fluency in language learning and use provided in this volume. As the frameworks and definitions have been commonly applied to the analysis of L2 speech, our discussion also focuses on speech. Then, we extend our perspective into the context of the three other basic skills in second language learning: listening, reading and writing, as accounts of fluency related to receptive skills (listening and reading) in particular are rare and need more emphasis. Finally, we provide an overview of the overall organisation of the present volume, and introduce the chapters included. In our presentation of the chapters, we highlight the original contributions to the study of L2 fluency. In many research fields, aspects of language use that can be understood as fluency-related phenomena have been acknowledged and studied without explicitly referring to theoretical fluency frameworks. Our volume brings these fields closer together to present a more comprehensive view of the multi-faceted phenomenon referred to as fluency.

## State-of-the Art: Current Frameworks and Definitions

### Basic definitions: Focus on speaking

Before discussing common definitions and frameworks of L2 fluency, it is necessary to define what we mean by L2: our perspective on L2 is nonrestrictive and contains all forms of additional language acquisition in both formal and informal contexts, including both second and foreign languages. We also acknowledge that, at present, L2 learning often takes place in hybrid contexts integrating characteristics of various kinds of ways to learn additional languages. In addition, the role of English as a global language challenges traditional views on formal foreign language learning, as learners of English, in most parts of the world, are also exposed to English and naturally acquire it in informal contexts (cf. Krashen's (1981) dichotomy between learning and acquisition).

In SLA studies, as well as in some neighbouring fields examining L2 learning and use, such as English as a lingua franca studies, fluency has been approached from various perspectives. Thus, the definitions adopted for specific purposes may emphasise different aspects of fluency (for previous overviews of different approaches to fluency, see Chambers, 1997; Koponen & Riggenbach, 2000). To contextualise the individual chapters of the volume approaching L2 fluency from different perspectives, we provide an overview of the current understanding of L2 fluency based on the most commonly employed definitions of L2 fluency.

In its broadest sense, fluency can refer to general language proficiency in any language, focus only on spoken language proficiency, or, in its most restricted sense, refer to certain temporal features of spoken language (see e.g. Tavakoli & Hunter, 2018). These senses form a hierarchy from general to more precise understandings of the concept.

Figure 1.1 summarises the most common approaches to L2 fluency and illustrates the links between them: the distinction between lower-order and higher-order fluency (Lennon, 2000) and Segalowitz' (2010) three senses of fluency (cognitive fluency, utterance fluency and perceived fluency; for cognitive fluency, see also Olkkonen, 2017: 18). We base our discussion on Segalowitz' (2010) three senses of fluency, starting with cognitive fluency, followed by utterance and perceived fluency. In addition, more specific aspects of each sense are presented: processing efficiency and automaticity as aspects of cognitive fluency, the speed, breakdown and repair dimensions as indicators of utterance fluency (e.g. Skehan, 2009, 2014; Tavakoli & Skehan, 2005), as well as potential features of L2 associated with perceived fluency based on Götz' (2013) synthesis. We will also introduce Lennon's (1990, 2000) distinction between narrow/lower-order and broad/higher-order fluency and discuss it in relation to Segalowitz' (2010) framework.

The notion of *cognitive fluency* precedes both utterance and perceived fluency: fluent (i.e. fast and efficient) underlying cognitive processing is a

## 4 Fluency in L2 Learning and Use

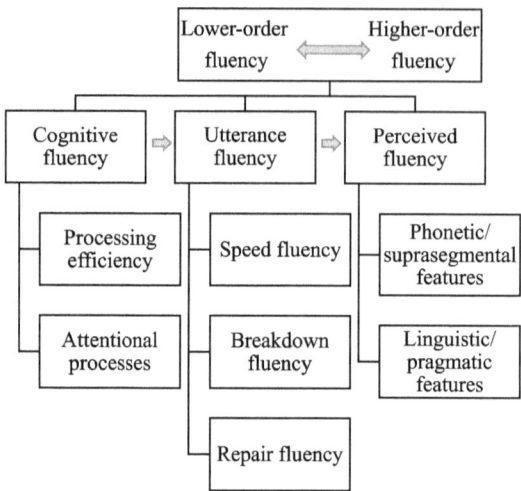

**Figure 1.1** Approaches to L2 fluency

prerequisite for smooth speech and thus also (indirectly) for perceptions of smooth speech (Segalowitz, 2010; Hilton, 2014). Cognitive fluency includes processing capacity (limitations of the working memory; see e.g. Just & Carpenter, 1992; Grabe, 2009) and the automaticity of sub-processes needed for producing basic language skills (reading, listening, speaking and writing). Lexical access (or retrieval), that is, how fast and accurately a language user can access words in their mental lexicon while performing a language task, can also be regarded as a key index of cognitive fluency. As presented in the model of lexical retrieval by Levelt *et al.* (1999: 3), lexical retrieval while speaking involves the following sequential stages from conceptual preparation of lexical concepts to articulation: conceptual preparation (lexical concepts) → lexical selection → morphological encoding → phonological encoding and syllabification → phonetic encoding → articulation. The more rapidly language users can access and produce the words they want to use, the more fluent their speaking is.

The model describes lexical retrieval in speech production, but similarities between cognitive levels of processing in speaking and writing have been discovered (see e.g. Olive, 2014). Reaction time measurements, for instance, in word retrieval tasks, can be interpreted to reveal the efficiency of cognitive processing while reading or listening to L2 production. Lexical retrieval has been found to be slower for bilinguals than monolinguals in picture naming tasks measuring retrieval speed (Sullivan *et al.*, 2017), but on the other hand, strategic competence, that is metalinguistic knowledge, might compensate and balance between speed and reading proficiency in L2 (e.g. Van Gelderen *et al.*, 2003). Cognitive processing becomes more efficient when learners become more proficient, that is, when cognitive processes become automatic and efficient. Studies have shown how exposure and training shorten reaction times, for instance, in phonetic sound perception tasks, and learners identify L2 sounds faster and more fluently (e.g. Tamminen *et al.*, 2015).

The degree of cognitive fluency is considered to be reflected in speech, in the form of, for instance, articulation rate, pausing and repair. These aspects capturing the smoothness and speed of L2 speech are aspects of *utterance fluency*, which in Lennon's (1990) terminology corresponds to the narrow sense of fluency. Lennon's (1990) distinction between *narrow* and *broad* senses of fluency (Lennon later referred to these as *lower-order fluency* and *higher-order fluency*, respectively; Lennon, 2000) can be regarded as the most influential and oft-cited approach to L2 fluency. When used in the broad sense (higher-order fluency), which is often the case in everyday contexts, fluency refers to general (oral) proficiency; for instance, someone can describe their proficiency in German as fluent, as opposed to basic skills in Swedish (Lennon, 1990). This sense of fluency, as described by Lennon (1990: 389), is also reflected in more formal contexts, for instance, in different types of scales used to assess one's (oral) proficiency in a foreign language, representing the highest level (see e.g. descriptors for assessment in CEFR; Council of Europe, 2001). Fluency as a term in the narrow sense (lower-order fluency) is more commonly used for research purposes and in L2 proficiency assessment to indicate a specific element of oral proficiency that refers to the speed, smoothness and effortlessness of speech (Chambers, 1997; Lennon, 1990). This narrow sense of fluency is also adopted in the current Complexity-Accuracy-Fluency (CAF) framework used to describe L2 oral and written proficiency and L2 productions; fluency captures one aspect of proficiency and can be distinguished from complexity and accuracy (Housen *et al.*, 2012).

An influential approach in L2 speech fluency studies for examining fluency in the narrow sense or, in other words, aspects of utterance fluency, has been Skehan's three-fold framework of the dimensions of fluency: *speed fluency, breakdown fluency* and *repair fluency* (see e.g. Skehan, 2009, 2014; Tavakoli & Skehan, 2005). The first dimension (speed fluency) includes temporal measures capturing the speed of talk, most importantly speech rate and/or articulation rate. The second dimension (breakdown fluency) contains different aspects of pausing, such as the frequency, duration and location (mid-clause/end-clause) of silent pauses (Skehan, 2009, 2014; for overviews of commonly used measures of L2 speech fluency, see De Jong, 2016; Kormos, 2006). Many studies indicate that for fluent language use, the location of pauses is particularly relevant (frequent mid-clause pausing indicating disfluency, e.g. Kahng, 2014), but the results related to pause length are more mixed. More research on pausing in L2, incorporating, for instance, potential crosslinguistic influences, is thus needed. Along with silent pauses, filled pauses are often included in the breakdown fluency dimension, although their status as indicators of 'breakdown' or disfluency in speech is not entirely straightforward even in L1 speech (e.g. O'Connell & Kowal, 2004). Finally, the third dimension (repair fluency) is measured as a separate dimension from speed and breakdown fluency, including, for instance, the frequency of false starts, repetitions and reformulations (Skehan, 2009, 2014). The use of several repairs, such as repetitions, in an utterance is usually considered a feature of disfluent speech.

One additional measure used as an indicator of fluency, combining dimensions of both speed and breakdown fluency, is the mean length of run (MLR; the mean number of syllables produced between silent pauses). Producing fluent runs is viewed as an essential part of fluency in L2 pronunciation research, where the appropriate use of suprasegmental features (prosody), especially intonation patterns and rhythm, is viewed as an integral element of fluency (e.g. Lintunen *et al.*, 2015; Wennerstrom, 2000). Importantly, formulaic sequences, that is, prefabricated stretches of speech that seem to be stored and retrieved as single units contribute to longer mean length of runs (Myles & Cordier, 2017). In other words, as learners are able to use formulaic sequences as complete chunks in an automatised way, they can be regarded as fluency-enhancing features. In addition to increasing the mean length of runs, they facilitate speed fluency in general (e.g. speech rate) while at the same time reducing features associated with disfluency in terms of breakdown (e.g. long and frequent pauses) and repair fluency (e.g. repetitions). As a whole, formulaic sequences seem to form an important element in enhancing utterance fluency.

Finally, *perceived fluency* can be examined to capture a more subjective, listener perspective on fluency. Perceived fluency refers to the listener's interpretations of utterance fluency features (Segalowitz, 2010). Perceived fluency is often studied by examining raters' assessments of fluency, which are then compared with objective fluency measures. While many studies have shown that, generally speaking, measured L2 fluency and ratings of fluency are connected (e.g. Bosker *et al.*, 2013), it has also been demonstrated that other aspects besides features of fluency in the narrow sense may influence the ratings (e.g. Iwashita *et al.*, 2008). Listeners can conceptualise fluency in different ways, resulting in variation in the ratings, especially if not given detailed instructions and/or definitions of fluency (e.g. Kormos & Dénes, 2004). In general, perceived fluency is often connected to intelligibility and even the pleasantness of the utterance (Lee *et al.*, 2019). Speech samples that are easy to understand are considered fluent. As exemplified in Figure 1.1, based on Götz' (2013: 9) summary of features, raters can take into account various features when assessing fluency, including linguistic/pragmatic features (e.g. accuracy, lexical diversity, sentence structure and idiomaticity) and phonetic/suprasegmental features (intonation and degree of perceived foreign accent; see also Préfontaine & Kormos, 2016; Rossiter, 2009). Therefore, besides relying on features associated with the narrow sense of fluency, they may also consider features associated with oral proficiency in general (the broad sense of fluency).

While our discussion so far has focused on L2 speech fluency, as fluency definitions and models are commonly applied to the study of L2 productions, fluency can also be approached from the perspectives of listening, reading and writing, which will be discussed next.

## Fluency from the perspective of listening, reading and writing

In the previous subsections, our focus has been on discussing the frameworks of fluency from the perspective of productive skills and in particular in relation to spoken language. However, fluency can also be approached from the perspective of receptive language skills, that is, listening and reading, even if these skills have rarely been explicitly linked to fluency (measures). When people listen to something, they have recourse to aural reception, whereas in reading they have recourse to visual reception. In language learning, these receptive skills are opposed to the productive skills, speaking and writing (Council of Europe, 2001: 57–61, 65–68). All four basic linguistic skills rely on active cognitive processes, which are distinct but also intertwined.

Listening involves mental processes of verbal cognitive activity; therefore, fluency in listening can be related to cognitive fluency in Segalowitz' terms. However, as Rost (2014: 281) points out, fluency in listening has not been as frequently discussed in research as other language skills. Even if language learners and users do not have overall control over the listening activity, they can regulate the mental processes involved in listening. Fluency in listening refers to the ability to decode incoming language (e.g. auditory-phonetic parsing from the speech stream) quickly and to 'deal with longer stretches of spoken discourse' (Rost, 2014: 281). Listening comprehension is an essential part of listening fluency (Tsai, 2014). In listening, two types can be distinguished: one-way listening and two-way listening, the latter being a social activity, that is, interaction with others (Nation, 2009a: 40). In consequence, listening is closely related to speaking, its speed, smoothness and complexity. Furthermore, in L2, recognising words from the continuous speech stream is affected, for instance, by the speaker's accent, use of reduced forms (e.g. contractions), lack of adequate vocabulary, or lack of effective decoding strategies (Hedevang, 2006: 124).

In the same way, fluency in reading can be related to cognitive fluency. Reading requires the skills to recognise orthographic forms, connect them to their phonemic representations, and understand the meaning, that is, decode the message. These skills can be measured by reading speed; increased fluency in this context indicates that the decoding and recognition of the units becomes faster (Nation, 2009b: 62–64). The development of computer and information technology has enabled online research of the reading process based on the reader's eye movements, for instance with eye-tracking equipment (Johansson *et al*., 2012; Kaakinen & Hyönä, 2005). During text reading, readers' eyes do not move linearly and smoothly from one word to another, but make 'a series of short stops [fixations] interleaved with quick jumps' instead, called saccades (Holmqvist *et al*., 2002: 103–104). Reading smoothly and rapidly is, however, not the only criterion for fluent reading – it also requires understanding of the text read. Reading comprehension is thus related to fluent lexical access (Verhoeven, 2000). Eye-movement studies have shown that deeper level comprehension is associated with longer fixation times as readers process the relevant information for them (Kaakinen & Hyönä, 2005). It should be noted that these kinds of psycholinguistic studies have mainly focused on first language performance, but studies on L2 performance are of recent interest.

Finally, while fluency is often considered to be related to the spoken mode, it is also essential in product- and process-oriented writing. Speaking and writing have different linguistic modalities, oral and written, but both involve an active production of verbal expressions. The inherent difference between speaking and writing is that in speaking the process and the product intermingle, whereas in writing the process and product are partly separated from each other in time. This is evident in traditional writing mode, for instance when writing by hand. In contrast, the use of digital writing devices and applications has created instances of online writing where the process and product overlap and could be approached in a different way; processing in speaking and writing converge in several aspects (e.g. pausing, hesitation and use of substitutions), even if the process of producing itself is slower in writing than in speaking. Therefore, Segalowitz' three fluency dimensions are differently distributed in writing, namely cognitive and production (i.e. utterance) fluency are evident during the writing processes, whereas perceived fluency can be evaluated from the final product as readers' perception of how fluent the text is. In the end product, fluency is defined by its audience, who evaluate how smoothly written the text is: is it coherent, logical, error free, with a well-structured layout (spelling, punctuation, presentation) (see e.g. Nation, 2009b: 126; Rose, 2018: 165–167)? That is, perceived fluency based on a written product can overlap with accuracy and appropriateness.

In this section, we have presented a thorough review of current frameworks and recent developments in the field. This book aims, however, to offer a new interdisciplinary approach by going beyond disciplinary boundaries, while also considering fluency as a feature of speaking, writing, listening and reading. The next section presents the contributions of the present volume, including empirical studies and review chapters on fluency by researchers who were encouraged to look at their specific subjects through a fluency lens.

## The Structure and Chapters of this Book

The present volume includes both review chapters and chapters presenting empirical research. The volume, as a whole, offers an overview of how fluency can be approached from a variety of new, unconventional perspectives and provides suggestions for further research. Covering a broad range of perspectives on fluency, including the four linguistic skills, the chapters of the present volume show the benefits of extending the point of view beyond specific skills when considering L2 fluency. All chapters adopt an integrative, interdisciplinary orientation to fluency and thus reach beyond traditional boundaries.

The volume consists of 12 chapters. The first two chapters introduce basic definitions; in addition to the current chapter, Chapter 2 focuses on learners' perceptions of fluency. After that, the balance shifts onto processing and cognitive fluency in Chapters 3–5. This is followed by new approaches to fluent production in L2 learning and use in Chapters 6–8, whereafter the following Chapters 9–11 focus on the teaching and assessment of fluency. The final chapter summarises and concludes the contributions of this book. The chapters will be presented in more detail in the following.

Following this introductory chapter and continuing the theme of fluency definitions, Lintunen and Peltonen focus on learners' perceptions of fluency in Chapter 2 'What is Fluency? Learner Perceptions of the Concept'. Learners' understanding of fluency has been less studied than researchers' L2 fluency definitions or, for instance, teachers' understanding of fluency. Conceptualisations of fluency were examined by analysing 71 university students' answers to fluency-related questions. The answers were analysed qualitatively and classified into four groups: aspects of proficiency to which fluency was related (including the language skills associated with fluency), the sub-components of fluency, differences in fluency across languages, and perceptions of how to improve fluency. The analysis showed that fluency was most commonly related to spoken language, but the learners also had a multifaceted and rich understanding of the concept, including other productive and receptive skills. Lintunen and Peltonen contribute to the general L2 fluency framework by increasing awareness of what learners understand by L2 fluency. Fluency definitions cannot be approached solely from teachers' and researchers' perspectives; we also need information from the learners themselves to narrow the potential gap between these groups.

Chapters 3–5 focus on processing and cognitive fluency in second language learning and use. In Chapter 3, 'Cognitive Fluency in L2: What Inaccuracies Can Reveal about Processing and Proficiency', Olkkonen and Mutta discuss the cognitive fluency framework in relation to L2 proficiency, utterance (or surface) fluency and perceived fluency. Cognitive fluency is determined in terms of working memory capacity and can be considered as the balance between automatic and controlled processing and the efficiency of processing. To study cognitive fluency, psycholinguistic methods, such as Stroop tasks, RAS and eye-tracking, are often used to reveal the distribution of cognitive resources between subprocesses. Among other factors, these tasks measure reaction times and accurate performance. Studying lexical access also provides information about participants' reading fluency. Problems in automaticity can materialise in slow performance or in inaccuracy, such as guessing the words in these tasks. By focusing on examples of lexical access, Olkkonen and Mutta argue that, from the cognitive perspective, inaccuracies are indices of disfluencies.

In Chapter 4, 'Fluency in L2 Listening', Anckar and Veivo explore fluency in listening, a skill that has been studied extensively but rarely associated with fluency. They discuss what is meant by a fluent listener in the process of listening. Listening comprehension can be understood as the outcome of this process. Fluency of the listening process implies the ability to recognise L2 sounds and words rapidly and link this information to already existing knowledge. As with other cognitive processes, these processes rely on effortlessness and automaticity, but they can also be influenced by orthographic forms when language users mentally transcribe the words they are listening to. Anckar and Veivo further discuss the possibilities for improving fluency in L2 listening, for instance by combining quantitative measures of online L2 listening processes and learners' qualitative self-evaluations.

In Chapter 5, 'L2 Fluency and Writer Profiles', Mutta discusses fluency in L2 writing and approaches it empirically by examining fluency both from the perspective of the writing process and the end product. She also creates writer profiles on the basis of writing process variables and studies the correlations between these variables. Eleven university students of French participated in the empirical experiment reported in this chapter. The general flow criteria were used to reveal aspects of cognitive fluency during the writing process (e.g. writers' pausal behaviour), whereas production (i.e. utterance) fluency was measured by features of the end product. The texts were evaluated by native French teachers with criteria related to grammatical and lexical accuracy, text coherence and global grading (i.e. perceived fluency). The results suggest that a fluent writing process does not correlate in a linear way with a fluent end product, which means that writers with different profiles can produce fluent texts.

In Chapters 6–8, fluency is approached from the perspective of production (utterance fluency). In Chapter 6, 'Fluency in English as a Lingua Franca Interaction', Hynninen approaches fluency from an ELF perspective, where the emphasis is on the smoothness and effortlessness of communication between speakers for whom English is not the first language. In this review chapter, Hynninen brings together two relatively separate strands of research: studies that have taken an interactional perspective on L2 fluency and studies in the ELF tradition. ELF studies have not usually referred to fluency explicitly, but nonetheless discuss phenomena that are related to the smoothness and effortlessness of communication. Thus, the chapter bridges the gap between fluency-oriented ELF research and L2 fluency research as well as provides important implications for future studies on L2 interactional fluency, a relatively unexplored aspect of L2 fluency.

In Chapter 7, 'Fluency in Sign Language', Kanto and Haapanen approach the concept of fluency from the perspective of sign language. As they point out, studies applying the concept of fluency to sign language have been rare; their chapter thus provides an important first step in conceiving what needs to be taken into account when fluency, a concept often associated with speech, is applied to languages produced in a different modality. In their review, Kanto and Haapanen address potential characteristics and patterns of fluency in sign language as well as discuss how fluency can be operationalised in sign language. The review points to significant implications not only for sign language research and how fluency should be taken into account from signers' perspective, but also provides insights into L2 (speech) fluency research regarding, for instance, the challenges in distinguishing fluent and disfluent language use.

In Chapter 8, 'Gestures as Fluency-enhancing Resources in L2 Interaction: A Case Study on Multimodal Fluency', Peltonen reports on an empirical study examining the use of gestures from the perspective of maintaining fluency in an interactional setting. In this exploratory study, gestures are approached as non-verbal fluency resources; their role in maintaining fluency and facilitating communication in addition to verbal fluency resources, such as communication strategies (e.g. paraphrases) and stalling mechanisms (e.g. repetitions and filler words) has not previously been studied in L2 speech fluency research, where the most common type of data are audio-recorded monologue speech. With a detailed examination of four learners' use of gestures during a problem-solving task, Peltonen shows how the flow of interaction is maintained multimodally. Overall, the chapter highlights the importance of incorporating analysis of non-verbal features along with verbal features in future L2 fluency studies.

Chapters 9–11 approach fluency from a broad, applied perspective, addressing fluency in L2 assessment, fluency in translation studies, and the effects of teaching on fluency development. In Chapter 9, 'Fluency in Language Assessment', Huhta, Kallio, Orhanen and Ullakonoja review how the concept of fluency is approached in spoken language assessment, which has traditionally used fluency as a criterion to measure L2 spoken proficiency. They examine studies that either focus on increasing language testers' understanding of fluency or use measures from fluency frameworks to assess learners' spoken language skills. In addition, they analyse practical language assessment instruments to discuss how fluency is operationalised in language assessment. The authors point out that the definition of fluency in rating scales may differ from how human raters use the scale and which parts they emphasise. Furthermore, they argue that in future techniques combining automated and human assessment will become more common.

In Chapter 10 'Fluency in Evaluating and Assessing Translations', Salmi discusses the concept of fluency from the perspective of Translation Studies, in particular professional translation. Salmi's perspective on translation studies relates to perceived fluency. She focuses on the assessment of written translations and translators; fluency in translation studies is closely related to accuracy in relation to both source and target text assessment. Two basic methods of assessment can be distinguished: error-based and criterion-based assessment. Translation scholars are not unanimous on how to apply theoretical knowledge in practice, and Salmi illustrates the phenomenon with examples of a selection of assessment grids.

In Chapter 11, 'The Effects of Songs on L2 Proficiency and Spoken Fluency: A Pedagogical Perspective', Heikkola and Alisaari report on a study on how to develop L2 fluency in formal classroom education. Their theoretical framework centres on the observation that music and singing have been found beneficial for L2 learning. The chapter complements the existing studies on fluency development in formal teaching by focusing on novel teaching methods. In their experiment, they examined how singing, listening to songs and reciting song lyrics affect L2 spoken fluency development. The participants ($n = 67$) attended two 4-week intensive courses in Finnish. According to their results, the most efficient teaching methods depend on the learners' overall proficiency level. The authors conclude that reciting song lyrics rhythmically seems to be a good way to promote both proficiency and spoken fluency.

In the final chapter of this volume, Lintunen, Mutta and Peltonen draw together the contributions of the individual chapters, summarise the main observations and present future directions for L2 fluency research in Chapter 12, 'Synthesising Approaches to Second Language Fluency: Implications and Future Directions'.

## Conclusion

In this chapter we have reviewed existing fluency frameworks and introduced the commonly used dimensions of L2 fluency that will be applied throughout this volume. We have emphasised that fluency, partly intuitively, is usually approached as a feature of spoken language, but most frameworks and operationalisations can also be applied to the written mode. In addition to the productive language skills, fluency is an essential quality measure for receptive language skills, listening and reading, as well.

Against this background, the following chapters present a range of perspectives on fluency in L2 learning and use. In sum, the volume combines a discussion of empirical findings and theoretical reflection; it brings together theoretical approaches and empirical case studies on fluency. The chapters adopt varied approaches, including mixed methods designs combining quantitative and qualitative analysis. Furthermore, various types of data are used to examine fluency, including written, spoken and interactional L2 productions to enlighten similarities between these modes. As a whole, the chapters in the volume examine a range of first (e.g. Finnish, French, Russian) and second languages (e.g. Finnish, English, French). Some of these languages have not previously been extensively researched from the perspective of fluency. With this multidisciplinary collection of chapters and representation of L2 fluency research from different fields, the volume provides a comprehensive overview of various approaches to L2 fluency. By providing novel insights into L2 fluency and demonstrating how these new openings reveal unmapped territories in terms of fluency research, this book paves the way for future fluency research with a more comprehensive grasp of the concept. Besides researchers, this book is beneficial for undergraduate and postgraduate students involved in SLA fluency research as well as L2 teachers and test-developers focusing on fluent L2 use. In the final concluding chapter of this book, we will summarise the observations made with these different users of the book in mind.

## References

Bosker, H.R., Pinget, A-F., Quené, H., Sanders, T. and De Jong, N.H. (2013) What makes speech sound fluent? The contributions of pauses, speed and repairs. *Language Testing* 30, 159–175.
Chambers, F. (1997) What do we mean by fluency? *System* 25, 535–544.
Council of Europe (2001) *Common European Framework of Reference for Languages. Learning, Teaching, Assessment.* Cambridge: Cambridge University Press. Retrieved from https://rm.coe.int/1680459f97.
De Jong, N.H. (2016) Fluency in second language assessment. In D. Tsagari and J. Banerjee (eds) *The Handbook of Second Language Assessment* (pp. 203–218). Berlin: De Gruyter Mouton.
Grabe, W. (2009) *Reading in a Second Language: Moving from Theory to Practice.* Cambridge: Cambridge University Press.
Götz, S. (2013) *Fluency in Native and Nonnative English Speech.* Amsterdam: John Benjamins.
Hedevang, L. (2006) La reconnaissance des mots dans la parole continue en L2: processus, facteurs et problèmes. [Word recognition in continuous L2 speech: process, factors and problems]. *Synergies Pays Scandinaves* 1, 114–131. https://gerflint.fr/synergies-pays-scandinaves.
Hilton, H. (2014) Oral fluency and spoken proficiency: Considerations for research and testing. In P. Leclercq, A. Edmonds and H. Hilton (eds) *Measuring L2 Proficiency: Perspectives from SLA* (pp. 27–53). Bristol: Multilingual Matters.
Holmqvist, K., Johansson, V., Strömqvist, S. and Wengelin, Å. (2002) Analysing reading and writing online. In S. Strömqvist (ed.) *The Diversity of Languages and Language Learning* (pp. 103–123). Lund: Lund University.
Housen, A., Kuiken, F. and Vedder, I. (eds) (2012) *Dimensions of L2 Performance and Proficiency: Complexity, Accuracy and Fluency in SLA.* Amsterdam: John Benjamins.

Iwashita, N., Brown, A., McNamara, T. and O'Hagan, S. (2008) Assessed levels of second language speaking proficiency: How distinct? *Applied Linguistics* 29, 24–49.
Johansson, R., Johansson, V., Wengelin, Å. and Holmqvist, K. (2012) Reading during text production. In M. Torrance, D. Alamargot, M. Castelló, F. Ganier, O. Kruse, A. Mangen, L. Tolchinsky and L. Van Waes (eds) *Learning to Write Effectively: Current Trends in European Research* (pp. 367–369). Studies in Writing, Volume 25. Bingley: Emerald Group Publishing Limited.
Just, M.A. and Carpenter, P.A. (1992) A capacity theory of comprehension: Individual differences in working memory. *Psychological Review* 99, 122–149.
Kaakinen, J.K. and Hyönä, J. (2005) Perspective effects on expository text comprehension: evidence from think-aloud protocols, eyetracking, and recall. *Discourse Processes* 40 (3), 239–257.
Kahng, J. (2014) Exploring utterance and cognitive fluency of L1 and L2 English speakers: Temporal measures and stimulated recall. *Language Learning* 64, 809–854.
Koponen, M. and Riggenbach, H. (2000) Overview: Varying perspectives on fluency. In H. Riggenbach (ed.) *Perspectives on Fluency* (pp. 5–24). Ann Arbor, MI: The University of Michigan Press.
Kormos, J. (2006) *Speech Production and Second Language Acquisition*. Mahwah, NJ: Lawrence Erlbaum Associates.
Kormos, J. and Dénes, M. (2004) Exploring measures and perceptions of fluency in the speech of second language learners. *System* 32, 145–164.
Krashen, S.D. (1981) *Second Language Acquisition and Second Language Learning*. Oxford: Pergamon Press.
Lee, J., Kim D.J. and Park H. (2019) Native listeners' evaluations of pleasantness, foreign accent, comprehensibility, and fluency in the speech of accented talkers. In J. Levis, C. Nagle and E. Todey (eds) *Proceedings of the 10th Pronunciation in Second Language Learning and Teaching Conference* (pp. 168–178). Ames, IA: Iowa State University.
Lennon, P. (1990) Investigating fluency in EFL: A quantitative approach. *Language Learning* 40, 387–417.
Lennon, P. (2000) The lexical element in spoken second language fluency. In H. Riggenbach (ed.) *Perspectives on Fluency* (pp. 25–42). Ann Arbor, MI: The University of Michigan Press.
Levelt, W.J.M., Roelofs, A. and Meyer, A.S. (1999) A theory of lexical access in speech production. *Behavioral and Brain Sciences* 22, 1–38.
Lintunen, P., Peltonen, P. and Webb, J. (2015) Tone units as indicators of L2 fluency development: Evidence from native and learner English. In J.A. Mompeán and J. Fouz-González (eds) *Investigating English Pronunciation: Current Trends and Directions* (pp. 196–218). Basingstoke: Palgrave Macmillan.
Myles, F. and Cordier, C. (2017) Formulaic sequence (FS) cannot be an umbrella term in SLA: Focusing on psycholinguistic FSs and their identification. *Studies in Second Language Acquisition* 39, 3–28.
Nation, I.S.P. (2009a) *Teaching ESL/EFL. Listening and Speaking*. New York: Routledge.
Nation, I.S.P. (2009b) *Teaching ESL/EFL. Reading and Writing*. New York: Routledge.
O'Connell, D.C. and Kowal, S. (2004) The history of research on the filled pause as evidence of *The Written Language Bias in Linguistics* (Linell, 1982). *Journal of Psycholinguistic Research* 33, 459–474.
Olive, T. (2014) Toward a parallel and cascading model of the writing system: A review of research on writing processes coordination. *Journal of Writing Research* 6 (2), 173–194.
Olkkonen, S. (2017) *Second and Foreign Language Fluency from Cognitive Perspective: Inefficiency and Control of Attention in Lexical Access*. Jyväskylä Studies in Humanities 314. Jyväskylä: University of Jyväskylä.

Préfontaine, Y. and Kormos, J. (2016) A qualitative analysis of perceptions of fluency in second language French. *International Journal of Applied Linguistics in Language Teaching* 54, 151–169.

Riggenbach, H. (ed.) (2000) *Perspectives on Fluency*. Ann Arbor, MI: The University of Michigan Press.

Rose, D. (2018) Evaluating the task of language learning. In T. Muller, J. Adamson, P.S. Brown and S. Herder (eds) *Exploring EFL Fluency in Asia* (pp. 161–181). Basingstoke: Palgrave Macmillan.

Rossiter, M.J. (2009) Perceptions of L2 fluency by native and non-native speakers of English. *The Canadian Modern Language Review* 65, 395–412.

Rost, M. (2014) Developing listening fluency in Asian EFL settings. In T. Muller, J. Adamson, P.S. Brown and S. Herder (eds) *Exploring EFL Fluency in Asia* (pp. 281–296). Basingstoke: Palgrave Macmillan.

Segalowitz, N. (2010) *Cognitive Bases of Second Language Fluency*. New York: Routledge.

Skehan, P. (2009) Modelling second language performance: Integrating complexity, accuracy, fluency, and lexis. *Applied Linguistics* 30, 510–532.

Skehan, P. (2014) The context for researching a processing perspective on task performance. In P. Skehan (ed.) *Processing Perspectives on Task Performance* (pp. 1–26). Amsterdam: John Benjamins.

Sullivan, M.D., Poarch, G.J. and Bialystok. E. (2017) Why is lexical retrieval slower for bilinguals? Evidence from picture naming. *Bilingualism: Language and Cognition* 21, 479–488.

Tamminen, H., Peltola, M.S., Kujala, T. and Näätänen, R. (2015) Phonetic training and non-native speech perception – New memory traces evolve in just three days as indexed by the mismatch negativity (MMN) and behavioural measures. *International Journal of Psychophysiology* 97 (1), 23–29.

Tavakoli, P. (2016) Fluency in monologic and dialogic task performance: Challenges in defining and measuring L2 fluency. *International Review of Applied Linguistics in Language Teaching* 54 (2), 133–150.

Tavakoli, P. and Hunter, A.-M. (2018) Is fluency being 'neglected' in the classroom? Teacher understanding of fluency and related classroom practices. *Language Teaching Research* 22 (3), 330–349.

Tavakoli, P. and Skehan, P. (2005) Strategic planning, task structure, and performance testing. In R. Ellis (ed.) *Planning and Task Performance in a Second Language* (pp. 239–273). Amsterdam: John Benjamins.

Tsai, Y.-C. (2014) Does autonomous listening increase fluency? In T. Muller, J. Adamson, P.S. Brown and S. Herder (eds) *Exploring EFL Fluency in Asia* (pp. 312–327). Basingstoke: Palgrave Macmillan.

Van Gelderen, A., Schoonen, R., de Glopper, K., Hulstijn, J., Snellings, P., Simis, A. and Stevenson, M. (2003) Roles of linguistic knowledge, metacognitive knowledge and processing speed in L3, L2 and L1 reading comprehension: a structural equation modeling approach. *International Journal of Bilingualism* 7 (1), 7–25.

Verhoeven, L. (2000) Components in early second language reading and spelling. *Scientific Studies of Reading* 4, 313–330.

Wennerstrom, A. (2000) The role of intonation in second language fluency. In H. Riggenbach (ed.) *Perspectives on Fluency* (pp. 102–127). Ann Arbor, MI: The University of Michigan Press.

Wright, C. and Tavakoli, P. (2016) New directions and developments in defining, analyzing and measuring L2 speech fluency. *International Review of Applied Linguistics in Language Teaching* 54 (2), 73–77.

# 2 What is Fluency? Learner Perceptions of the Concept

Pekka Lintunen and Pauliina Peltonen

## Introduction

Second language (L2) fluency has been studied from numerous perspectives in different fields, including L2 learning, teaching and assessment. As outlined in the introductory chapter to this volume, L2 fluency is a notoriously difficult concept to define; it can be approached broadly as general (oral) proficiency or more narrowly as a dimension of oral proficiency that includes the smoothness and effortlessness of speech (Lennon, 1990, 2000). Furthermore, despite often being associated with speaking, fluency can also be linked to other L2 skills, that is, listening, reading and writing. While studies often acknowledge the variation in L2 fluency definitions and operationalisations (e.g. Chambers, 1997; Koponen & Riggenbach, 2000), few studies have focused on the concept itself (but see Préfontaine & Kormos, 2016; Tavakoli & Hunter, 2018). The recent exceptions provide important insights into an under-researched area by examining teachers' perceptions of fluency; nevertheless, more research is needed on how language learners themselves understand the concept of fluency (on self-assessments of fluency, see Préfontaine, 2013).

The purpose of this study is to focus on learners' understanding of fluency; in particular, how advanced learners (first year university students of English) define fluency or fluent use of language in their own words. In this sense, we approach fluency as a concept from a phenomenographic perspective; that is, our aim is to capture people's experience of a certain phenomenon (Marton, 1981; Sin, 2010; Tight, 2016) and thus identify their conceptual understanding of fluency. To shed more light on the issue, we also asked the learners to evaluate their own language skills and consider how they could improve their fluency. Presenting a qualitative analysis of the learners' answers, this study thus not only contributes to the growing body of research on L2 fluency perceptions but, more specifically, complements the existing findings on teachers' perceptions with learners' perceptions. While it is important to consider learning objectives, including fluency, from the teachers' perspective, the goals should also be clear to learners themselves to support their learning process. As fluency is a commonly used concept in L2 learning and assessment, it is essential to examine how fluency is understood from the researchers', teachers' and learners' perspectives to avoid possible misunderstandings regarding what is meant by fluency. Additionally, the present study contributes to the development of L2 fluency research more broadly by increasing awareness of what is understood by L2 fluency and facilitates conceptualising L2 fluency in a more nuanced manner.

## Perceptions of Fluency in Previous Research

As highlighted in the introductory chapter to this volume, L2 fluency is a multifaceted concept that can be defined in various ways. In addition, definitions in different fields (including psycholinguistics, L2 assessment and L2 teaching and learning) may vary. To contextualise our study, we will first briefly present the most commonly used definitions and frameworks for conceptualising L2 fluency. As these definitions and frameworks have been formulated to describe L2 speech fluency and have mostly been applied to the analysis of L2 speech, we also focus on speech in our discussion. Nonetheless, the definitions and frameworks can be applied to the other productive skill, that is, writing fluency, and even to receptive skills, that is, listening and reading (see also Chapter 1 in this volume). We will then move on to presenting relevant empirical studies examining connections between fluency measures and fluency assessments, which provide insights into listeners' or raters' understanding of fluency. As these studies have not directly focused on fluency perceptions, we end our discussion by presenting two recent studies in which the main focus is on (teacher) perceptions of L2 fluency.

First, for many studies on L2 fluency, the starting point is Lennon's (1990, 2000) influential distinction between the two senses of fluency: the broad sense of fluency (he referred to this later as higher-order fluency) and the narrow sense of fluency (later named as lower-order fluency). The former refers to 'all-round oral proficiency' (Lennon, 2000: 25), while the latter captures a particular element of the more general oral proficiency, namely 'the speed and smoothness of oral delivery' (Lennon, 2000: 25). Different types of temporal phenomena, for instance, speech rate and aspects of pausing, as well as repair features (see e.g. Skehan, 2009) can be considered elements of fluency in the narrow sense and are often used as a basis for measuring fluency from spoken productions. Thus, according to the narrow sense of fluency, smoothness and effortlessness of speech can be viewed as one aspect of oral proficiency, excluding aspects such as grammatical accuracy or lexical variation. This view is also reflected in the current Complexity-Accuracy-Fluency (CAF) framework of L2 oral proficiency: fluency can be approached as a separate component of proficiency along with accuracy and complexity (see e.g. Housen *et al.*, 2012). While especially in task-based research the dimensions are often measured separately, due to the ambiguous use of fluency as a near-synonym for proficiency, on the one hand, and as a distinct dimension of proficiency, on the other, it will be interesting to see to what extent the participants of the present study treat fluency and accuracy, for instance, as separate concepts.

While Lennon's broad sense of fluency mainly refers to the overall command of spoken language and not, for instance, proficiency in writing, it can also refer to other aspects of language use. Recently, based on teachers' perceptions of L2 fluency, Tavakoli and Hunter (2018: 14) suggested that a 'very broad' definition can be distinguished from Lennon's (1990) 'broad' sense of fluency: when fluency is used to refer to overall mastery or general proficiency in a language, it reflects an even broader understanding of fluency than understanding fluency as a general speaking ability. Since these two views could be identified based on teachers' perceptions, we assume that the learner perceptions focused on in our study can allude to both of these senses as well. As exemplified by Segalowitz' (2010) framework of three different dimensions of fluency, besides the broad/narrow distinction, fluency can also be considered from the following viewpoints: utterance fluency, perceived fluency and cognitive fluency. The first includes identifiable and measurable fluency-related features from (speech) samples, being closely related to the narrow sense of fluency. The second involves listeners' interpretations of utterance fluency features (Segalowitz, 2010). The third aspect relates to effortless underlying cognitive processing; a prerequisite for smooth speech (i.e. utterance fluency; Segalowitz, 2010). While the learners in our study are probably not familiar with this specific terminology, it is likely that they are referring to these aspects in their comments in some way or another.

In L2 speech fluency studies, perceptions of fluency have commonly been explored through fluency assessment. In these studies, the focus has often been on the connections between objective fluency measures and more subjective listener perceptions of fluency (i.e. on the connections between utterance and perceived fluency, Segalowitz, 2010; e.g. Lennon, 1990; Riggenbach, 1991; Freed, 1995; Kormos & Dénes, 2004; Rossiter, 2009). These studies have demonstrated variation in raters' understanding of fluency: especially when not given guidelines on how to approach fluency, the ratings can be based on a variety of factors besides the temporal aspects associated with the narrow sense of fluency (e.g. Riggenbach, 1991; Freed, 1995; Kormos & Dénes, 2004). For instance, Kormos and Dénes (2004: 160) observed that six (non-native and native) teacher raters in their study interpreted fluency differently: some associated it with temporal phenomena, while others included, for instance, accuracy and lexical diversity in their assessments. Similarly, Freed (1995) found variation in six native speakers' justifications for their fluency assessments: fluency was understood in a rather broad sense, incorporating aspects such as varied vocabulary, accent and confidence, in addition to temporal features. Despite these differences in fluency conceptualisations across raters found in many studies, others have demonstrated more homogeneity, especially if the raters have been instructed to assess fluency according to the narrow sense (e.g. Rossiter, 2009).

While the studies presented above have provided insights into raters' perceptions of fluency, their main focus has not been to examine different understandings of fluency. In the following, we will thus present the two recent studies (Préfontaine & Kormos, 2016; Tavakoli & Hunter, 2018) that are particularly relevant for the present study as they have focused specifically on the perceptions of fluency. Préfontaine and Kormos' (2016) study examined three native speaker teachers' perceptions of L2 French fluency and Tavakoli and Hunter's (2018) study mapped language teachers' perceptions and classroom practices related to L2 fluency in England. While Préfontaine and Kormos (2016) elicited perceptions of fluency in conjunction with ratings of concrete speech samples (capturing perceived fluency in Segalowitz' 2010 terminology), our study follows the broader approach adopted in Tavakoli and Hunter (2018), which involved teachers reporting their understanding of the concept of L2 fluency on a more general level without reference to specific samples. The raters in Préfontaine and Kormos' (2016) study viewed fluency mainly in terms of temporal spoken language features, in accordance with the narrow definition of fluency (mentioning aspects such as speed, pause phenomena, efficiency/effortlessness and target-like rhythm), but also referred to other aspects, for instance, grammatical competence, albeit to a lesser extent. In contrast, Tavakoli and Hunter's (2018) study, based on a frequency analysis of the most often recurring items in the responses ($n = 452$), showed that the teachers ($n = 84$) understood fluency more broadly. Only 13.4% of the responses contained items related to fluency in the narrow sense, while a clear majority involved items referring to fluency as a general speaking ability (43.8%; e.g. speaking confidently, ability to communicate, correct pronunciation) or even more broadly to general L2 proficiency (32.5%; e.g. correct grammar, a wide range of vocabulary; Tavakoli & Hunter, 2018). We assume that this variation in responses will also be reflected in the present study on learner perceptions as the participants were given no definition of fluency. Against this background, we will present the methodology of our study in the following section.

## Methodology

To investigate the learner perspective on fluency, we collected learner opinions on L2 fluency from L1 Finnish first-year university students who studied English language and culture as their major or minor ($n = 71$). The participants can be considered advanced learners of English, as they studied the subject at university level and had passed a competitive admission test, largely focusing on language skills, to enter university studies. We collected the responses at the very beginning of the learners' first academic year at university to avoid the influence of analytical, research-led university-level teaching, which could have geared their opinions towards what is being taught based on earlier research; students who had started their studies earlier were excluded from the sample. Their earlier education has been teacher-led and guided by course books, which do not systematically discuss speech fluency (Tergujeff, 2013). All participants were native speakers of Finnish and knew English and Swedish as additional languages; native speakers of other languages, for example exchange students, were excluded from the sample. Many participants also knew some other additional languages to varying degrees.

We collected our data by means of a short questionnaire. Mainstream phenomenographic research usually focuses on interview data (Sin, 2010), but we used open-ended questions in a paper-and-pencil questionnaire to collect more material in a relatively short period of time at the beginning of a compulsory lecture series. Our questions reflected interview-type questions, and the participants had about 20 minutes to answer them. The participants were able to ask for clarifications if they found the questions unclear. The first set of questions focused on the definition of fluency: *What does it mean if someone uses a language fluently? What does it include and refer to? What are fluent language skills?* To make the learners think beyond the language they studied at the time of the questionnaire, the second set of questions consisted of the following questions: *How fluent do you consider your language skills in the languages that you know? How could you improve your fluency?* We allowed the students to respond either in English or in their native language (Finnish). The examples in the following section that were originally written in Finnish have been translated into English.

The answers were categorised qualitatively to establish the participants' perspectives on fluency (qualitative content analysis; see Dörnyei, 2007: 245–256). The data set comprised 5903 words (424 sentences). We did not define fluency in the questionnaire as we approached the concept phenomenographically with the aim of capturing how learners intuitively understand the concept and how our participants as a group express qualitatively different interpretations of the phenomenon. The answers were grouped according to the following four broader themes that emerged from the data: (1) aspects of proficiency that fluency is related to (including the language skills associated with fluency), (2) sub-components of fluency, (3) differences across languages in fluency and (4) perceptions of how to improve fluency further. We will discuss each of these in a separate section in the following; however, it should be noted that the answers often combined these themes, and the boundaries in our classification are flexible. Therefore, the frequencies of answers mentioned should be considered as approximations to roughly show which themes were more common than others.

## Findings and Discussion

### Fluency in relation to aspects of proficiency and language skills

The first theme identified in the responses focused on the aspects of proficiency and language skills that were mentioned in connection with fluency. The starting point in most answers was to approach fluency as a feature of speech, writing, communication, or processing. Often the answers also combined these topics and discussed the concept from different perspectives. Almost all participants discussed speech fluency in some way (in total 69 participants, 97%); in their opinion, when someone is fluent, their speech is fluent. Two participants had different approaches: one focused on structures of language and one on native-speaker capacity. However, it should also be noticed that the verb 'to speak' can refer to generally understanding or knowing a language as in 'Do you speak English?' The corresponding verb in Finnish (Fin. 'puhua') can be used similarly. Nevertheless, a clear majority of the answers discussed general spoken proficiency in a second language. This common approach to fluency is in line with, for example, Lennon's (1990) broad sense of fluency (higher-order fluency), which links fluency to oral proficiency. In addition, Segalowitz' utterance fluency encompasses 'the fluency characteristics that a *speech* sample can possess' (2010: 48, added emphasis). However, in many definitions, the learners added more perspectives or expressed some reservations that implied that they could understand some other perspectives on fluency as well, as illustrated in Example 1, which represents a very common type of initial response in our data set.

(1) For me fluency is mostly speech-related: pronunciation and the natural flow of speech. Of course, written skills (grammar) etc. have to be considered as well though. (Participant 28)

In addition to fluency as a feature of spoken language, another domain that was discussed by 12 participants (17%) was fluency in written language, often in combination with speaking. In this connection, writing fluency was also associated with accuracy, the ability to produce error-free texts (Example 2), or with reading, the receptive skill related to written language (Example 3).

(2) Can write without significant errors. (Participant 11)
(3) If a person is fluent in a given language he can read most non-academic texts with ease. (Participant 46)

These examples could be interpreted as alluding to the 'very broad' sense of fluency (Tavakoli & Hunter, 2018: 14), since they address proficiency related to writing and reading, not speaking. Overall, learners still explicitly associated fluency most commonly with the productive skills of speaking and writing, whereas the number of times that fluency was mentioned as a part of receptive skills was rare (reading mentioned by three participants, 4%, and listening mentioned by one participant, 1%). While listening is an essential part of communication, listening was the skill that learners intuitively most seldom linked to the concept of fluency.

Skilful listening could, nevertheless, be viewed as an implied aspect of fluency in answers discussing fluency broadly from the perspective of communication. Although the word 'speaker' was used in many answers, the context showed that both speaking and listening were included as aspects of fluency. In fact, fluency was commonly understood as the smoothness of communication as a whole (25 participants, 35%). For instance, the answers referred to the ability to participate in conversations in L2 (Examples 4 and 5) and the general ease of communication (Example 6).

(4) In my opinion fluent language skills mean that you can communicate without big troubles. (Participant 16)
(5) To be a fluent speaker means that you can participate in a conversation (understand and be understood). (Participant 10)
(6) Communicating should be effortless. (Participant 16)

These examples illustrate a broader, communicative approach to fluency that has so far not been common in empirical L2 fluency studies examining L2 (utterance) fluency; L2 speech fluency has often been examined from monologue speech and even if interactional data have been used (e.g. Götz, 2013; Tavakoli, 2016), the collaborative aspects of fluency have rarely been the focus of analysis. Nonetheless, some researchers have recently called for a broadening of the scope of fluency as a concept and as an object of study; fluency should also cover the interactive aspects and be approached from a broader, interactional and communicative perspective (e.g. Segalowitz, 2016; Wright & Tavakoli, 2016). The fact that many participants in our study also intuitively associated fluency with this more communicative perspective is in line with the recent developments in L2 fluency research.

Finally, in 11 answers (15%) the participants discussed fluency in the context of processing: fluency was associated with effortless processing (Example 7) and automaticity of language use (Example 8). As these reflect an understanding of fluency as a general process in language use not necessarily belonging to a certain skill area, those comments referring to fluency as creativity in language use (Example 9; see also Fillmore, 1979) were grouped in the same category.

(7) To use a language fluently means that you can transform your thoughts into words without having to pay too much attention to it. (Participant 7)
(8) It means that you know the language 'by heart'. (Participant 34)
(9) A fluent speaker is able to use the language freely and creatively. (Participant 15)

These examples illustrate an understanding of fluency that has been commonly applied in more psycholinguistically oriented L2 fluency studies (e.g. Olkkonen, 2017; Olkkonen & Mutta, this volume); yet viewing fluency in terms of efficient underlying cognitive processing forms the basis for Lennon's (2000: 26) oft-cited definition of (lower-order) fluency as 'the rapid, smooth, accurate, lucid, and efficient translation of thought or communicative intention into language under the temporal constraints of on-line processing' and corresponds to the cognitive fluency component in Segalowitz' (2010) three-fold fluency framework.

To summarise, the answers revealed that learners intuitively associated fluency with general oral proficiency. The learners described fluency as a multifaceted phenomenon that can be associated with all aspects of language use, yet emphasised productive skills. The importance of communication, including a good command of receptive skills, was also relatively commonly discussed. Those aspects of proficiency and language skills that were identified in the learners' answers provided the context and starting point for the more detailed descriptions of the fluency features that were discussed in their answers. In the following, we will scrutinise the answers further to look at the ingredients of fluency associated with these broader contexts.

## The subcomponents of fluency

The aspects of fluency mentioned in the answers were grouped into the following categories (the percentages show the proportion of participants mentioning the aspect in question): vocabulary (59%); pronunciation and temporal features (45%); grammar (42%); intelligibility (41%); accommodation (23%); accuracy (8%); strategic language use (8%); and non-verbal communication (3%). The first five categories (vocabulary, pronunciation and temporal features, grammar, intelligibility and accommodation) were discussed fairly frequently by the participants; the remaining categories were less common. Often these categories were discussed in combination, such as grammar and vocabulary, and there are many links between them, but they can also be considered different aspects of fluency. While vocabulary was the most often mentioned aspect of fluency, we will begin our discussion with pronunciation and temporal features, such as speech rhythm, hesitations and pauses, because they were two closely related themes that were often combined in the answers. Therefore, we also combined them into one subcomponent.

Commonly the definitions focused on matters related to spoken language and pronunciation: pronunciation was mentioned by 32 participants (45%) as an important aspect of fluency and was also often associated with nativelikeness, as illustrated in Example 10. Some participants, on the other hand, emphasised that pronunciation need not be nativelike but simply easily understood by the listener (Example 11). As aspects of pronunciation, the participants included, for instance, phonemes, intonation, linking and speech rhythm. That is, pronunciation included both segmental and suprasegmental features of speech.

(10) Pronunciation is close to native speakers' pronunciation. (Participant 6)
(11) Being fluent in a language means ... having such a pronunciation that it's easily understood. (Participant 9)
(12) a person who can speak a language almost accent-free, without hesitation and pauses (to try to remember a word) is a fluent speaker. (Participant 71)

Example 12 shows how hesitations or pauses were often discussed together with pronunciation. The absence of pauses or hesitation phenomena was discussed in 25 definitions (35%). This implies that automatic lexical retrieval was also considered an important factor in fluent language use and partly explains why vocabulary was so often discussed as a subcomponent of fluency. Example 12 further illustrates how the perspectives of utterance and cognitive fluency can be considered within a single answer: searching for words, a cognitive process, can be reflected in disfluencies, for example pauses, in the spoken production. Similarly, in Préfontaine and Kormos' (2016) study, lexical retrieval was one of the themes identified in the qualitative analysis: whereas lexical retrieval problems affected perceptions of fluency negatively, the use of communication strategies to overcome lexical retrieval problems was viewed positively (Préfontaine & Kormos, 2016: 160–161; see also Example 20 below).

In addition to matters mostly related to spoken language, aspects of linguistic competence that can be linked either to spoken or written language were also discussed. For instance, adequate lexical (including phrases, idioms and lexical retrieval; Example 13) and grammatical competence (Example 14) were viewed as subcomponents of fluency by 42 participants (59%) and 30 participants (42%), respectively.

(13) The language user also has a wide vocabulary and understands / can use expressions and phrases typical of the language in question. (Participant 25)
(14) The language you produce is grammatically correct (not necessarily 100% but close to it). (Participant 70)

Grammar was also often associated with accuracy, but, as Example 14 shows, perfect mastery was not expected, which was emphasised in some answers (for more on accuracy, see also Examples 18 and 19). These views reflect a broad understanding of fluency as general L2 proficiency. In a similar manner, in Tavakoli and Hunter's (2018) study, a relatively high proportion of items (32.5%) in the teachers' answers reflected this view (referred to as a 'very broad' definition of fluency by the researchers).

In addition to referring to aspects of linguistic competence when naming the ingredients of fluency, another perspective was focusing on intelligibility (29 answers, 41%), either regarding the language user's ability to understand spoken or written texts with ease (Example 15) or regarding the speaker being easy to understand from the listener's perspective (Example 16; see also Example 11). That is, the participants also considered perceived fluency when defining fluent language use. We included in this category answers reflecting intelligibility (the actual understanding of the intended message) and comprehensibility (how easy or difficult listeners find understanding the message) (see e.g. Derwing & Munro, 2015: 5).

(15) you should also be able to understand the 'gist' of each sentence spoken, or written, even if the sentence in question is 'academic' (Participant 22)
(16) A fluent speaker gets understood with ease. (Participant 32)

Accommodation (the ability to adapt to different language use situations or the ability to accommodate one's language use to secure maximal intelligibility, Giles & Ogay, 2007; see also Fillmore, 1979) was also relatively often mentioned as an ingredient of fluency (Example 17).

(17) A fluent language user can adapt to different speaking situations with word choices and speaking style. (Participant 14)

A total of 16 participants (23%) mentioned the context-specific nature of fluency. The answers discussing accommodation are in line with the fluency research literature highlighting task-based effects on fluency and demonstrating context-based variation in fluency. For instance, in a recent study, Tavakoli (2016) demonstrated differences in the speakers' fluency in monologue and dialogue contexts (on the influence of social context on fluency, see also Fillmore, 1979; Segalowitz, 2010). Thus, as illustrated in Example 17, fluent language users should be able to vary their performance and understand the optimal style of language use from the context. This includes, according to the responses, the mode of language use, genres and cultural differences. Accommodation was also associated with variation in native and non-native language use, as the ability to understand different accents and dialects of the target language was also mentioned. This also demonstrates that learner intuitions on fluency are often related to L2 proficiency as a whole, or fluency in the very broad sense.

In addition to the relatively commonly mentioned subcomponents of fluency discussed above, three other aspects were mentioned in a few students' answers: accuracy, strategy use and non-verbal communication. In many models of L2 proficiency, accuracy is seen as a separate dimension from fluency (e.g. the CAF-framework; Housen *et al.*, 2012). In the very broad sense, however, fluency refers to general language proficiency (Tavakoli & Hunter, 2018). This was also characteristic of six participants' (8%) answers that discussed the number of mistakes in language use and how (almost) error-free language use is associated with fluency (Examples 18 and 19; see also Example 14). As accuracy was not only considered from the grammatical perspective, but also as a more general attitude towards language norms or in terms of lexical accuracy, we identified it as a separate category. That said, it should be acknowledged that there is some degree of overlap between the categories grammar and accuracy.

(18) [ability] to talk without grammatical errors. (Participant 67)
(19) Fluency doesn't mean 'perfection'. One doesn't have to be a native speaker in order to speak a language fluently. (Participant 69)

Six participants (8%) focused on strategic language use, that is, overcoming a limited language capacity when faced with situations that require the use of words that they do not yet know properly or when they are unable to retrieve certain words. In these participants' answers, fluent language users were viewed as being able to paraphrase their ideas if they notice lexical gaps in their knowledge, as illustrated in Example 20 (see also Préfontaine & Kormos, 2016).

(20) If a word is unknown to the speaker they are able to explain the meaning of the word using other words. (Participant 19)

Example 20 shows how speech fluency can be linked to strategy use. While fluency analysis has rarely been linked to the analysis of communication strategies in empirical L2 fluency studies (but see Peltonen, 2017), it has been suggested that an efficient use of problem-solving mechanisms, such as communication strategies, can help to reduce the number of hesitations and pauses, which are usually considered signs of disfluent language use (Dörnyei & Kormos, 1998).

The final category the participants discussed was non-verbal features (two participants; 3%). As an example, these participants mentioned appropriate gestures and facial expressions as important elements of fluent spoken language use (see also Peltonen, this volume). In addition, non-verbal features were connected with confident language use, implying that a certain kind of non-verbal behaviour was associated with nervousness.

All in all, the participants' definitions revealed a multifaceted view of the subcomponents of fluency: while almost half of the answers incorporated pronunciation and temporal features as ingredients of fluency, reflecting an orientation towards lower-order fluency, vocabulary and grammar were also frequently mentioned, demonstrating a broader, higher-order understanding of fluency (not necessarily only restricted to spoken language, echoing what is known as a very broad understanding of the concept). In fact, vocabulary was the most frequently discussed aspect of language skills in the answers, emphasising the central role of vocabulary size and fast lexical access in fluent L2 use. The relatively many answers highlighting intelligibility and accommodation as ingredients of fluency also demonstrated the participants' communicative view on fluency, incorporating aspects of both utterance fluency (the producer's perspective) and perceived fluency (the receiver's perspective).

## Fluency in different languages

As part of the questionnaire, we also asked the participants to consider how fluent they are in different languages. Our motivation was to investigate whether the participants understood fluency as a feature of foreign languages alone or whether native language fluency was also discussed. In second language acquisition studies, learners have traditionally been compared to (idealised) native-speaker norms; while native speakers' language use has been viewed as error-free and fluent, L2 production, in comparison, has been evaluated as deficient or disfluent (Cook, 2012). Today, however, variation is more widely acknowledged in native speaker use, especially in corpus-oriented research. In the responses, the participants mostly discussed and compared their fluency in various foreign languages, but some also mentioned their native language.

Native language fluency was mentioned as a starting point by 23 participants (32%). Fluency was thought of as a native speaker feature, and other additional languages were, therefore, considered less fluent (Example 21). However, some participants also questioned their fluency even in their native language: while they generally considered their native language use fluent, they also acknowledged that expressing one's opinions in a concise and intelligible form was sometimes challenging or that they cannot produce their native language fluently in all situations (Example 22).

(21) I think I'm fluent in my native language but the languages I study (Swedish and English) are not fluent because I cannot speak as a native Swedish or English person. (Participant 53)

(22) My [native language] Finnish skills are fluent in written but not in spoken language. My English language skills are quite fluent in written and spoken language, but there is room for improvement. (Participant 13)

In particular, Example 22 illustrates learners' acknowledgement of native speakers' variation in fluency. As discussed in the previous section, fluency can vary according to context and, as pointed out by Fillmore as early as in 1979, not even native speakers are equally fluent in all situations. While several other researchers after Fillmore have also raised the point about native speaker variation in fluency (e.g. Lennon, 1990; Riggenbach, 1991), a homogenous group of ideally fluent native speakers is often assumed as an implied reference group for L2 speakers in L2 fluency research. However, while not specifically focusing on native speaker variation, some empirical studies comparing a learner group or learner groups to a native speaker control group have observed variation also among native speakers (e.g. Kahng, 2014; Peltonen & Lintunen, 2016).

In half of the answers, the participants discussed how fluent their L2 was (35 participants; 49%). While the participants were university level advanced learners of English, they did not think that their fluency in English meant that they had a perfect command of the language. Rather, they often mentioned that despite some inaccuracies, they still thought their English was fluent. English was often considered the only fluent additional language although many participants knew other languages as well and compared these languages to English (Example 23). English is usually the first additional language in Finland, and therefore the language that the participants had studied the most (Example 24).

(23) Fluent in English, average in Swedish and (an advanced) beginner in Japanese. (Participant 2)
(24) I'm fluent in English but not really in the other languages that I've studied because I still get very nervous when I have to communicate in those languages. (Participant 57)

There were nine participants (13%) who mentioned that they spoke more than one language fluently (Example 25). According to the participants, it was possible to speak two or three additional languages fluently. That is, there was a lot of variation in the number of languages that the participants considered fluent, which may reflect their background and skill level in different languages. On the other hand, four participants (6%) did not name any language explicitly or wrote that they need to improve their language skills to become fluent (Example 26). Examples 25 and 26 also show how 'fluent' and 'fluently' were understood as gradable words modified by 'rather' or 'very'. That is, fluency is seen as a quality of language that can be present to different degrees.

(25) I speak English and Swedish rather fluently. (Participant 3)
(26) I don't think my English is very fluent right now. (Participant 21)

To summarise, fluency was mainly viewed as a characteristic of foreign languages; only approximately a third of the participants discussed fluency as a feature of native language and in that context often as a default. Nonetheless, some of the answers also reflected an awareness of context-based variation in native language fluency. With respect to foreign languages, many participants considered themselves fluent in the language they were studying at university (English), yet some also mentioned other languages. Generally speaking, the answers discussed here mostly reflect a broad understanding of fluency, fluency being 'the highest point on a scale that measures spoken command of a foreign language' (Lennon, 1990: 389).

## Improving fluency

We also asked the participants to discuss how they could develop their skills further and improve their fluency. In these answers, the participants focused on means for improving general language proficiency as well as which aspects of language or language skills to improve. This was the final part of the questionnaire, and 12 participants (17%) did not discuss this aspect at all. In general, the participants emphasised the role of input, active language use and informal learning as methods to become more automatic and fluent in their language use.

To improve general language proficiency, the participants emphasised active language use (35 participants; 59% of those who answered this question). That is, more than half of the answers mentioned that language should be used as much and as often as possible (Example 27). Spending time in a target language environment was considered a good solution as it increases the opportunities to use the target language (Example 28). Spending time in target language environments was explicitly discussed by 11 participants (19%).

(27) The best way to improve one's fluency is to use that language! (Participant 17)
(28) The best way to improve your fluency is to spend time in a country where they speak the language you want to learn. The more and more you speak in a language, [the] more fluent you'll get. (Participant 57)

Those answers highlighting the benefits of spending time in target language environments for fluency development are in line with the empirical studies demonstrating that studying abroad facilitates fluency development (e.g. Freed, 1995; Lennon, 1990; Mora & Valls-Ferrer, 2012), which is often explained as resulting from increased opportunities for authentic language use in communicative situations.

When the aspects of language were discussed in the context of fluency development, most participants specifically mentioned pronunciation (6 participants; 10%) or spoken language in general (20 participants; 34%) as their starting point and stated that the lack of automatisation of some phonemes slowed down their spoken performance and made it disfluent. Other phonetic features, such as word stress and intonation, were also mentioned. Furthermore, lack of spoken language practice is a general worry in formal education, which is reflected in answers emphasising the need to improve spoken language skills (Example 29).

(29) Speaking more in English will definitely improve my fluency. (Participant 27)

Two participants (3%) mentioned grammar and nine (15%) vocabulary as aspects that they could develop to improve their fluency (Example 30). This also reflects the fact that most answers discussed higher-order fluency development. Considering the fact that grammar and vocabulary were very commonly mentioned subcomponents of fluency, they were surprisingly rarely discussed as areas to focus on to improve fluency.

(30) The things that I need to improve the most are my lexical and grammatical correctness. (Participant 66)

Some participants discussed different skills; in answers referring to different skills, productive language skills were mentioned more frequently than receptive skills. As observed above, speaking skills were most often discussed, and five participants (8%) also mentioned writing as an area they need to develop. The receptive skills of listening (11 participants; 19%) and reading (8 participants; 14%) were also considered in many answers (Examples 31 and 32). For instance, watching TV was mentioned as a good way to practise listening skills and learn new words.

(31) Improving happens by studying and listening to English-speaking media. (Participant 22)
(32) I can expand my vocabulary by reading, but for spoken production I need to spend time in an English-speaking country. (Participant 38)

Fluency development was also viewed as requiring adequate contexts to improve the proficiency level already reached, as one participant mentioned that they would need more practice with formal language use, implying that they are more familiar with informal contexts. Finally, some answers mentioned affective factors as crucial for improving one's fluency. A lack of motivation was mentioned by one participant as a factor that hinders their development.

In conclusion, the developmental aspect revealed that fluency was mostly approached from a very broad sense (corresponding to general language proficiency), reflected in the variety of methods of language learning discussed in the answers. A similar focus on developing fluency with general (oral) practice was found in Tavakoli and Hunter's (2018) study: when asking teachers about activities for developing fluency, activities developing specifically temporal fluency only covered 10.4% of the mentioned activities, while the majority of the activities mentioned were communicative (oral) activities (53.6%); activities aimed at improving other language skills covered 13.5%. In our study, the emphasis on a very broad understanding of fluency when asked about its development was even more prominent: the participants believed they needed practice with different domains of language use and needed to work on different levels of language to develop their fluency further. In this context, practising both productive and receptive language skills was viewed as beneficial for fluency development, although productive skills and especially spoken language skills were more frequently discussed.

## Conclusion

Our goal was to examine how advanced learners of English define and understand the concept of fluency and fluent language use. To a large extent, we approached our research objective phenomenographically to qualitatively map our participants' perceptions of fluency. As our analysis showed, advanced learners had a multifaceted and rich understanding of the concept. Fluency was most commonly associated with spoken language, but was also approached as a feature of written language, communication, or language processing. Fluency included pronunciation and other spoken-language specific features, but lexical and grammatical aspects were also discussed, implying that many learners had a very broad understanding of fluency that can be interpreted as general language proficiency (see also Tavakoli & Hunter, 2018). Fluency was discussed more as a feature of productive language skills, but receptive skills were also often mentioned as fluent interaction requires both. To complement our findings based on open-ended questionnaire answers, learners' fluency definitions could be methodologically further investigated with interviews.

As our analysis showed that fluency can be understood in different ways, ranging from narrow to very broad definitions, it is very important to define fluency when it is addressed in research (see also the concluding chapter of this volume). In a similar vein, in language assessment more research is needed to investigate the phenomenon further. The challenge for language teaching and assessment is to bring researchers' and learners' perspectives closer (see also Tavakoli & Hunter, 2018). In particular, to support the learners in their learning process, it is important that their understanding of the assessment criteria matches teachers' and testers' understandings. Many fluency definitions in this study reflected non-technical, very broad understandings of the concept. Pre-service foreign language teachers could thus benefit from familiarising themselves with the more technical features of fluency, focusing on specific aspects of the spoken utterance. This would offer them concrete approaches to teaching learner fluency in the classroom. On the other hand, the learner understandings of fluency observed in this study were more geared towards communication or language proficiency as a whole than those that earlier fluency studies have commonly used as their primary perspective. This further underscores the importance of clarifying the concept of fluency – it benefits both fluency researchers as well as in-service teachers applying the concept in teaching.

## References

Chambers, F. (1997) What do we mean by fluency? *System* 25, 535–544.
Cook, V. (2012) Going beyond the native speaker in language teaching. *TESOL Quarterly* 33 (2), 189–209.
Derwing, T. and Munro, M. (2015) *Pronunciation Fundamentals: Evidence-based Perspectives for L2 Teaching and Research*. Amsterdam: John Benjamins.
Dörnyei, Z. (2007) *Research Methods in Applied Linguistics*. Oxford: Oxford University Press.
Dörnyei Z. and Kormos, J. (1998) Problem-solving mechanisms in L2 communication: A psycholinguistic perspective. *Studies in Second Language Acquisition* 20, 349–385.
Fillmore, C.J. (1979) On fluency. In C.J. Fillmore, D. Kempler and W.S.-Y. Wang (eds) *Individual Differences in Language Ability and Language Behavior* (pp. 85–102). New York: Academic Press.
Freed, B.F. (1995) What makes us think that students who study abroad become fluent? In B.F. Freed (ed.) *Second Language Acquisition in a Study Abroad Context* (pp. 123–148). Amsterdam: John Benjamins.
Giles, H. and Ogay, T. (2007) Communication accommodation theory. In B.B. Whaley and W. Samter (eds) *Explaining Communication: Contemporary Theories and Exemplars* (pp. 293–310). Mahwah, NJ: Lawrence Erlbaum.
Götz, S. (2013) *Fluency in Native and Nonnative English speech*. Amsterdam: John Benjamins.
Housen, A., Kuiken, F. and Vedder, I. (eds) (2012) *Dimensions of L2 Performance and Proficiency: Complexity, Accuracy and Fluency in SLA*. Amsterdam: John Benjamins.
Kahng, J. (2014) Exploring utterance and cognitive fluency of L1 and L2 English speakers: Temporal measures and stimulated recall. *Language Learning* 64, 809–854.
Koponen, M. and Riggenbach, H. (2000) Overview: Varying perspectives on fluency. In H. Riggenbach (ed.) *Perspectives on Fluency* (pp. 5–24). Ann Arbor, MI: The University of Michigan Press.
Kormos, J. and Dénes, M. (2004) Exploring measures and perceptions of fluency in the speech of second language learners. *System* 32, 145–164.
Lennon, P. (1990) Investigating fluency in EFL: A quantitative approach. *Language Learning* 40, 387–417.
Lennon, P. (2000) The lexical element in spoken second language fluency. In H. Riggenbach (ed.) *Perspectives on Fluency* (pp. 25–42). Ann Arbor, MI: The University of Michigan Press.
Marton, F. (1981) Phenomenography: Describing conceptions of the world around us. *Instructional Science* 10, 177–200.
Mora, J.C. and Valls-Ferrer, M. (2012) Oral fluency, accuracy, and complexity in formal instruction and study abroad learning contexts. *TESOL Quarterly* 46, 610–641.
Olkkonen, S. (2017) *Second and Foreign Language Fluency from a Cognitive Perspective: Inefficiency and Control of Attention in Lexical Access*. Jyväskylä Studies in Humanities 314. Jyväskylä: University of Jyväskylä.
Peltonen P. (2017) Temporal fluency and problem-solving in interaction: An exploratory study of fluency resources in L2 dialogue. *System* 70, 1–13.
Peltonen, P. and Lintunen, P. (2016) Integrating quantitative and qualitative approaches in L2 fluency analysis: A study of Finnish-speaking and Swedish-speaking learners of English at two school levels. *European Journal of Applied Linguistics* 4, 209–238.
Préfontaine, Y. (2013) Perceptions of French fluency in second language speech production. *The Canadian Modern Language Review* 69 (3), 324–348.
Préfontaine, Y. and Kormos, J. (2016) A qualitative analysis of perceptions of fluency in second language French. *International Journal of Applied Linguistics in Language Teaching* 54, 151–169.

Riggenbach, H. (1991) Toward an understanding of fluency: A microanalysis of nonnative speaker conversations. *Discourse Processes* 14 (4), 423–441.

Rossiter, M.J. (2009) Perceptions of L2 fluency by native and non-native speakers of English. *The Canadian Modern Language Review* 65, 395–412.

Segalowitz, N. (2010) *Cognitive Bases of Second Language Fluency*. New York: Routledge.

Segalowitz, N. (2016) Second language fluency and its underlying cognitive and social determinants. *International Review of Applied Linguistics in Language Teaching* 54, 79–95.

Sin, S. (2010) Considerations of quality in phenomenographic research. *International Journal of Qualitative Methods* 9 (4), 305–319.

Skehan, P. (2009) Modelling second language performance: Integrating complexity, accuracy, fluency, and lexis. *Applied Linguistics* 30, 510–532.

Tavakoli, P. (2016) Fluency in monologic and dialogic task performance: Challenges in defining and measuring L2 fluency. *International Review of Applied Linguistics in Language Teaching* 54, 133–150.

Tavakoli, P. and Hunter, A.-M. (2018) Is fluency being 'neglected' in the classroom? Teacher understanding of fluency and related classroom practices. *Language Teaching Research* 22 (3), 330–349.

Tergujeff, E. (2013) *English Pronunciation Teaching in Finland*. Jyväskylä: University of Jyväskylä.

Tight, M. (2016) Phenomenography: The development and application of an innovative research design in higher education research. *International Journal of Social Research Methodology* 19 (3), 319–338.

Wright, C. and Tavakoli, P. (2016) New directions and developments in defining, analyzing and measuring L2 speech fluency. *International Review of Applied Linguistics in Language Teaching* 54, 73–77.

# 3 Cognitive Fluency in L2: What Inaccuracies Can Reveal about Processing and Proficiency

Sanna Olkkonen and Maarit Mutta

### Introduction

In this chapter, the focus is on the cognitive aspects of second language (L2) fluency, the idea being that the concept of cognitive fluency and the psychology-oriented framework may present new approaches and understanding of the surface fluency phenomena (i.e. utterance fluency in Segalowitz's terms, 2010). To the study of the relationship between fluency and L2 proficiency, the cognitive fluency framework can, furthermore, offer novel tasks that help to avoid overlap between oral proficiency and fluency assessment. The different aspects of cognitive fluency are illustrated, and the concept of disfluency (i.e. inaccuracy in the context of cognitive fluency) is discussed in the empirical part of this chapter, with some examples of L2 lexical access in visually presented tasks by Russian learners of Finnish as a second language (L2). The relevance of cognitive fluency and disfluency are briefly discussed in relation to a wider framework of fluency (cognitive, utterance and perceived).

The main focus of this chapter is to present a review of how cognitive fluency can be defined. It is, in addition, accompanied by an empirical section with the purpose of illustrating the theoretical framework with relevant examples on lexical access. The examples are a part of the data gathered with the study design from Olkkonen (2017), but with a previously unreported population. The chapter is divided into two main sections: the review part (Definition and Aspects of Cognitive Fluency) and empirical part (Relationship between Cognitive Fluency and Lexical Access). The first section introduces different aspects of cognitive fluency, namely those of automatic and controlled processes. The second section provides examples of inaccuracies in lexical access processing.

Furthermore, the relationship between cognitive fluency, disfluencies and L2 proficiency are discussed.

## Definition and Aspects of Cognitive Fluency

The overall concept of cognitive fluency is somewhat under-defined and elusive, and researchers have explored it in varying ways, for instance, with working memory capacity (Georgiadou & Roehr-Brackin, 2016), the size of vocabulary (De Jong & Bosker, 2013), or stimulated recall of disfluencies with retrospective interviews (Kahng, 2014). However, these are not straightforward fluency measures as Segalowitz (2016) points out: vocabulary measures an aspect of knowledge, interviews are highly indirect and capture only certain conscious aspects of cognitive processing and, while working memory capacity influences the fluency of language use, it is not a sufficient measure by itself. Figure 3.1 illustrates the diversity of the concept of fluency related to cognitive processing (Olkkonen, 2017: 18).

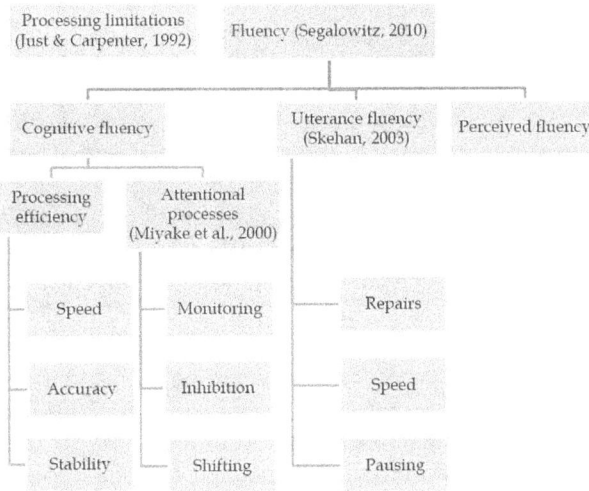

**Figure 3.1** Construction of the fluency concept

Segalowitz (2010: 165) uses the description of cognitive fluency as 'the efficiency of operation of the underlying processes' of utterance production, and the important question is how these are reflected in the measurable surface level of fluency (see also, Schmidt, 1992). Cognitive fluency is closely related to the utterance fluency, that is, the surface fluency, which is thought to reflect the cognitive fluency (e.g. Segalowitz, 2010). The difference between cognitive studies on the one hand and Second Language Acquisition (SLA) and utterance fluency studies on the other hand is that in SLA cognitive processes are seen as a background factor, but in the cognitive perspective, they are the object of study – but, on the other hand, cognitive fluency usually cannot be measured without some sort of surface realisations (Olkkonen & Peltonen, 2017). For measuring the efficiency or fluency of these underlying processes, a valuable insight comes from Lennon (2000: 27), who states that 'for most speakers in most situations, processing demands, rather than deficient knowledge, will limit fluency'. The limits of cognitive processing are, for their part, determined by the capacity of working memory, as is described by Just and Carpenter (1992) in their influential theory of information processing. These capacity limitations mean that the basic low-level processes (e.g. phonological processing) have to operate mostly automatically for the resources to be available for higher, controlled mental processes (e.g. planning and revising in writing, Olive & Kellogg, 2002; in reading, see Grabe, 2009). Therefore, the study of cognitive fluency may be understood as the balance between the automatic and controlled processes in language use (Segalowitz, 2010: 91), which we shall examine next.

## Automatic processing and efficiency

Automatically operating low-level processes are a prerequisite for a fluent performance. These low-level, automatic processes include, for example, phonological processing, word recognition, syntactic parsing and forming links between the grammatical categories and conceptual interpretations (Schmidt, 1992; Segalowitz & Frenkiel-Fishman, 2005). They are quick, accurate and mostly immune to interference from outside sources, but at the same time they are unconscious, unintentional and involuntary (Grabe, 2009). Automaticity is often used interchangeably with efficiency, which is described as the speed and accuracy of performance (see also Figure 3.1). Lack of cognitive resources may be seen in the trade-off between these, especially at the beginning of language learning, and language users may prefer either quick or accurate performance (Grabe, 2009; Jeon, 2012). These differences in preferences affect fluency and the types of disfluencies that are produced: for instance, in L2 reading, someone who wants to read quickly may skip words, and another person may repeat them in order to be sure of their accuracy. Therefore, Segalowitz (2010) has stressed that efficiency and automaticity are not synonymous, and that automaticity requires more than speeding-up of the operation. There should be mental restructuring as well, which is reflected in the stability of performance (decrease in the variability of reaction times). Support for the measurement of stability, however, remains somewhat meagre (Hulstijn *et al.*, 2009). To sum up, fluent cognitive processing is automatic and efficient, which can be measured (at least to a degree) by the speed and accuracy of performance. Automaticity and efficiency develop gradually with repetition and training, which then in turn releases (i.e. this gradual development) cognitive resources for the attention-requiring controlled actions.

## Controlled processes and executive functions

Controlled processes are conscious and flexible actions that are needed in all proficient performance, in monitoring, maintaining goals and making decisions that ascertain successful communication in real-life environments (Schmidt, 1992). For instance, verbal protocols (e.g. think-aloud methods) are used to reveal mental processes to which people are paying conscious attention ('heeded' information) during carrying out different kind of activities (e.g. Ericsson & Simon, 1996). Segalowitz and Frenkiel-Fishman (2005) propose that the ability to control attention is one of the most important mechanisms that differentiate expert language users from beginners, and as the control of attention requires cognitive resources, it has an influence on the surface-level fluency (i.e. utterance fluency) as well. Control of attention can be operationalised in many ways (see Segalowitz, 2010: 93) and, for example Segalowitz and Frenkiel-Fishman (2005) have measured it with the control of attention-directing functions of language (reaction times to categorising time adverbials and connectors such as *despite, because*). On the other hand, in cognitive psychology, attention and its control have also been examined under the concept of working memory and its central executive (Baddeley, 1996; Grabe, 2009: 35), which are closely related and correlated to neuropsychological counterparts, executive functions (McCabe *et al.*, 2010). An advantage of these concepts is that they can be examined at the neural level, as the neuroimaging studies have placed the executive functions in the frontal lobe areas and studies can be conducted on how, for example, word retrieval tasks influence the activation in these areas (Bialystok *et al.*, 2008).

Executive functions are often divided into monitoring/updating, inhibition and switching (Miyake *et al.*, 2000; see also Figure 3.1). First, monitoring is used for upcoming information, updating and revising it for its relevance and replacing old information with new. This feature is active and dynamic, and it is sometimes conflated with working memory (e.g. Drijbooms *et al.*, 2015). Controlled attention is required, for example, in monitoring one's own speech for errors as well as other's understanding, and correcting the output accordingly (Engle *et al.*, 1999).

Second, inhibition is the ability to suppress information that is irrelevant or distracting in the current situation; for example, inhibiting word activation in the first language (L1) requires cognitive resources (see e.g. Veivo, 2017). Eye-tracking studies on reading have revealed that fluent readers pre-process the upcoming material, and this activation has to be suppressed sufficiently, as well as the activation of the previous item (Jones *et al.*, 2008). Inhibition is often studied with a Stroop task, which requires participants to name the colour of the ink of written words while ignoring the word. When the ink is incongruent with the word, reaction times are slower because of the automatic activation of the word that has to be suppressed (Stroop, 1935; for a review, MacLeod, 1991). Marian *et al.* (2013) found a stronger Stroop effect for L1 and L2 than for L3 (the least proficient foreign language). This was explained by a weaker activation of the least proficient language, which was easier to inhibit than the activation of the stronger languages. Bialystok *et al.* (2008) found that bilinguals performed better than monolinguals in letter fluency tasks, where participants were asked to name as many things in categories (animals) or beginning with a certain letter (while inhibiting words from the same word family). The explanation for this result was that the task required both monitoring and inhibition, which are supposed to be more developed for bilinguals who have to inhibit other languages constantly.

Third, fluent performance requires efficient shifting between different tasks, by controlling attention actively. Segalowitz and Frenkiel-Fishman (2005) found that the reaction times in shifting between categorising time adverbials and connectors were slower in L1 than in L2. Meuter and Allport (1999) reported similar findings and, in addition, that when switching between the languages, the switch-cost (i.e. slower reaction time) was consistently stronger when switching from L2 to L1 than vice-versa. This is explained as a greater need to suppress the stronger language in order to be able to perform in the L2 in the first place. These results displaying the balance between fluent and disfluent cognitive processing have an influence on the interpretation of the surface fluency features, as we shall see next.

## Cognitive fluency, disfluencies and L2 proficiency

One major difference between the utterance and cognitive fluency perspectives, as pointed out by De Jong (2016), lies in how they approach disfluencies. In SLA studies, they are often seen as something negative – however, a more positive approach to disfluencies can be seen in recent SLA studies (e.g. Peltonen, 2017); in psycholinguistics, they have had a positive role, e.g. for a listener's understanding in interaction. As Lennon (1990) has concluded, L1 speech is not without interruptions either, and includes pausing, self-corrections and repetitions. This is in line with Ehri's (1991) remark that certain types of errors may also be connected to the development of language skills, appearing only after a certain proficiency threshold (also e.g. Engelhardt *et al.*, 2010). This should be borne in mind when assessing disfluencies in any language. Approaching the use of utterance fluency features from a cognitive fluency perspective (i.e. the balance between automatic and controlled processes) may offer answers to why certain utterance fluency phenomena have been found to be related to proficiency, while some have not (De Jong *et al.*, 2015; Kahng, 2014; Kormos, 2000). This is because the disfluencies resulting from automatic and controlled processes may not relate to language proficiency in a similar manner.

The problems in automaticity can be thought of as inefficient performance, which should be mostly related to low proficiency. This means that the low-level processes (e.g. decoding, lexical access) use the resources instead of the more global planning and monitoring processes, and speed and accuracy may also compete for the same limited resources, thus creating a trade-off situation. In the context of rapid naming and word list reading tasks, the cognitive disfluency may then materialise on the utterance level in either a slow performance, or an inaccurate one, such as guessing the words in a text, skipping difficult-looking items, or not correcting errors.

On the other hand, the phenomena related to control of attention may produce quite different kind of disfluencies. For example, monitoring own and others' speech and comprehension can produce self- or other-corrections. Kormos (2000) found that people corrected a larger proportion of their errors in L1 and some types of repairs were more prevalent in L1 than L2 (see also, Kahng, 2014). She concludes that 'monitoring for errors is generally more efficient in L1 than L2' (Kormos, 2000: 368); furthermore, correcting seems to be a conscious process, in which the speaker has to decide whether to engage or not (see also, Georgiadou & Roehr-Brackin, 2016), and these findings point to more strategic than proficiency-related factors in the distribution of corrections.

As was shown in the previous section, switching and inhibition are often more difficult in a more proficient language for which the activation is more automatic, whether an L1 or an L2 compared to a one less-developed (Marian *et al.*, 2013; Meuter & Allport, 1999). Therefore, as a result, a more proficient language may include disfluencies that a language with less strong activation does not and where the need to suppress irrelevant material is less pronounced. As these examples highlight, the different disfluencies can also be a result of a conscious control of attention, and, as a result, the term 'inaccuracy' seems a more appropriate term for them as it covers more aptly these conscious aspects and different functions. This term also serves in drawing a distinction with how the term 'disfluency' is used in utterance fluency studies, with somewhat different connotations (see De Jong *et al.*, 2015; Kahng, 2014). It is important to note that in SLA studies, accuracy is usually related to the CAF (complexity, accuracy, fluency) framework, where fluency and accuracy are separate but related concepts (Housen & Kuiken, 2009). From the cognitive viewpoint, accuracy and fluency are more complementary concepts, combining into fluency (e.g. Grabe, 2009: 292).

In addition to the differences in how disfluencies can be interpreted, cognitive and utterance fluency also differ in the kind of tasks that are used in measuring them. Whereas the latter is usually examined from spoken material, the former has often been measured by visual tasks (Segalowitz, 2016). For example, in the Stroop task, rapidly presented words and animacy judgment tasks are based on visually presented material. The majority of the tasks measuring cognitive processing and executive functions are, furthermore, word-level tasks and mostly rely on efficient lexical access; consequently, in L1 studies, fluent lexical access has been shown to play an important role in further language learning, and its importance in, for example, reading development has been demonstrated widely (see e.g. Ehri, 1991; Georgiou *et al.*, 2013).

In the L2 environment, the importance of fluent lexical access has been shown in relation to reading comprehension, and this connection seems to be even stronger than in L1 reading (Verhoeven, 2000). Furthermore, it is substantial in different phases of the writing process (Drijbooms *et al.*, 2015; Manchón *et al.*, 2007) and in speaking in order to attain 'normal speech rate' (Schmidt, 1992); in other words, not pausing excessively to find appropriate words during speaking. Interestingly, oral lexical access (reading words aloud) has been shown to be a better predictor of reading comprehension than silent reading tasks (Fuchs *et al.*, 2001; see also Košak-Babuder *et al.*, 2019). This suggests that the interaction between lexical access and reading comprehension does not stem solely from the ability to read; as a consequence, Wolf (1986) has proposed that the connection might stem from the executive functions (inhibition and control of attention) needed in performing both lexical retrieval and reading comprehension (also Drijbooms *et al.*, 2015). Therefore, as opposed to speaking tasks, visually presented lexical access tasks (e.g. rapid naming, RAN or RAS, tasks which measure the speed of lexical retrieval) may offer standardised measures that tap into cognitive operations rather than into speaking skills. The RAS task together with word list reading can be used to measure fluency of lexical access, which is also related to the proficiency level of different linguistic skills, such as reading comprehension (Olkkonen, 2017; Verhoeven, 2000), writing process (Drijbooms *et al.*, 2015; Manchón *et al.*, 2007), L2 spoken word recognition (Veivo *et al.*, 2016) and speaking (Schmidt, 1992; also, Kormos, 2000). For capturing cognitive fluency, the advantage of the RAS task together with word list reading seems to be that they are less dependent on individual speaking styles or conversational skills than speaking tasks, meaning that there is less overlap between cognitive fluency measures and proficiency measures. The role of lexical access is further discussed in the following section with some concrete examples from an L2 corpus.

## Relationship between Cognitive Fluency and Lexical Access

In a study by Olkkonen (2017), cognitive fluency was studied in lexical access tasks with Finnish-speaking learners of English from three age groups (age 10, 14 and 17; $n = 563$). The aim was to see how inefficient lexical access on the one hand and control of attention on the other were associated with the different proficiency levels. The proportions of the inaccuracies (i.e. disfluencies) revealed that in a task with the most automatised items (rapid naming, i.e. RAS task), most of the inaccuracies in all groups were related to attention control and their proportion was quite stable across the proficiency levels. In a more challenging task, reading a word list with less-automatised lexicon, the beginning learners corrected themselves significantly less in both L1 and L2 than the older students. All the groups, furthermore, had a tendency to correct themselves more often in L1 than in L2 (e.g. correcting skipped words). Therefore, the lower proficiency in a language could mean that fewer resources are available for attention direction, whether within individuals when comparing their L1 and L2, or between groups of different proficiency levels (see also, Kormos, 2000). In an ideal case, if the lower-level processes (i.e. decoding and word recognition) behind lexical retrieval are fluent and effortless, they result in accurate and rapid task performance. In this section, the following examples are examined according to the same framework, with a further data set of Russian-speaking second language learners of Finnish ($n = 184$, aged 8–13, $M = 11$). Their data will be discussed in order to illustrate the balance between fluent and disfluent cognitive processing in lexical access.[1]

Learners of a second (i.e. language of the place of residence) and a foreign language (i.e. language learned in classroom) are quite often treated as a one group (see Grabe, 2009: 4; Segalowitz, 2010: 2) and in most instances that may be quite valid. However, it is evident that the learning situations do differ, and when examining the applicability of a framework, it is of interest whether there are differences between the two learning environments and how this might affect the overall fluency profiles (see e.g. Jeon & Yamashita, 2014). The Russian learners of Finnish are, in addition to classroom learning context, learning the language in a natural context, and therefore, their language skills in both L1 and L2 were very varied. Lexical access fluency was measured in both L1 and L2 with two visual tasks: a rapid naming task RAS (colours, numbers, letters, objects; Rapid Alternating Stimulus, from Ahonen *et al.*, 2003), in which the participant has to rapidly name items following each other in line (in five rows on a paper), and a reading aloud from a Word List (105 words on a paper) in just one minute (from Häyrinen *et al.*, 1999; Russian versions by DIALUKI project). The time-pressure in the tasks was thought to ensure both the speed and accuracy components of the overall cognitive fluency measure. The answers were analysed according to a procedure from Olkkonen (2017), by which the inaccuracies or disfluencies were categorised as resulting either from inefficiency (guessing, skipping, same-category and pronunciation problems) or from attention-control (self-corrections, inhibition and shifting problems).

In these illustrative data, the overall accuracy rates (percentages of accurately and fluently produced items in the tasks) revealed that these second language learners performed more accurately in their L2 tasks than in L1 (RAS L1 95% and L2 96%, Word List L1 77% and L2 81%). The results highlight the problem of the L1–L2 division regarding the L2 speakers, especially when studying second language learners, and show the difficulty of drawing a clear-cut line between those who could be treated as a L1 or L2 speaker of a certain language. In this data set, 90% of the participants reported Russian as the most used language at home, which offers some support for treating them as (bilingual) Russian speakers. The executive control benefits usually assigned to bilinguals are an important factor as well, but the question is how balanced a bilingual the language user has to be and whether the L1 skills in general are on a sufficient level for these benefits (Bialystok *et al.*, 2008). For example, the exposure to L1 for second language learners may be quite limited in their new societal context, and the students in the current study produced considerable amounts of inaccuracies in their L1 tasks as well. Therefore, controlling for the L1 behaviour is even more relevant for a more grounded assessment of fluency of second than of foreign language learners (see e.g. De Jong *et al.*, 2015; Lennon, 1990; Segalowitz & Frenkiel-Fishman, 2005).

When looking at the differences between the types of inaccuracy, either relating to inefficiency or attention-control, the largest proportion of the inaccuracies in the current data (see Figure 3.2) was related to inefficiency in RAS L1 (62% of L1 inaccuracies) and in both Word Lists (85–88% of all inaccuracies); see Appendix, Table 3.1 for frequencies and percentages of types of inaccuracies by task and language in the illustrative data.

The inefficiency inaccuracies are often due to pronunciation problems; in this case they constituted most of the inefficiency inaccuracies, which is especially interesting in the case of RAS L1, a task with vocabulary that should be well automatised for students of this age. In the Word List, the students needed to have command of two different writing systems (Latin vs Cyrillic alphabet), and for reading aloud Russian words, in general, the stress placement is particularly difficult: it is not fixed, it is distinctive, and it affects the quality of the vowels. These were the major challenges with the most error-prone words. Also, several consecutive consonants caused difficulties for pronunciation (most difficult words being *должный*

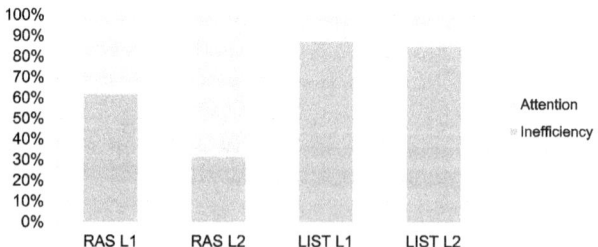

**Figure 3.2** Proportion of inaccuracies relating to attention and inefficiency in the tasks

[dolszhnyj] 'due, indebted' and *являться* [javljat'sja] 'to appear'). Difficulties in the L2 pronunciation were, first of all, related to the nature of Finnish as an agglutinative language, with considerable inflection and derivation. The resulting long words posit challenges to sight-word reading (the longest word in the list being a 22-letter *prosessikirjoittaminen* 'process writing'; for sight-word reading, see Ehri 1991). Another source of difficulties can be the quality of letters, as in L2 Finnish the quantity of vowels and consonants was especially problematic being a distinctive property in Finnish but not in Russian (Ylinen *et al.*, 2005): e.g. p*u*ro 'creek' > p*uu*ro 'porridge'; *elektr*o*niikka* 'electronics' > elektr*oo*ni*k*a; *ranni*k*ko* 'coast' > ranni*k*o; and also the articulation locations, such as *sääri* ['sæːri] 'leg' > *saari* ['sɑːri] 'island'. Noteworthy here is that even beginning readers of L1 Finnish rarely make these kinds of mistakes, with the exception of dyslexics, who often have difficulties with quantity as well (e.g. Richardson *et al.*, 2003).

Of the other categories of inefficiency, the phenomenon of guessing (based on the form of the target language) in the RAS task included, for example, 'A' interpreted as '4'. This phenomenon was not very frequent in the RAS task (see Appendix); however, it was quite prevalent in both Word Lists. Guessing usually results in real, more frequent words (Balota *et al.*, 2006), which graphemically resemble the target words. These were either conjugated or were in some other way a modified form of the target words, or completely different words or even novel creations. Most often the non-target words were more familiar or frequent words, as was expected, and, interestingly, often similar to the ones produced by the L1 Finnish speakers, such as *liian* 'too' > *liina* 'cloth', and *kiulu* 'pail' > *kuilu* 'gorge', *kiukku* 'anger'. For its part, the skipping of items means that these are not uttered, and this can happen either accidentally (due to too rapid a performance) or purposefully (avoiding difficult-looking items). This distinction could not be distinguished with our tasks, but could be examined with study designs using, for instance, eye-tracking. In this corpus, a considerable number of inaccuracies in the RAS task were within-category inaccuracies, such as green uttered as blue, or six as seven. Their proportions did not differ between L1 and L2, and it can be hypothesised that this kind of error can happen due to the speed requirement (trade-off phenomenon), and perhaps a strategic decision on whether to pause to correct or not (Georgiadou & Roehr-Brackin, 2016; Kormos, 2000).

Turning to the attention-control inaccuracies, self-corrections were here the second most common type of inaccuracy in both Word Lists and the most common inaccuracy in RAS L2. RAS is by nature an automatic task, designed to diagnose severe learning problems rather than distinguishing normally developing children, and differences at these levels of proficiency should already be minimal (Wolf, 1986). Therefore, the substantial role of attention-control inaccuracies in RAS was in line with the initial hypothesis when compared to the more challenging and resource-demanding Word List reading. However, the finding that the students had more attention-control inaccuracies in L2 than in L1 was not expected; on the other hand, when taking into account their better overall accuracy scores in L2 than L1 (see above), this seems again to support the overall resource theory.

Inaccuracies related to inhibition problems mean that some distracting information is not properly suppressed. For instance, there were some occasions in the Word List task, when, from the succeeding word, a plural ending was attached to the target word; targeted words under each other were *kyynel* (singular) – *pyyhkeet* (plural), but a participant produced:

42. kyynel > kyynel/eet 'tear – tear/s'
43. pyyhk/eet 'towel/s'

This may mean that the reading occurs so fast that the readers' eyes are already scanning the next word when uttering the previous one. The eye-tracking methodology could be used to reveal this kind of pre-processing of up-coming material (Jones *et al.*, 2008). The last category, problems in shifting or switching, applied only to the RAS task and the inaccuracies resulted from the task demand of switching between the categories (alternating between numbers, letters and colours). An example of this would be a number '6', that is followed by a letter 'S', and because of difficulty in switching from the activated category of numbers, the letter is instead read as 'seven'. These two last categories of attention-control, namely inhibition and shifting problems are not well presented in the data as these tasks were not designed to measure these phenomena. Instead, Stroop or letter fluency tasks should be used (Bialystok *et al.*, 2008; McCabe *et al.*, 2010; Miyake *et al.*, 2000); however, the close to equal proportions of shifting problems in L1 and L2 hint again that not all disfluencies are signs of low language skills.

## Conclusion

The review part of the current chapter discussed the fluency and disfluency phenomena by defining them from the cognitive perspective: as a question of balance between automaticity and efficiency, and attention-control phenomena. The measurement of cognitive fluency was also related to the concept of utterance fluency as we discussed its relationship with the utterance fluency phenomena, and how these two relate to L2 proficiency. The framework was illustrated with examples of lexical access measured by two visual tasks in the empirical part of this chapter. The lower-level processes, such as word recognition and retrieval, should be accurate and rapid in order to perform in an efficient and automatic way. This automatic and effortless processing creates the fundamental basis for fluent surface realisations, that is, oral and written language performance. Thus, it is closely related to utterance fluency in Segalowitz's

(2010) terms. However, also discussed was the issue that as the effortless processing frees up resources, more controlled processing aspects can be applied and this may produce inaccuracies that are not indicative of low proficiency but of strategic and conscious language use (e.g. Marian *et al.*, 2013; Meuter & Allport, 1999).

The discussion and illustrative examples presented offer support for the hypothesis that a more individual, cognition-related analysis may offer novel ways to explain the variable findings between surface fluency phenomena and L2 proficiency (see De Jong, 2016) and that the easy, visual tasks designed to tap into the cognitive processing may be able to tease out differences in L2 proficiency profiles that the broader speaking tasks miss. The distributions of types of inaccuracies or disfluencies related to inefficiency (guessing, skipping, within-category, pronunciation problems) or to attention-control (self-corrections, inhibition and shifting problems) seem to vary according to different learning contexts and this should be taken into account when studying these phenomena. As has been shown with some of the other repair disfluencies, such as repetitions (Kahng, 2014; Olkkonen & Peltonen, 2017) these attention-related inaccuracies seem not to be consistently related to proficiency or the lack of it, but should be studied in the more individual, functional and strategical frameworks (De Jong *et al.*, 2015; Kormos, 2000). Therefore, for future studies, designs tapping into the executive functions in a more targeted way than was possible in the empirical part of the current example, such as Stroop tasks, or eye-tracking, would contribute to further understanding of how cognitive fluency functions. Furthermore, a longitudinal setting would charter the possible changes in processing profiles within individuals. Overall, the aim of this discussion was to highlight the benefits of a multi-disciplinary approach to fluency, both in terms of methods and theory building.

## Note

(1) The data were a part of a larger DIALUKI project (see Alderson *et al.*, 2014), aimed at diagnosing reading and writing in a second and foreign language.

## References

Ahonen. T., Tuovinen, S. and Leppäsaari, T. (2003) *Nopean sarjallisen nimeämisen testi* [The test of rapid serial naming. Research reports.]. Jyväskylä, Finland: Haukkaranta school & Niilo Mäki Institute.

Alderson, J.C., Haapakangas, E.-L., Huhta, A., Nieminen, L. and Ullakonoja, R. (2014) *The Diagnosis of Reading in a Second or Foreign Language*. New York: Routledge.

Baddeley, A. (1996) Exploring the Central Executive. *The Quarterly Journal of Experimental Psychology Section A* 49, 5–28.

Balota, D.A., Yap, M.J. and Cortese, M.J. (2006) Visual word recognition: The journey from features to meaning (A travel update). In M. Traxler and M.A. Gernsbacher (eds) *Handbook of Psycholinguistics* (2nd edn, pp. 285–375). Amsterdam: Academic Press.

Bialystok, E., Craik, F.I.M. and Luk, G. (2008) Lexical access in bilinguals: Effects of vocabulary size and executive control. *Journal of Neurolinguistics* 21, 522–538.

De Jong, N.H. (2016) Fluency in second language assessment. In D. Tsagari and J. Banerjee (eds) *Handbook of Second Language Assessment* (pp. 203–218). Berlin: De Gruyter Mouton.

De Jong, N.H. and Bosker, H.R. (2013) Choosing a threshold for silent pauses to measure second language fluency. In R. Eklund (ed.) *Proceedings of Disfluency in Spontaneous Speech* (pp. 17–20). Stockholm: Royal Institute of Technology (KTH).

De Jong, N.H., Groenhout, R., Schoonen, R. and Hulstijn, J.H. (2015) Second language fluency: Speaking style or proficiency? Correcting measures of second language fluency for first language behavior. *Applied Psycholinguistics* 36, 223–243.

Drijbooms, E., Groen, M.A. and Verhoeven, L. (2015) The contribution of executive functions to narrative writing in fourth grade children. *Reading & Writing: An Interdisciplinary Journal* 29, 989–1011.

Ehri, L. (1991) Development of the ability to read words. In R. Barr, M. Kamil, P. Mosenthal and P.D. Pearson (eds) *Handbook of Reading Research* (pp. 383–417). NY: Longman.

Engelhardt P.E., Corley, M., Nigg, J.T. and Ferreira, F. (2010) The role of inhibition in the production of disfluencies. *Journal of Memory & Cognition* 38, 617–628.

Engle, R.W., Tuholski, S.W., Laughlin, J.E. and Conway, A.R.A. (1999) Working memory, short-term memory and general fluid intelligence: A latent variable approach. *Journal of Experimental Psychology: General* 128, 309–331.

Ericsson, K.A. and Simon, H.A. (1996) *Protocol Analysis. Verbal Reports as Data* (1st edn) 1984. Cambridge, MA: The MIT Press.

Fuchs, L.S., Fuchs, D., Hosp, M.K. and Jenkins, J.R. (2001) Oral reading fluency as an indicator of reading competence: A theoretical, empirical, and historical analysis. *Scientific Studies of Reading* 5, 239–256.

Georgiadou, E. and Roehr-Brackin, K. (2016) Investigating executive working memory and phonological short-term memory in relation to fluency and self-repair behavior in L2 speech. *Journal of Psycholinguistic Research* 46, 877–895.

Georgiou, G.K., Parrila, R., Cui, Y. and Papadopoulos, T.C. (2013) Why is rapid automatized naming related to reading? *Journal of Experimental Child Psychology* 115, 218–225.

Grabe, W. (2009) *Reading in a Second Language: Moving from Theory to Practice.* Cambridge: Cambridge University Press.

Häyrinen, T., Serenius-Sirve, S. and Korkman, M. (1999) *Lukilasse. Lukemisen, kirjoittamisen ja laskemisen seulontatestistö peruskoulun ala-asteen luokille 1–6.* [The Lukilasse graded achievement package for comprehensive school age children.] Helsinki: Psykologien Kustannus Oy.

Housen, A. and Kuiken, F. (2009) Complexity, accuracy, and fluency in second language acquisition. *Applied Linguistics* 30, 461–473.

Hulstijn, J., Van Gelderen, A. and Schoonen, R. (2009) Automatization in second-language acquisition: What does the coefficient of variation tell us? *Applied Psycholinguistics* 30, 555–582.

Jeon, E.H. (2012) Oral reading fluency in second language reading. *Reading in a Foreign Language* 24, 186–208.

Jeon, E.H. and Yamashita, J. (2014) L2 reading comprehension and its correlates: A meta-analysis. *Language Learning* 64, 160–212.

Jones, M.W., Obregón, M., Kelly, M.L. and Branigan, H.P. (2008) Elucidating the component processes involved in dyslexic and non-dyslexic reading fluency: An eye-tracking study. *Cognition* 109, 389–407.

Just, M.A. and Carpenter, P.A. (1992) A capacity theory of comprehension: Individual differences in working memory. *Psychological Review* 99, 122–149.

Kahng, J. (2014) Exploring utterance and cognitive fluency of L1 and L2 English speakers: Temporal measures and stimulated recall. *Language Learning* 64, 809–854.

Kormos, J. (2000) The role of attention in monitoring second language speech production. *Language Learning* 50, 343–384.
Košak-Babuder, M., Kormos, J., Ratajczak, M. and Pižorn, K. (2019) The effect of read-aloud assistance on the text comprehension of dyslexic and non-dyslexic English language learners. *Language Testing* 36 (1), 51–75.
Lennon, P. (1990) Investigating fluency in EFL: A quantitative approach. *Language Learning* 40, 387–417.
Lennon, P. (2000) The lexical element in spoken second language fluency. In H. Riggenbach (ed.) *Perspectives on Fluency* (pp. 25–42). Ann Arbor, MI: University of Michigan.
MacLeod, C. (1991) Half a century of research on the Stroop effect: An integrative review. *Psychological Bulletin* 109, 163–203.
Manchón, R.M., Murphy, L. and Roca de Larios, J. (2007) Lexical retrieval processes and strategies in second language writing: A synthesis of empirical research. *International Journal of English Studies* 7, 149–174.
Marian, V., Blumenfeld, H.K., Mizrahi, E., Kania, U. and Cordes, A.-K. (2013) Multilingual Stroop performance: Effects of trilingualism and proficiency on inhibitory control. *International Journal of Multilingualism* 10, 82–104.
McCabe, D.P., Roediger, H.L., McDaniel, M.A., Balota, D.A. and Hambrick, D.Z. (2010) The relationship between working memory capacity and executive functioning: Evidence for a common executive attention construct. *Neuropsychology* 24, 222–243.
Meuter, R.F.I. and Allport, A. (1999) Bilingual language switching in naming: Asymmetrical costs of language selection. *Journal of Memory and Language* 40, 25–40.
Miyake, A., Friedman, N.P., Emerson, M.J., Witzki, A.H., Howerter, A. and Wager, T.D. (2000) The unity and diversity of executive functions and their contributions to complex 'frontal lobe' tasks: A latent variable analysis. *Cognitive Psychology* 41, 49–100.
Olive, T. and Kellogg, R.T. (2002) Concurrent activation of high- and low-level production processes in written composition. *Memory & Cognition* 30, 594–600.
Olkkonen, S. (2017) *Second and Foreign Language Fluency from Cognitive Perspective: Inefficiency and Control of Attention in Lexical Access*. Jyväskylä Studies in Humanities 314. Jyväskylä: University of Jyväskylä.
Olkkonen, S. and Peltonen, P. (2017) Mitä on toisen kielen sujuvuus? Näkökulmia kognitiivisen ja puhetuotoksen sujuvuuden tutkimuksesta. [What is second language fluency? Perspectives from cognitive and utterance fluency research.] In M. Kuronen, P. Lintunen and T. Nieminen (eds) *Näkökulmia toisen kielen puheeseen – Insights into Second Language Speech*. AFinLA-e: Soveltavan kielitieteen tutkimuksia 10. Jyväskylä: Finnish Association of Applied Linguistics AFinLA, 234–257.
Peltonen, P. (2017) Temporal fluency and problem-solving in interaction: An exploratory study of fluency resources in L2 dialogue. *System* 70, 1–13.
Richardson, U., Leppänen, P., Leiwo, M. and Lyytinen, H. (2003) Speech perception of infants with high familial risk for dyslexia differ at the age of 6 Months. *Developmental Neuropsychology* 23, 385–397.
Schmidt, R. (1992) Psychological mechanisms underlying second language fluency. *Studies in Second Language Acquisition* 14, 357–385.
Segalowitz, N. (2010) *Cognitive Bases of Second Language Fluency*. New York: Routledge.
Segalowitz, N. (2016) Second language fluency and its underlying cognitive and social determinants. *International Review of Applied Linguistics in Language Teaching* 54, 79–95.
Segalowitz, N. and Frenkiel-Fishman, S. (2005) Attention control and ability level in a complex cognitive skill: Attention-shifting and second language proficiency. *Memory & Cognition* 33, 644–653.
Skehan, P. (2003) Task-based instruction. *Language Teaching* 36 (1), 1–14.
Stroop, J.R. (1935) Studies of interference in serial verbal reaction. *Journal of Experimental Psychology* 18, 643–662.

Veivo, O. (2017) *Orthographe et reconnaissance des mots parlés chez les apprenants tardifs de L2*. [Orthography and spoken-word recognition in late L2 learners]. Turku: University of Turku.

Veivo, O., Järvikivi, J, Porretta, V. and Hyönä, J. (2016) Orthographic activation in L2 spoken word recognition depends on proficiency: Evidence from eye-tracking. *Frontiers in Psychology* July 2016.

Verhoeven, L. (2000) Components in early second language reading and spelling. *Scientific Studies of Reading* 4, 313–330.

Wolf, M. (1986) Rapid Alternating Stimulus naming in the developmental dyslexias. *Brain and Language* 27, 360–379.

Ylinen, S., Shestakova, A., Alku, P. and Huotilainen, M. (2005) The perception of phonological quantity based on durational cues by native speakers, second-language users and nonspeakers of Finnish. *Language and Speech* 48, 313–338.

## Appendix: Example of inaccuracies in the illustrative data (L2)

Table 3.1 Frequencies and percentages of types of inaccuracies by task and language

| | RAS | | | | Word List | | | |
| --- | --- | --- | --- | --- | --- | --- | --- | --- |
| | L1 (Russian) | | L2 (Finnish) | | L1 (Russian) | | L2 (Finnish) | |
| | n | % | n | % | n | % | n | % |
| Inefficiency | | | | | | | | |
| Guessing | 6 | 1.39% | 1 | 0.43% | 380 | 15.65% | 145 | 8.73% |
| Skipping | 22 | 5.10% | 15 | 6.41% | 3 | 0.12% | 1 | 0.06% |
| Within-category | 67 | 15.55% | 37 | 15.81% | n/a | n/a | n/a | n/a |
| Pronunciation | 172 | 39.91% | 21 | 8.97% | 1742 | 71.75% | 1265 | 76.20% |
| % | | 61.95% | | 31.62% | | 87.52% | | 85.00% |
| Attention | | | | | | | | |
| Self-correction | 103 | 23.90% | 113 | 48.29% | 252 | 10.38% | 174 | 10.48% |
| Repetition | 34 | 7.89% | 28 | 11.97% | 38 | 1.57% | 60 | 3.61% |
| Inhibition | 1 | 0.23% | 3 | 1.28% | 13 | 0.54% | 15 | 0.90% |
| Shifting | 26 | 6.03% | 16 | 6.84% | n/a | n/a | n/a | n/a |
| % | | 38.05% | | 68.38% | | 12.48% | | 15.00% |

n/a = non-applicable to this task

# 4 Fluency in L2 Listening

Joanna Anckar and Outi Veivo

## Introduction

Among the four language skills, listening is probably least often associated with fluency. While it seems quite intuitive to describe a language user as a fluent speaker or writer, or as a fluent reader in his or her first language (L1) or in a second or foreign language (L2), it is less common to refer to someone as a fluent listener. However, although listening in your L1 is usually easy and effortless, listening in your L2 can be challenging in many ways. For instance, it can be difficult to recognise L2 sounds or words, or to understand the syntax of L2 phrases. Listening is a complex active process which requires receiving, constructing, negotiating and creating meanings and matching new information with existing knowledge (Rost, 2002). It does not result in any concrete or measurable products, such as utterances or texts. In this chapter, we use the term *listening* to refer to the listening process, the ability to process spoken language in real time. We use the term *listening comprehension* to refer to the outcome of this process, the understanding of overt and covert linguistic information, (Buck, 2001: 114). Another distinction to be made is that of one-way listening and interactive listening (see e.g. Vandergrift & Goh, 2012: 28). In one-way listening, listeners only listen, whereas in interactive listening, listeners alternate as listener and speaker. In the present chapter, our focus is on one-way listening, although we will also mention examples referring to interactive listening situations. How could fluency be defined in the context of L2 listening? What are the factors that can affect fluency in L2 listening? How could listening fluency be taught or assessed? These are the questions that we set out to answer in the present chapter.

## Listening in L2

In all listening, the listener has to be able to analyse the acoustic signal in order to understand the intended meanings of spoken utterances. This means recognising different sounds and words, understanding syntactic structures, analysing prosodic features such as stress and intonation, and

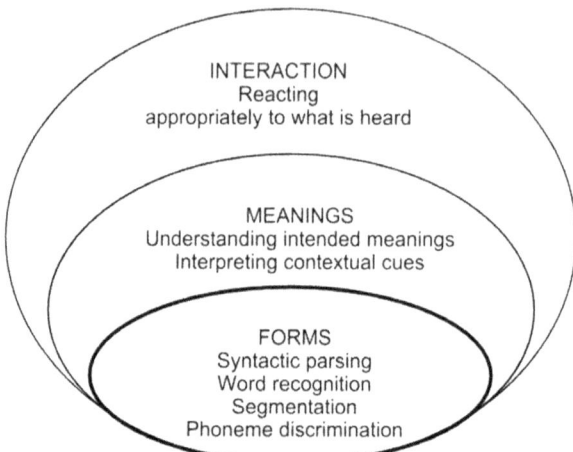

**Figure 4.1** Levels of processing in L2 listening

interpreting the communicative context (Wipf, 1984). The different levels of processing in L2 listening (based on e.g. Segalowitz, 2010; Vandergrift & Goh, 2012) are presented in Figure 4.1.

In the listening process, information can flow between the levels of forms, meanings and interaction in a bottom-up or top-down manner (e.g. Rost, 1990). In bottom-up processing, each lower level unit, for example a phoneme, has to be recognised before a higher level unit, for example a word, can be recognised. Bottom-up processing is based on linguistic knowledge only, whereas top-down processing also relies upon the listeners' prior experiential, pragmatic, cultural and discourse knowledge and on cues from a larger linguistic context. In listening, these two types of processing alternate and interact depending on the purpose of the listening task. If the task demands focusing on details in the speech flow, it is more likely that the listener will rely on bottom-up processing, whereas if the task demands the creation of an overall picture, the listener is more likely to rely on top-down processing (Flowerdew & Miller, 2005). Therefore, it is also possible to make a distinction between bottom-up fluency and top-down fluency in L2 listening, with bottom-up fluency referring to 'the ability to decode speech automatically' and top-down fluency to the ability to use knowledge, experience as well as strategies to facilitate the listening task (Rost, 2014: 282–285).

L2 listening is different from L1 listening because the entire auditory perception system as well as the syntactic and semantic decoding systems are shaped by linguistic experience with the L1. In the following section, we will discuss different aspects of fluency in L2 listening focusing especially on the possible influence of the L1 on L2 listening.

## Defining Fluency in L2 Listening

Segalowitz (2003: 384) defines fluency in an L2 as 'an ability in the second language to produce or comprehend utterances smoothly, rapidly, and accurately'. According to this definition, the three fundamental components of L2 fluency are smoothness, speed and accuracy (see also Segalowitz, 2000). Although fluency in an L2 often refers to speaking, Segalowitz does not distinguish between productive and receptive language skills. Taguchi *et al.* (2006: 1) define fluency in reading, the other receptive language subskill, as the ability 'to identify words in the text quickly and accurately with a minimal amount of attention'. Their definition shares the key components of Segalowitz' definition of speaking fluency: speed and accuracy. Further, a minimal amount of attention can be interpreted as referring to automaticity, just like smoothness. In what follows, we take as our hypothesis that these same key components could also be used to define fluency in L2 listening. To underline the experience of the listener, we will use the term effortlessness for smoothness, and discuss it together with the concept of automaticity which is often associated with fluency.

## Speed

Listening is fundamentally different from other language subskills because listeners cannot control the speed of processing themselves. Language processing in other subskills can be submitted to similar time constraints (e.g. speaking with many people in a debate, writing in an online chat or reading film subtitles), but in speaking, writing and reading language users can usually control the speed of processing more than in listening. This means that fluency in L2 listening always refers to the ability to cope with a speed defined by others, not by the listeners themselves. We will continue by exploring different factors which can influence the speed of processing spoken utterances.

First, to be able to recognise spoken words, the L2 listener must recognise the sounds they consist of. In continuous speech, such phenomena as assimilation, reduction, omission and elision can make this task difficult. The speed of discrimination of L2 sounds can also be influenced by previously existing L1 sound categories (Best, 1995; Flege, 2003) which can lead, for instance, to interpreting unfamiliar L2 sounds as belonging to L1 sound categories (Weber & Cutler, 2004). Second, the L2 listener has to be able to detect word boundaries from the speech flow rapidly. This segmentation process is based on language specific phonotactic cues and phonological knowledge (Carroll, 2004). It can be slowed if L1 segmentation strategies are transferred to L2 listening (Cutler *et al.*, 1992). Third, to comprehend the global meanings of utterances quickly, L2 listeners have to recognise spoken word forms rapidly and then associate these forms with their correct meanings. This process, too, can be slowed if the spoken words are confused with homophones or other similar-sounding L2 words (e.g. Rüschemeyer *et al.*, 2008), or L1 words (Spivey & Marian, 1999). If L2 listeners have problems in recognising L2 sounds, even phonologically more distant words in both L2 and L1 can be activated and retard the recognition process (see e.g. Weber & Cutler, 2004).

The speed of the listening comprehension process can also be affected by the listener's capacity to parse syntactic structures in L2. However, there is evidence that L2 listeners rely less on syntactic than on lexical cues in sentence processing (Papadopoulou & Clahsen, 2003). Additionally, other factors that can influence the speed of the listening process include textual features, for example being able to follow the semantic thread from one phrase to another, being able to understand non-literal meanings such as metaphors and idiomatic expressions, or being able to understand references to facts that are not explicitly mentioned by the speaker (see Dickinson, 1987). Speed is also essential in the top-down process of activating relevant and ignoring irrelevant stored information (Rost, 2014: 283). Last, in interactive listening situations speed can also refer to the ability to react immediately and appropriately to what is heard and thereby show that the message has been understood.

Taken together, we consider that fluent listening implies the ability to recognise L2 sounds and L2 words rapidly, and to make appropriate references to stored information quickly in order to understand the meaning of longer stretches of speech.

## Accuracy

Accuracy in listening can be defined as referring to the capacity to process spoken language with a sufficient degree of precision at different levels of processing, but also as the outcome of the listening process, that is, the ability to comprehend the meaning intended by the speaker accurately (cf. the 'default listening construct' described by Buck, 2001: 93). To be able to do this, the listener has to be successful at all the levels of processing described in the previous section: discriminating sounds, segmenting and recognising words, parsing sentences and interpreting contextual cues. Problems with accuracy at one level can lead to accuracy problems at another level. For instance, if new L2 sounds are misheard and interpreted as belonging to familiar L1 sound categories, it can result in the formation of non-accurate, or fuzzy, lexical representations in L2, which can slow down word recognition (Darcy *et al.*, 2013). Accuracy also includes a successful analysis of the communication situation in order to be able to identify contextual factors influencing the communication (see Council of Europe, 2001: 44–49; Dickinson, 1987). Further, we consider that accuracy also implies the listener's ability to adjust her/his processing to the demands of the listening task, and to use contextual cues to compensate for possible problems in lower level processing.

## Effortlessness and automaticity

There are no simple direct methods to obtain information about the listening process. Therefore, its effortlessness can best be evaluated by the listeners themselves, for example using verbal protocols (e.g. Cohen, 2014). Effortlessness relates to automaticity (e.g. Nation, 2014a; Rost, 2014; Tsai, 2014). It has also been used as a synonym for fluency, but we share Segalowitz' (2000: 403) view that automaticity and fluency are not synonyms because fluency in L2 listening is likely also to require controlled processing just as does fluency in L2 speaking. This view is also shared by Rost (2014), who underlines that L2 listeners can learn to regulate the processes involved in L2 listening and thereby become more fluent listeners. This includes the use of appropriate strategies to overcome processing challenges. Automaticity can refer to fast, effortless, ballistic processing which does not require conscious attention and which is not affected by the amount of information to be processed (Segalowitz, 2003). In L2 listening, we consider automaticity and effortlessness to be related: automaticity refers to an aspect of the listening process and effortlessness refers to the experience that the listener has of an automatic listening process.

Speed and accuracy in L2 listening can be affected by the activation of written word forms. For instance, Rost (2014: 288) mentions that the main goal of bottom-up listening is the ability to recognise phonological patterns directly and in longer chunks without 'mentally transcribing' them into written form. There is ample evidence that orthography can play a role in L1 listening (e.g. Ziegler & Ferrand, 1998), but its role in L2 listening has been less studied. However, orthography can have an even more important role in L2 listening if L2 learners have been exposed to written language in parallel to spoken language from the initial stages of L2 acquisition. Extensive exposure to written language may even lead to an imbalance with written L2 word forms being more familiar to the learners than spoken word forms (Veivo *et al.*, 2015). There is evidence that the orthographic systems of both L2 (e.g. Bartolotti *et al.*, 2013) and L1 (e.g. Hayes-Harb *et al.*, 2010) can interfere at multiple levels of L2 speech processing. This may have significant consequences for bottom-up fluency in L2 listening. For instance, the knowledge of the grapheme-to-phoneme correspondences of L1 can influence the perception of L2 sounds. Recent studies have also shown that orthographically similar words in both L2 and L1 are activated in the recognition of isolated spoken words in L2 (Veivo *et al.*, 2016, 2018). Whether this activation of orthography affects the speed and accuracy, and thereby fluency of L2 listening in more naturalistic listening situations is an interesting question for future studies.

To resume, we consider that the characteristics of speaking or reading fluency – speed, accuracy and effortlessness – also seem appropriate for defining fluency in L2 listening. Moreover, we assume that fluent listening in L2 implies the use of different strategies to overcome processing difficulties, for example the challenges of listening in a noisy environment. Therefore, we suggest that fluency in L2 listening could be defined as the ability to decode auditory input in L2 effortlessly, accurately and rapidly in order to comprehend the meanings intended by the speaker, and to use different strategies to overcome processing deficits. More empirical studies are needed to refine and to operationalise this definition, especially as far as effortlessness is concerned.

## Improving Fluency in L2 Listening

The goal of fluency in L2 listening can be considered to be the ability to deal with long stretches of speech in a wide range of discourse situations (Rost, 2014: 281). This ability is a part of a learner's proficiency in L2. Although listening in L2 can be challenging, fluency in listening can be improved in various ways with sufficient practice (Rost, 2014: 282). In what follows, we will discuss the relationship between fluency in listening and L2 proficiency, and present different methods that have been used to improve fluency in L2 listening.

### L2 proficiency and fluency in listening

The relationship between L2 proficiency and fluency invites differing views. Even if Nation (2014b: 38) takes the viewpoint that 'at every stage of language proficiency right from the very beginning lessons, you need to be fluent in using what you have already learnt', fluency is often used to describe only highly proficient L2 learners. Following Nation, we consider that listeners can be fluent at all proficiency levels. There are, however, some differences in listening between lower and higher proficiency learners.

Lower proficiency listeners typically focus more on bottom-up processing. They may believe that they need to focus on every single syllable or word in the flow of speech (Tsui & Fullilove, 1998). They often get stuck on unknown vocabulary, become frustrated and easily give up listening (Tsai, 2014: 314) instead of trying to infer and elaborate on the basis of the parts of the stream of speech that they have understood. In test situations, this can lead to missing the key information altogether, and thereby to answering test questions with random guesses, as was revealed by Anckar (2011), who used introspective responses to study L2 French listeners' behaviour in a multiple-choice listening test. However, it would be useful for a L2 listener to treat speech as lexical chunks or formulaic sequences, because they can be accessed as whole units in memory, thereby reducing the cognitive load in language processing (Herder & Sholdt, 2014: 38; Kirk, 2014: 105).

Higher proficiency listeners rely more on top-down processing and are able to use different listening strategies efficiently and interactively. They can predict information, take account of the rhetorical organisation of the text, guess the meanings of words, draw inferences and relate what they hear to previous knowledge and experiences (Berne, 2004; Rost, 2002; Vandergrift & Goh, 2012). Metacognitive capacities associated with more proficient listeners include monitoring one's own performance and areas of uncertainty, formulating clarifying questions about necessary information and evaluating how well one has understood (idem.). Therefore, in test situations, higher proficiency listeners are able to focus on global meanings and to eliminate unlikely and impossible answer options (Anckar, 2011). Although learners at different proficiency levels may be different listeners, they are likely to gain from various listening activities.

## Activities promoting bottom-up and top-down listening fluency

How could listening fluency be taught? If we consider that speed and automaticity of lower-level processes are important components of listening fluency, the first goal would be to find activities which allow the practising of discriminating sounds, segmenting the speech flow and recognising spoken words. As repetition is crucial for developing processing speed (Nation, 2014b: 39), this practice should be added to frequent and abundant exposure to spoken language (Chang, 2011). However, in order for the listening process to flow smoothly, and to overcome potential disfluencies, learners also need the capacity to use contextual cues and their world knowledge and experiences for faster and more efficient access to mental linguistic representations (Bybee, 2006, 2008; Ellis, 2002). Thereby, training top-down processing and the use of strategies becomes useful. Since motivation factors are essential, and since the use of a variety of activities in class promotes 'a holistic listening ability' (Siegel, 2014: 30), a combination of both bottom-up and top-down activities is likely to give best learning results.

Rost (2014: 282–289) proposes different activities for improving bottom-up fluency, especially to focus on different 'fast speech' phenomena, such as assimilation, elision and reductions. Bottom-up activities include word grab (identifying words and phrases after listening to a passage); partial dictation (listening to text passages and filling in gaps) and 3-2-1 listening (listening to a passage at different speed versions) (Rost, 2014). Another activity related to gap-filling, aiming at becoming familiar with connected speech, is using songs as a means to practise listening to typical patterns in spoken language (Carreira, 2014: 302). This activity can also reduce the anxiety which beginning learners may feel when faced with fast natural spoken discourse. An example of a process-oriented bottom-up activity is 'discovery listening' (Wilson, 2003). In this activity, learners are taken through a process of reconstructing a listening passage, and discovering what features on the level of sounds and vocabulary have been challenging for them and why.

Top-down fluency can be improved by different pre-listening, while-listening and post-listening activities (Rost, 2014). Pre-listening tasks aim at creating a conceptual or lexical framework to aid the actual listening process. While-listening and post-listening tasks include, for instance, note-taking combined with giving a presentation, or associating pictures with text content. For top-down fluency, it is beneficial to use authentic texts and tasks, to encourage learners' curiosity about new ideas, active engagement in listening tasks and the use of listening strategies (Rost, 2014). Extensive listening, which refers to 'all types of listening activities that allow learners to receive a lot of comprehensible and enjoyable listening input' (Renandya & Farrell, 2011: 56), and autonomous listening have also been found efficient in developing L2 listening fluency (Tsai, 2014: 315; cf. Ghaniabadi & Hashemi, 2016). Autonomous listening is based on the idea that learners can listen to spoken text passages at home as many times as they wish during one week and thereby gain opportunities to increase their processing speed.

Listening strategy use and preferences vary from one individual to another. When learners are presented with a variety of bottom-up and top-down strategies, they can select those that fit their personality and the specific task at hand (Yeldham & Gruba, 2016). Strategy instruction can also promote a greater sense of control of the listening process for L2 learners (Graham *et al.*, 2011). Bottom-up strategies include focusing on stressed words and discourse markers to facilitate comprehension, whereas top-down listening strategies include, for example, predicting text content, guessing the meaning of unfamiliar words, or inferring meaning with the help of the context (Yeldham & Gruba, 2016: 14). However, the usefulness of teaching listening strategies has also been questioned (Newton, 2017; Swan & Walter, 2017). This debate relates to the way strategies are taught. To actually gain from strategies, learners should have opportunities to practise them and feel that there is an advantage in using them (Rost, 2002: 157–158). Further, Field (2003) suggests that perceptual and segmentation processes should be focused on before strategy instruction.

Interactive listening fluency is based on cooperation and negotiation of meaning (Rost, 2014). It can be improved by activities such as the use of speaking circles, interactive stories and pair reconstruction (Rost, 2014: 289–292). These goal-oriented activities are likely to be meaningful and motivating to learners and thereby lead to more successful learning. All in all, motivational factors should always be considered when selecting activities and methods to improve fluency in L2 listening (see e.g. the 'affective frame' discussed in Flowerdew & Miller, 2005: 91–92; Rost & Wilson, 2013; Vandergrift & Goh, 2012: 72–73).

As stated above, L2 learners can be more familiar with written than spoken word forms. Chang (2009, 2011) and Chang and Millett (2014, 2016) suggest that fluency in L2 listening could be improved by using activities in which spoken word forms are presented together with their written counterparts. According to Chang (2011), using this 'reading-while-listening' method (R/L) before focusing on listening only can potentially improve comprehension, help learners acquire linguistic knowledge and motivate students to enjoy listening in the L2. Chang (2009) compared the listening-only and the R/L method in a classroom-based experiment with listeners on two proficiency levels and his results suggest that the R/L method also enhances students' confidence and motivates them to listen more carefully. A related method, but which includes an interactive element of peer cooperation, is the dictogloss method (suggested for example in Prince, 2013). The learners listen to a text twice, taking notes the second time, and then recreate the text in pairs or groups trying to arrive as close as possible to the original text, which they are eventually given to compare their production with. This type of activity combines bottom-up and top-down processing with the use of different strategies (Prince, 2013: 488).

After discussing the possibilities for improving fluency in L2 listening, we continue with a discussion of how listening fluency could be assessed.

### Assessing Fluency in L2 Listening

How then could fluency in L2 listening be assessed? Because fluency is not commonly associated with listening, it has not been operationalised as such. The different processing levels of L2 listening (see Figure 4.1 on p. 50) form what Buck (2001) calls the 'default listening construct'. In language proficiency assessment scales, these levels are referred to, for example, as the ability to recognise specific words and phrases in rapid speech, the ease of continuous listening and recall of main ideas; and the smoothness of listening behaviour in face-to-face interaction (Rost, 2014: 282). A systematic analysis of listening proficiency scales is not within the scope of the present article, but, as an example, the term 'fluency' is not mentioned explicitly in the descriptors of overall listening comprehension in the proficiency scales of *The Common European Framework of Reference for Languages* (CEFR) (Council of Europe, 2001). However, its sub-components are referred to at the three highest levels of the CEFR proficiency scale (B2, C1, C2). For example, at level C2, processing speed is mentioned: 'Has no difficulty in understanding any kind of spoken language, whether live or broadcast, delivered at fast native speed' (Council of Europe, 2001: 66). Although fluency is often associated with the processing of fast speech, even a less proficient L2 learner can be relatively fluent in L2 listening if the speech rate of the interlocutor is sufficiently slow.

Like listening comprehension, fluency in listening can only be assessed and tested indirectly. Although the result of the listening process, that is accuracy of comprehension, can be targeted fairly easily with comprehension tests, it is more difficult to evaluate the underlying fluency components of automaticity and effortlessness of an individual learner. In addition, the assessment situation can influence how L2 listeners behave. They may use their cognitive capacity for more controlled processes and strategies, not only to interpret the spoken input accurately, but also to cope with the assessment situation (Buck, 2001; Rost, 2002). According to Buck (2001: 113), spoken texts used for assessing L2 listening need to be (1) of sufficient length, (2) spoken at a sufficiently fast pace, (3) delivered in a 'real-time'-manner, and only listened to once, if possible and (4) 'genuine' with regard to such typical spoken language features as stress, intonation and the syntax of spoken discourse. These general conditions for assessing listening in the communicative framework seem essential also from the point of view of assessing listening fluency, since they imply automaticity and rapidity in the listening process. The communicative approach implies a purpose for using language, and a replication of the target-language use situation in the tasks used in an assessment situation. (On test task creation, see e.g. Buck, 2001: 134–153; Flowerdew & Miller, 2005: 198–209; Rost, 2002: 169–183).

Tasks used to assess bottom-up listening at the level of forms typically focus on only a limited part of an utterance. These include phonemic discrimination (e.g. minimal pairs), paraphrase recognition (e.g. meaning of idioms) and response evaluation (Buck, 2001: 62–65). The problem with these tasks is that they are rarely based on 'natural' streams of speech, in which sounds are affected by their phonological context, utterances contain hesitations as well as redundant elements, and meanings are constructed in a larger communicative context. Moreover, speed and automaticity do not seem to be challenged in these types of tasks. Within the integrative approach, listening tasks require learners to process sequences of speech in context (Buck, 2001: 67). These tasks, such as dictation, cloze-tests or other gap-filling tasks, combine the need for bottom-up fluency and top-down fluency. Buck (2001: 73) points out that in gap-filling tasks the construct measured depends on what information is demanded to be filled in the gaps. The listener may have to recognise and reproduce phonetic, lexical or syntactic elements, but even discourse knowledge and inferencing skills may be challenged.

Assessment tasks can also be chosen on the basis of the 'cognitive load' that they represent (Brown, 1995). To target L2 listening fluency, test tasks could thus be deliberately based on spoken texts presenting challenges for listening fluency, such as several speakers, speakers with less distinctive voices or events told in a non-chronological order. However, the challenge presented by a test task is not exclusively dependent on its cognitive complexity, but also on the test-taker's familiarity with a specific type of task (Oxford *et al.*, 2004: 12; cf. the notions of code, cognitive and communicative complexity defined by Skehan, 1996). Both the fluency of the input comprehension as well as its accuracy level and the complexity of the stored information are affected by the characteristics of the listening task and the possibility of advance planning (Oxford *et al.*, 2004: 13).

The sub-component of effortlessness in listening fluency can only be assessed by the L2 learners themselves, through their own experiences. Combining self-evaluations of effortlessness with think-aloud protocols or retrospective interviews and with objective assessment of listening fluency at different processing levels would give interesting insights to what effortlessness in listening consists of. This type of triangulation would be an interesting option for future studies.

The level of interaction is probably the most challenging to assess, since it implies the presence of at least two interlocutors. It could be assessed by simulating the interactional situation in a task that demands spoken reactions to oral prompts (e.g. Saleva, 1997), but this type of task can never represent the negotiation of meaning in authentic face-to-face interaction.

In any assessment framework, it is necessary to evaluate the validity of the assessment instruments. In the present framework, this means evaluating whether the listeners' performance in the suggested tasks reflects fluency in L2 listening. More research is needed to evaluate the nature of this construct. For instance, to determine whether a L2 listener's fluency improves linearly or whether it can be divided into different stages with specific cut-off points.

## Conclusion

In the present chapter, we have presented an overview of different aspects of fluency in L2 listening. We have explored the possible main components of fluency in L2 listening with a special focus on the influence of L1 and of the written modality. We have also evaluated some possibilities for teaching and assessing fluency in L2 listening, underlining the importance of different listening strategies. In the context of speaking fluency, Segalowitz (2010) identifies three subcategories of speaking fluency: utterance fluency, cognitive fluency and perceived fluency. Because one-way listening is a process with no outcome comparable to utterances which could be perceived by others, we have defined listening fluency mainly in terms of processing fluency, i.e. cognitive fluency. As we have seen, this aspect of L2 listening has been extensively studied, although it has not always been directly associated with the concept of fluency. Therefore, a more thorough review of studies on different fluency-related characteristics of L2 listening would be useful. Further, the definition and operationalisation of fluency in interactive listening situations, which was beyond the scope of the present article, would be necessary to complement the picture of fluency in L2 listening. Another dimension of listening fluency that could be explored in future studies is the contrasting of measurable listening fluency with experienced listening fluency. By experienced listening fluency, we mean the effortlessness of the listening process as evaluated by L2 listeners themselves. Although metacognitive aspects of listening have gained more interest recently (e.g. Cohen, 2014; Vandergrift & Goh, 2012), to our knowledge, they have not commonly been combined with processing studies. Therefore, combining quantitative measures of learners' online L2 listening processes and qualitative self-evaluations of these processes could provide interesting new insights into fluency in L2 listening.

### References

Anckar, J. (2011) *Assessing Foreign Language Listening Comprehension by Means of the Multiple-choice Format: Processes and Products.* Jyväskylä Studies in Humanities 159. Jyväskylä: University of Jyväskylä.

Bartolotti, J., Daniel, N. and Marian, V. (2013) Spoken words activate cross-linguistic orthographic competitors in the absence of phonological overlap. *Proceedings of the Annual Meeting of the Cognitive Science Society* 35, 1827–1832.

Berne, J. (2004) Listening comprehension strategies: A review of the literature. *Foreign Language Annals* 37 (4), 521–531.

Best, C.T. (1995) A direct realist perspective on cross-language speech perception. In W. Strange (ed.) *Speech Perception and Linguistic Experience: Theoretical and Methodological Issues in Cross-language Speech Research* (pp. 167–200). York: Timonium, MD.

Brown, G. (1995) Dimensions of difficulty in listening comprehension. In D.J. Mendelsohn and J. Rubin (eds) *A Guide for the Teaching of Second Language Listening* (pp. 59–69). Carlsbad: Dominie Press, Inc.

Buck, G. (2001) *Assessing Listening.* Cambridge: Cambridge University Press.

Bybee, J.L. (2006) From usage to grammar: The mind's response to repetition. *Language* 82 (4), 711–733.

Bybee, J. (2008) Usage-based grammar and second language acquisition. In P. Robinson and N.C. Ellis (eds) *Handbook of Cognitive Linguistics and Second Language Acquisition* (pp. 226–246). New York: Routledge.

Carreira, J.M. (2014) How can we enhance EFL learners' listening fluency? Teaching connected speech to Japanese university students using songs. In T. Muller, J. Adamson, P.S. Brown and S. Herder (eds) *Exploring EFL Fluency in Asia* (pp. 297–311). Basingstoke: Palgrave Macmillan.

Carroll, S.E. (2004) Segmentation: Learning how to 'hear words' in the L2 speech stream. *Transactions of the Philological Society* 102 (2), 227–254.

Chang, A.C-S. (2009) Gains to L2 listeners from reading while listening vs. listening only in comprehending short stories. *System* 37 (4), 652–663.

Chang, A.C-S. (2011) The effect of reading while listening to audiobooks: Listening fluency and vocabulary gain. *Asian Journal of English Language Teaching* 21, 43–64.

Chang, A.C-S. and Millett, S. (2014) The effect of extensive listening on developing L2 listening fluency: Some hard evidence. *ELT Journal* 68 (1), 31–40.

Chang A.C-S. and Millett, S. (2016) Developing L2 listening fluency through extended listening-focused activities in an extensive listening programme. *RELC Journal* 47 (3), 349–362.

Cohen, A.D. (2014) *Strategies in Learning and Using a Second Language.* New York: Routledge.

Council of Europe. (2001) *The Common European Framework of Reference for Languages: Learning, Teaching, Assessment.* Cambridge: Cambridge University Press. Retrieved from https://rm.coe.int/1680459f97.

Cutler, A., Mehler, J., Norris, D.G. and Segui, J. (1992) The monolingual nature of speech segmentation by bilinguals. *Cognitive Psychology* 24 (3), 381–410.

Darcy I., Daidone D. and Kojima C. (2013) Asymmetric lexical access and fuzzy lexical representations in second language learners. *Mental Lexicon* 8, 372–420.

Dickinson, L. (1987) *Self-instruction in Language Learning*. Cambridge: Cambridge University Press.

Ellis, N.C. (2002) Frequency effects in language processing: A review with implications for theories of implicit and explicit language acquisition. *Studies in Second Language Acquisition* 24 (2), 143–188.

Field, J. (2003) Promoting perception: Lexical segmentation in L2 listening. *ELT Journal* 57 (4), 325–333.

Flege, J. (2003) Assessing constraints on second-language segmental production and perception. In A. Meyer and N. Schiller (eds) *Phonetics and Phonology in Language Comprehension and Production, Differences and Similarities* (pp. 319–355). Berlin: Mouton de Gruyter.

Flowerdew, J. and Miller, L. (2005) *Second Language Listening: Theory and Practice*. Cambridge: Cambridge University Press.

Ghaniabadi, S. and Hashemi H.R. (2016) Enhancing listening fluency through well-beaten path approach. *Theory and Practice in Language Studies* 6 (3), 592–595.

Graham, S., Santos, D. and Vanderplank, R. (2011) Exploring the relationship between listening development and strategy use. *Language Teaching Research* 15 (4), 435–456.

Hayes-Harb, R., Nicol, J. and Barker, J. (2010) Learning the phonological forms of new words: Effects of orthographic and auditory input. *Language and Speech* 53 (3), 367–381.

Herder, S. and Sholdt, G. (2014) Employing a fluency-based approach to teach the TOEFL iBT: An action research project. In T. Muller, J. Adamson, P.S. Brown and S. Herder (eds) *Exploring EFL Fluency in Asia* (pp. 26–41). Basingstoke: Palgrave Macmillan.

Kirk, S. (2014) Addressing spoken fluency in the classroom. In T. Muller, J. Adamson, P.S. Brown and S. Herder (eds) *Exploring EFL Fluency in Asia* (pp. 101–119). Basingstoke: Palgrave Macmillan.

Nation, P. (2014a) Developing fluency. In T. Muller, J. Adamson, P.S. Brown and S. Herder (eds) *Exploring EFL Fluency in Asia* (pp. 11–25). Basingstoke: Palgrave Macmillan.

Nation, P. (2014b) *What do you need to know to learn a foreign language?* School of Linguistics and Applied Language Studies Victoria University of Wellington New Zealand. 11 August 2014.

Newton, J. (2017) Comprehending misunderstanding. *ELT Journal* 71 (2), 237–244.

Oxford, R., Cho, Y., Leung, S. and Kim, H-J. (2004) Effect of the presence and difficulty of task on strategy use: An exploratory study. *International Review of Applied Linguistics* 42 (1), 1–47.

Papadopoulou, D. and Clahsen, H. (2003) Parsing strategies in L1 and L2 sentence processing: A study of relative clause attachment in Greek. *Studies in Second Language Acquisition* 25 (4), 501–528.

Prince, P. (2013) Listening, remembering, writing: Exploring the dictogloss task. *Language Teaching Research* 17 (4), 486–500.

Renandya, W.A. and Farrell, T.S.C. (2011) 'Teacher, the tape is too fast!' Extensive listening in ELT. *ELT Journal* 65 (1), 52–59.

Rost, M. (1990) *Listening in Language Learning*. London: Longman.

Rost, M. (2002) *Teaching and Researching Listening*. Harlow: Pearson Education.

Rost, M. (2014) Developing listening fluency in Asian EFL settings. In T. Muller, J. Adamson, P.S. Brown and S. Herder (eds) *Exploring EFL Fluency in Asia* (pp. 281–296). Basingstoke: Palgrave Macmillan.

Rost, M. and Wilson, J.J. (2013) *Active Listening*. New York: Routledge.

Rüschemeyer, S.A., Nojack, A. and Limbach, M. (2008) A mouse with a roof? Effects of phonological neighbors on processing of words in sentences in a non-native language. *Brain and Language* 104 (2), 132–144.

Saleva, M. (1997) *Now They're Talking – Testing Oral Proficiency in a Language Laboratory*. Studia Philologia Jyväskyläensia 43. Jyväskylä: University of Jyväskylä.

Segalowitz, N. (2000) Automaticity and attentional skill in fluent performance. In H. Riggenbach (ed.) *Perspectives on Fluency* (pp. 200–219). Ann Arbor, MI: University of Michigan Press.

Segalowitz, N. (2003) Automaticity and second language acquisition. In C. Doughty and M. Long (eds) *The Handbook of Second Language Acquisition* (pp. 382–408). Oxford: Blackwell Publishers.

Segalowitz, N. (2010) *The Cognitive Bases of Second Language Fluency*. New York: Routledge.

Siegel, J. (2014) Exploring L2 listening instruction: Examinations of practice. *ELT Journal* 68 (1), 22–30.

Skehan, P. (1996) A framework for the implementation of task-based instruction. *Applied Linguistics* 17, 38–62.

Spivey, M. and Marian, V. (1999) Cross talk between native and second languages: Partial activation of an irrelevant lexicon. *Psychological Science* 10 (3), 281–284.

Swan, M. and Walter, C. (2017) Misunderstanding comprehension. *ELT Journal* 71 (2), 228–236.

Taguchi, E., Bunka, D., Gorsuch, G. and Sasamoto, E. (2006) Developing second and foreign language reading fluency and its effect on comprehension: A missing link. *The Reading Matrix* 6 (2), 1–18.

Tsai, Y.-C. (2014) Does autonomous listening increase fluency? In T. Muller, J. Adamson, P.S. Brown and S. Herder (eds) *Exploring EFL Fluency in Asia* (pp. 312–327). Basingstoke: Palgrave Macmillan.

Tsui, A.B. and Fullilove, J. (1998) Bottom-up or top-down processing as a discriminator of L2 listening performance. *Applied Linguistics* 19 (4), 432–451.

Vandergrift, L. and Goh, C. (2012) *Teaching and Learning Second Language Listening, Metacognition in Action*. New York: Routledge.

Veivo, O., Järvikivi, J., Porretta, V. and Hyönä, J. (2016) Orthographic activation in L2 spoken word recognition depends on proficiency: Evidence from eye-tracking. *Frontiers in Psychology* 7 (1120), 1–15.

Veivo, O., Porretta, V., Hyönä, J. and Järvikivi, J. (2018) Spoken second language words activate native language orthographic information in late second language learners. *Applied Psycholinguistics* 39 (5), 1011–1032.

Veivo, O., Suomela-Salmi, E. and Järvikivi, J. (2015) Orthographic bias in L3 lexical knowledge learner-related and lexical factors. *Language, Interaction and Acquisition* 6, 271–294.

Weber, A. and Cutler, A. (2004) Lexical competition in non-native spoken-word recognition. *Journal of Memory and Language* 50 (1), 1–25.

Wilson, M. (2003) Discovery listening – improving perceptual processing. *ELT Journal* 57 (4), 335–343.

Wipf, J.A. (1984) Strategies for teaching second language listening comprehension. *Foreign Language Annals* 17 (4), 345–348.

Yeldham, M. and Gruba, P. (2016) The development of individual learners in an L2 listening strategies course. *Language Teaching Research* 20 (1), 9–34.

Ziegler, J.C. and Ferrand, L. (1998) Orthography shapes the perception of speech: The consistency effect in auditory word recognition. *Psychonomic Bulletin & Review* 5 (4), 683–689.

# 5 L2 Fluency and Writer Profiles

Maarit Mutta

**Introduction**

Fluency in writing can be studied at the process level, the product level or by combining these two. There is a lack of studies on L2 writing fluency that use both product and process data to describe this complex phenomenon. In this chapter, to study fluency in foreign language (L2) writing, a multi-perspective approach comparing writing processes and products is used (cf. Ellis & Yuan, 2004; Gunnarsson, 2012). The analysis of the processes contained variables such as pause length and median transition times, while the quality of the final product was assessed via the evaluation of the texts by native speakers. To study the writers' pausal behaviour and to create thus their individual writer profiles (cf. Van Waes, 1992; Van Waes & Schellens, 2003), two different pause criteria were defined: a stipulated pause criterion automatically provided by the tool ($\geq 2$ and $\geq 5$ seconds) and individual pause states.

This chapter presents the results of a small-scale experiment in which the data were collected by using the keystroke recording tool *ScriptLog* (versions 1.07f and 1.07i), a computer program which allows one to carry out research on the online process of writing. The online data were produced by 11 Finnish university students of French. To summarise, the objective of this research was to examine how writer profiles are linked to L2 fluency during writing process and what their relationship is to the quality of the end product. The following research questions were formulated to shed light on this issue: How fluent is the participants' writing process in L2? What is the relationship between fluency and the final product in L2? How are writer profiles related to fluency? These different aspects of fluency will also be illustrated from the perspective of the SLA fluency framework proposed by Segalowitz (2010, 2016), namely effortless processing (i.e. cognitive fluency), performance (i.e. utterance fluency) and reader experience (i.e. perceived fluency).

## Writing Processes and Profiles

Fluency in second language learning and use is a complex phenomenon usually related to oral language use indicating a certain level of language proficiency (e.g. Lennon's broad sense, 1990). From a cognitive perspective, it refers to the effortless and unconscious processing of language based on the automaticity of processes (Segalowitz, 2010). Segalowitz (2010, 2016) divided fluency into three types: cognitive (i.e. fluid operation of relevant cognitive processes), utterance (i.e. fluidity of observable processes) and perceived fluency (i.e. subjective judgements of fluent processes). Fluency is also one of the central concepts in writing studies, in both product- and process-oriented approaches. In the end product, fluency is related to the reader perception, which means, for instance, how coherent, logical, error-free and well-structured the layout is (see e.g. Crossley *et al.*, 2016; Nation, 2009; Rose, 2018). In process-oriented studies, writing fluency is viewed as being based on the relationships between the three primary cognitive functions, namely the planning, formulation and revision phases (Ellis & Yuan, 2004; Roca de Larios *et al.*, 2006; Roca de Larios *et al.*, 2008; Sasaki, 2004) and can be analysed based on pauses, especially their location and duration (Gunnarsson, 2012; Olive, 2010; Spelman Miller, 2000).

Fluency in writing processes is closely related to the writer's textual organisation at micro- and macrostructural levels, which happens in the working memory during the writing process. Adult L2 writers' processes do not differ enormously from L1 writers', but there are some differences related to limitations due to, for instance, lexical access, memory capacity and L2 proficiency (e.g. Ellis & Yuan, 2004; Levelt *et al.*, 1999; Sasaki, 2004). One indication of differences is the use of pauses. The pause is a basic unit, as it seems to reflect covert cognitive activity. Therefore, pause length, location and frequency are studied in online or temporal studies: automatised lower-level processes induce short pauses, whereas higher-level processes invite longer pauses (e.g. Janssen *et al.*, 1996; see also Olkkonen & Mutta's chapter on cognitive fluency, this volume). It is assumed that writing in an L2 makes, for instance, the pauses even longer at every location compared to L1 writing, and that there are more pauses within words, which should be the most fluent location in writing (see e.g. Spelman Miller, 2000); in other words, long pauses are not likely to emerge within words during writing when processes are fluent.

When writing on a computer, one sign of fluency could be a rapid transition between keystrokes (cf. mean transition times; Kowal, 2014). Expertise on a keyboard relies on practice and thereby automatised processes due to an encoding of motor memory or motor activity (Gaonac'h & Larigauderie, 2000). Fluency could also be measured by calculating the words produced per unit of composition time; for instance, words per minute of writing time provide an average measure of a certain kind of fluency (Kellogg, 1996; see also Chenoweth & Hayes, 2001; Ellis & Yuan, 2004). Several researchers have, however, taken a broader view of fluency in writing by combining several aspects of writing to yield a more complex image of the multifaceted phenomenon, such as Wengelin (2002), Ellis and Yuan (2004) and Gunnarsson (2012), among others. Wengelin (2002) studied L1 text production by adults with reading and writing difficulties. She made a triple analysis of her data: error analysis, textual analysis and analysis of processes (*ScriptLog*). Wengelin did not determine the concept of fluency directly in her study, but when studying time distribution, pauses and the word-production rate, she alluded to the concept of fluency as speed of typing. For their part, Ellis and Yuan (2004) and Gunnarsson (2012) studied fluency, complexity and accuracy in L2 productions. Ellis and Yuan (2004) studied the effects of planning on fluency (e.g. syllables per minute and number of disfluencies), complexity (e.g. the ratio of clauses to T-units, syntactic variety and mean segmental type-token ratio) and accuracy (e.g. error-free clauses and correct verb forms) in a paper-and-pencil task in L2 English. Gunnarsson (2012) analysed L2 French competence by means of 'log' files (*ScriptLog*) and video-filmed thinking-aloud protocols. She understood fluency and complexity in the same way as Ellis and Yuan (2004), whereas accuracy was apprehended in particular morphosyntactic contexts: finiteness, subject-verb agreement and past tense.

Furthermore, when studying writing processes, a distinction between writing profiles and writer profiles can be made: according to Van Waes (1992), the former can be used to describe variation in the organisation of writing processes, whereas the latter are specific to each individual writer (see also Van Waes & Schellens, 2003). Therefore, as the two above-mentioned profiles intertwine, in the present chapter, the concept of writer profiles is used in both senses to describe each writer's pausal behaviour. More than 35 years ago, Hayes and Flower (1980), the writing modelling pioneers, distinguished writing profiles in college students writing, but these used the pencil and paper mode. Van Waes and Schellens (2003) compared the pencil and paper mode to computer mode with a subcategory of two different screen formats (25 lines vs 66 lines of text); they had recourse to a keystroke recording program called *Keytrap*. In the present study, a keystroke recording tool (*ScriptLog*) was used which differed from *Keytrap*, but as the logging provides information such as total duration of the writing process, number and length of pauses, their categorisation was adopted.

Van Waes (1992; Van Waes & Schellens, 2003: 836–837) proposes a typology of five writer profiles on the basis of three aspects, namely (a) time taken and final product – total duration of the writing process, duration of each phase (e.g. phase I starts from the beginning and ends at the completion of the first draft), ratio of time spent pausing to time spent actively writing, number of words in the final text; (b) pausing behaviour (number, duration, types of pauses); and (c) revision behaviour (number, level, purpose, location, remoteness and temporal location of revision):

- *Initial planners* make a rather small number of revisions, most of them occurring in the second phase. They have the relatively longest initial planning phase, and their average pause length is relatively long, since the longest and total pause times are significantly higher than the average.
- *Fragmentary first-phase writers* have a revision attitude that heavily concentrates on the first phase. The total number of revisions is higher than that of other groups, but the second phase contains few revisions, the time for initial planning is restricted, and pauses are manifold and relatively short, which makes the process strongly fragmented.
- *Second-phase writers*' revision is concentrated in the second writing phase and this allows for ample attention to changes above word level. They have a long initial planning phase but once they start writing, they pause relatively little, even if the pauses are relatively long.
- *Non-stop writers*, on the other hand, revise least of all the groups, pause less than others and the total pause time clearly lies below average, their processing time is shorter, and they spend little time on initial planning.
- *Average writers*' profile shows values that are closest to the average values of each of the variables of the total group.

The last category, average writers, was excluded from the analysis, as even if some writers seemed to have average values for some variables, they differed elsewhere.

## Methodology

Eleven multilingual Finnish university students studying French participated in the small-scale experiment.[1] In addition, five of them, randomly chosen, participated in the verbalisation session (see below). All the students were female and between 20 and 23 years of age (mean age = 21.6 years). They were mainly third-year students and participated in the test voluntarily. Despite the small number of participants, the amount of data collected on pausal behaviour by means of the *ScriptLog* tool was sufficient to permit some conclusions to be made regarding their L2 pausal behaviour. The data collected were described next.

The data were collected in two sessions: a writing session, which was carried out by means of the *ScriptLog* keystroke recording tool (permitting research on the online process of writing); and a verbalisation with a stimulated recall verbal protocol. Verbalisations are not studied in this chapter, but discussed elsewhere (see e.g. Mutta, 2007, 2017a). The participants wrote an expository essay in French on the topic of the single European currency, the euro (the prompt: *Give your opinion on the given subject*), which invited implicitly the writers to argue either for or against the use of the euro. They were asked to write approximately 150 to 200 words on the topic within one hour, but were not penalised if they wrote more words or slightly exceeded the time limit – they were given one hour to avoid the time pressure which some students might have experienced. In fact, their total writing time varied from 29.51 to 63.31 minutes (mean, $\bar{x}$ = 46.25 minutes), and the number of words between 184 and 631 ($\bar{x}$ = 288). They were not allowed to use dictionaries or other resources.

Fluency was examined by combining two aspects: the analysis of processes and the quality of the final product. The latter was assessed via the evaluation (i.e. grading) of the texts and some other quality criteria (e.g. number of words, average length of sentences). Evaluation of the final product consisted of three grading values given by two to four native French teachers: grammatical and lexical accuracy, text coherence (e.g. structure, argumentation, style) and holistic evaluation according to the *Common European Framework of Reference for Languages* (2001). The first score concerning the grammatical and lexical accuracy provided a maximum of 36 points, the second on text coherence also 36 points, and the third score, a global grade, 24 points (A1 = 1, A2 = 2, B1 = 3, B2 = 4, C1 = 5, C2 = 6 × 4). The variables on processes differed slightly from Van Waes and Schellens (2003: 836–837): first, instead of duration of each phase, the length of time spent on writing different paragraphs and on initial and revision writing phases were measured. This is because it was difficult to make a clear distinction between the writing phases, as these processes are of a cyclical nature, and thus dynamic and overlapping (see Roca de Larios *et al.*, 2008; Olive, 2014). Second, instead of using types of pauses, the number of pauses automatically provided by the tool were totalled, as were individual pauses, and each of these was then considered in relation to the total writing time. The analysis of the general flow of the processes and the quality contained the following variables:

(1) General flow of processes
- Pause length ($\geq$ 2 and $\geq$ 5 seconds) given by ScriptLog and individual pause length by Hidden Markov Model (HMM)
- Number of intra-lexical pauses
- Median transition time
- Total writing time
- Pause time in relation to total writing time
- Number of editions
- Number of deleted characters
- Length of initial writing phase
- Length of revision phase
- Pause location
(2) Criteria of quality
- The number of words

- The number of sentences
- The number of clauses
- The average length of words and sentences
- The number of characters and words in relation to total writing time
- Type/token ratio
- Evaluation of the final product by native teachers (max 96 points)
    - Grammatical and lexical accuracy (max 36 points)
    - Text coherence (max 36 points)
    - A global grade according to the *Common European Framework of Reference for Languages* (CEFR) (max 24 points)

To study the relationship between the values and scores correlation tests (Pearson, r) were used.

In the present experiment, two pause lengths were used: stipulated pause criteria automatically provided by the *ScriptLog* tool (≥ 2 and ≥ 5 seconds) to compare the results with earlier studies, and an individual pause criterion. *ScriptLog* enables one to define a pause length even shorter, but it was decided to rely on the automatically provided durations used in other studies (e.g. Gunnarsson, 2012). This stipulated criterion aims to cover all pauses that should really be considered as pauses, and exclude, for instance, so-called 'technical pauses', which are due to correcting typographical errors. A pause that is ≥ 2 seconds long is thus considered short, whereas a pause that is ≥ 5 seconds long can be treated as a long pause, reflecting the cognitive load of processes behind writing activities in working memory. An individual pause criterion for each writer was also defined by using a HMM on the basis of ScriptLog (≥ 2 seconds) durations (for further information, see Mutta, 2007, 2017b; see also Olive, 2014).[2] The three states were: state of fluent writing (state 1), state of thinking writing (state 2) and state of reflective writing (state 3). Median values of these states were used because, for instance, participant P8 had a mean pause length of 15.85 seconds, and a median pause length of 7.11 seconds; the median value reveals the central tendency more accurately as individual very long pauses affect the mean value.

## Results

### Pausal behaviour and flow of processes

When writing on a computer, median transition time measures how writers proceed between letters in a word (e.g. Kowal, 2014) and reflects typing fluency in general. This measure generated values varying between 0.156 and 0.281 milliseconds ($\bar{x} = 0.212$), which shows quite normal individual variation in L2 writing speed (cf. Mutta, 2007; also Wengelin, 2002). This value is related to automaticity of writing and how

**Table 5.1** Number and duration of pauses related to total writing time

| P | Number of pauses | | Writing time | Pause time per writing time | |
|---|---|---|---|---|---|
| | ≥ 2 | ≥ 5 | | ≥ 2/% | ≥ 5/% |
| 1. P1 | 134 | 61 | 33.57 | 21.44/64% | 18.00/53% |
| 2. P2 | 115 | 67 | 55.07 | 45.42/83% | 43.12/78% |
| 3. P3 | 104 | 54 | 39.44 | 23.49/60% | 21.24/54% |
| 4. P4 | 97 | 54 | 29.44 | 19.47/67% | 17.49/60% |
| 5. P5 | 285 | 124 | 63.31 | 37.40/59% | 29.20/46% |
| 6. P6 | 176 | 111 | 52.35 | 39.50/76% | 36.11/69% |
| 7. P7 | 97 | 40 | 29.51 | 12.29/42% | 9.24/32% |
| 8. P8 | 196 | 98 | 58.03 | 31.29/54% | 26.20/45% |
| 9. P9 | 182 | 92 | 47.18 | 34.17/73% | 29.44/63% |
| 10. P10 | 195 | 111 | 57.01 | 45.21/80% | 40.55/72% |
| 11. P11 | 157 | 88 | 43.45 | 32.44/75% | 28.58/66% |
| M | 158 | 82 | 46.25 | 31.21/68% | 27.23/59% |

Time is indicated in minutes and seconds. Pause times of ≥ 2 and ≥ 5 seconds are compared to the total time. The pauses of ≥ 2 seconds also include the ≥ 5 second pauses. P = participant M = mean

experienced the writer is in using a computer keyboard (cf. Kowal, 2014). The values for the number of pauses and pause lengths compared with the total writing time are shown in Table 5.1.

As shown in Table 5.1, the number pauses (≥ 2) ranged from 97 to 285, whereas the number of long pauses (≥ 5) varied between 40 and 124. The percentages show that the pausing time covers from 42% to 83% (≥ 2 pauses) of the total writing time ($\bar{x}$ = 68%) and from 32% to 78% (≥ 5 pauses) of the total writing time ($\bar{x}$ = 59%); in other words, during L2 writing, the keyboard activity, for instance, concrete writing time is about a third of the total writing time. At the individual level, for instance, P8 seemed to allocate a long time to the writing process (58.03 min), and her writing process accordingly contained 196 pauses (short 98 and long 98), whereas P4 allocated half of that time to her writing process (29.44 min) and had accordingly fewer pauses 97 (43 and 54, respectively). However, their pauses per writing time show that P8 had relatively less keyboard inactivity during her writing time than P4. The individual pause states refine the participants' pausal behaviour; this is illustrated in Table 5.2 – the percentages are related to the number of pauses of each state (for more detail, see Mutta, 2017b).

Table 5.2 shows that the fluent state pauses ranged from 2.65 to 3.47 seconds, the thinking state pauses from 6.77 to 8.32 seconds, and finally, the reflective state pauses from 18.83 to 42.61 seconds. Some writers remained almost continuously in a fluent state of writing (P7, P8), whereas

**Table 5.2** Individual states of pauses according the Hidden Markov Model

| Participant | State 1 | % | State 2 | % | State 3 | % |
|---|---|---|---|---|---|---|
| 1. P1 | 3.10 | 45% | 7.68 | 38% | 23.56 | 17% |
| 2. P2 | 3.09 | 43% | 7.22 | 42% | 42.61 | 15% |
| 3. P3 | 2.83 | 57% | 8.19 | 29% | 24.26 | 14% |
| 4. P4 | 2.65 | 52% | 6.77 | 33% | 25.29 | 15% |
| 5. P5 | 3.07 | 56% | 7.02 | 29% | 19.14 | 15% |
| 6. P6 | 3.47 | 42% | 8.32 | 34% | 21.10 | 24% |
| 7. P7 | 3.22 | 60% | 7.09 | 32% | 18.83 | 8% |
| 8. P8 | 3.08 | 60% | 8.10 | 34% | 29.85 | 6% |
| 9. P9 | 3.05 | 42% | 7.62 | 39% | 22.87 | 19% |
| 10. P10 | 3.12 | 41% | 7.07 | 40% | 26.31 | 19% |
| 11. P11 | 3.23 | 48% | 7.04 | 39% | 24.52 | 13% |
| M | 3.08 | 50% | 7.47 | 35% | 25.30 | 15% |

Pause durations are indicated in seconds. State 1 = state of fluent writing (short pauses), State 2 = state of thinking writing (medium pauses), and State 3 = state of reflective writing (long pauses).

some others spent proportionally almost as much time in the fluent as in the thinking state (P2, P10); in other words, their writing behaviour differs, the first ones' writing activity contains mainly short pauses, whereas the latter ones seems to accelerate and slow down their activity in turn. Pauses are related to the other values that create the flow of processes. Table 5.3 shows the number of intra-lexical pauses, the number of editions (i.e. how many times they edited the text) and deletions (i.e. how many deletions) done during the process, as well as the number of words in the end product; the last number shows how many words they wrote in a minute, that is the number of words was divided by the total time spent in writing.

These values also indicate the acceleration and slowing down of the writing process; intra-lexical pauses slow down the process as this should be the most fluent location in writing (see e.g. Spelman Miller, 2000) and there was in fact a significant correlation between these values, as can be expected: total writing time vs intra-lexical pauses ($\geq 2$), $r = 0.622$ ($p \leq 0.05$) and total writing time vs intra-lexical pauses ($\geq 5$), $r = 0.647$ ($p \leq 0.05$). However, at the individual level, there is a great deal of variation; for instance, P2 paused several times inside words, made a lot of deletions and wrote the shortest text at a speed of 3.34 words per minute; P1 also made intra-lexical pauses and proportionally more deletions compared to the mean percentage, but could write 7.03 words per minute; P4 made no intra-lexical pauses and deleted less than average, but in her case, she often used the mouse instead of keyboard (mouse events), which diminished backspace deletions; and

Table 5.3 Intra-lexical pauses, editions, deletions and words

| P | Number of intra-lexical pauses | | Number of editions | Number of deletions | Number of words in the end product | Total writing time | W/TWT |
|---|---|---|---|---|---|---|---|
| | ≥ 2 | ≥ 5 | | /% | | | |
| 1. P1 | 7 | 2 | 93 | 52/56% | 236 | 33.57 | 7.03 |
| 2. P2 | 10 | 3 | 82 | 48/59% | 184 | 55.07 | 3.34 |
| 3. P3 | 4 | 2 | 155 | 72/47% | 319 | 39.44 | 8.09 |
| 4. P4 | 0 | 0 | 91 | 37/41% | 252 | 29.44 | 8.56 |
| 5. P5 | 21 | 4 | 343 | 156/46% | 277 | 63.31 | 4.38 |
| 6. P6 | 3 | 4 | 167 | 90/54% | 211 | 52.35 | 4.03 |
| 7. P7 | 0 | 1 | 93 | 49/53% | 631 | 29.5 | 21.39 |
| 8. P8 | 4 | 1 | 443 | 235/53% | 241 | 58.03 | 4.15 |
| 9. P9 | 6 | 1 | 65 | 33/45% | 275 | 47.18 | 5.83 |
| 10. P10 | 5 | 4 | 176 | 85/48% | 232 | 57.01 | 4.07 |
| 11. P11 | 9 | 0 | 65 | 35/54% | 312 | 43.45 | 7.18 |
| Mean | 6.3 | 2 | 161 | 81/51% | 288 | 46.25 | 6.23 |

Time is indicated in minutes and seconds. W = words, TWT = words per total writing time. The intra-lexical pauses of ≥ 2 seconds are calculated separately from the ≥ 5 seconds intra-lexical pauses. The percentage of deletion is related to number of editions.

finally P7 wrote the longest text and achieved a speed of 21 words per minute. In her case, I would argue that a part of her writing processes has been automatised in such a way that she could operate fluently and perform an effortless writing process in L2 (cf. cognitive fluency; Segalowitz, 2010, 2016; see, however, below).

In addition to pausal behaviour, editing and deleting, the flow of writing processes is related to the architecture of the text, that is, how the text is structured in time. Table 5.4 illustrates the length of initial writing phase, revision writing phase (= revision of the whole text at the end) and time spent on different paragraphs.

Table 5.4 shows that some writers structure their text in several paragraphs, whereas others reviewed and corrected their text the whole time with no distinctive revision phase at the end. Furthermore, writers concentrate on different parts of their text (introduction, body paragraphs and conclusion) and did not always create their text linearly and could add a paragraph between other paragraphs or add text at the end during the revision phase. This illustrates the dynamic and overlapping natures of writing processes (e.g. Roca de Larios *et al.*, 2008; Olive, 2014), which concretises the variability in individual writing paths. All values presented in this sub-section indicate aspects of fluency in writing processes, for instance, the general flow and smoothness of processing.

**Table 5.4** Time spent on writing different phases

| P | Initial | Paragraphs | | | | | Revision | Total writing time |
|---|---|---|---|---|---|---|---|---|
| | | I | II | III | IV | V | | |
| 1. P1 | 2.19 | 8.22 | 14.56 | **25.52** | 33.57 | | 8.45 | 33.57 |
| 2. P2 | 13.50 | **29.27** | 47.53 | | | | 7.14 | 55.07 |
| 3. P3 | 1.48 | 8.17 | 22.52 | 29.28 | **34.51** | | 6.47 | 39.44 |
| 4. P4 | 1.35 | 3.16 | 13.34 | **26.58** | 28.16 | | 7.59 | 29.44 |
| 5. P5 | 2.21 | 9.49 | 25.24 | **46.30** | 58.25 | | 5.06 | 63.31 |
| 6. P6 | 3.56 | 20.0 | **40.03** | 44.57 | | | 7.38 | 52.35 |
| 7. P7 | 0.31 | **29.51** | | | | | 0.00 | 29.51 |
| 8. P8 | 1.45 | 22.43 | 36.05 | **46.27** | | | 11.36 | 58.03 |
| 9. P9 | 4.12 | 11.41 | **24.39** | 34.56 | 47.18 | | 0.00 | 47.18 |
| 10. P10 | 2.33 | 6.15 | **40.20** | 57.01 | | | 0.00 | 57.01 |
| 11. P11 | 0.39 | 5.22 | 17.15 | 21.36 | 23.26 | **43.45** | 0.00 | 43.45 |

The initial phase is calculated from the start until the beginning of the second sentence. The revision phase corresponds to the reviewing of the text after finishing it. Time in bold indicates the paragraph to which the writer allocated most time.

### Writer profiles and the end product

To answer the question of how writer profiles, based on writing processes, are related to fluency, they will be discussed in comparison to the end product. Writer profiles were created on the basis of van Waes's categorisation, with some modifications (see above). The writers were distributed into four groups in the following way:

- Initial planners: P2, P9
- Fragmentary first-phase writers: P4, P5, P8, P10
- Second-phase writers: P6
- Non-stop writers: P1, P3, P7, P11

It is to be noted that the classification is not clear-cut, which means that, for instance, P11 has mainly the characteristics of a non-stop writer, but her pauses are quite long. P7 is a fine example of a non-stop writer: compared to the other groups, they revise least of all the groups, pause less than others and the total pause time clearly lies below average. Their processing time is shorter, and they spend little time on initial planning. On the other hand, P7 and P8 have a lot of similarities according to their pausal behaviour, for instance, their respective pause stages are 60% fluent, 32% thinking and 8% reflective state (P7) vs 60% fluent, 34% thinking and 6% reflective state (P8) (cf. Mutta, 2017b). However, when studying all the values, P8 is classified as a fragmentary first-phase writer who revises a lot in the first phase, pauses are manifold and relatively short, which makes

**Table 5.5** Number of words, clauses, sentences, average length of sentences and type/token ratio

| P | Words | Clauses | Sentences | Average length of sentences | Type/token ratio |
|---|---|---|---|---|---|
| 1. P1 | 236 | 28 | 18 | 13.1 | 51.5 |
| 2. P2 | 184 | 15 | 8 | 23.0 | 59.8 |
| 3. P3 | 319 | 36 | 22 | 14.5 | 48.2 |
| 4. P4 | 252 | 26 | 12 | 21.0 | 56.8 |
| 5. P5 | 277 | 20 | 15 | 18.5 | 47.5 |
| 6. P6 | 211 | 18 | 10 | 21.1 | 54.0 |
| 7. P7 | 631 | 65 | 23 | 27.4 | 43.3 |
| 8. P8 | 241 | 25 | 12 | 20.1 | 45.6 |
| 9. P9 | 275 | 31 | 14 | 19.6 | 58.0 |
| 10. P10 | 232 | 21 | 19 | 12.2 | 57.6 |
| 11. P11 | 312 | 33 | 16 | 19.5 | 54.1 |
| Mean | 288 | 28 | 15 | 19.2 | 52.4 |

the process strongly fragmented. From the point of view of cognitive fluency, her fragmentary writing process appeared markedly disfluent, but she performed quite well when her final product was evaluated. On the other hand, P7's writing processes indicated a certain cognitive fluency as she could operate fluently and carry out an effortless writing process (cf. Segalowitz, 2010, 2016), but the end result invites some discussion. For their part, initial planners (P2, P9) have a relatively long planning phase and they make few revisions, whereas the second-phase writer (P6) plans at the beginning but once having started to write she pauses relatively little.

The fluency of the end product was related to values such as number of words, clauses, sentences, the average length of sentences, the number of words in relation to the total writing time (presented in Table 5.3), type/token ratio (TTR, indicating lexical variation) and evaluation of the product by native teachers. These values are presented in Tables 5.5 and 5.6 – the average length of sentences (i.e. number of words) and TTR given to an accuracy of one decimal place.

These values illustrate some quality values of the end product; for instance, TTR indicates the lexical variation in the text, but it is influenced by the text length, which is seen in P7's value: her text is the longest, therefore, TTR is low. On the other hand, the average length of sentences is high, which also indicates a certain quality of her text. A well-structured text is a sign of quality (e.g. Fayol, 1997), but ultimately quality is related to reader perception (cf. perceived fluency; Segalowitz, 2010, 2016); for instance, text coherence can be a subjective measure as it depends on readers' earlier knowledge of the subject matter (on aspects of cohesion/coherence, see, for instance, Council of Europe, 2001; Fayol, 1997).

**Table 5.6** Scores of the evaluation of the end product

| | Evaluation of the end product | | | |
|---|---|---|---|---|
| P | Grammar and lexis max 36 | Coherence 36 | CEFR 24 | Total (96/%) |
| 1. P1 | 24 | 22 | 16 | 62/65% |
| 2. P2 | 22 | 24 | 14 | 62/65% |
| 3. P3 | 26 | 24 | 18 | 68/71% |
| 4. P4 | 22 | 20 | 14 | 56/58% |
| 5. P5 | 24 | 24 | 14 | 62/65% |
| 6. P6 | 26 | 30 | 16 | 72/75% |
| 7. P7 | 36 | 20 | 19 | 75/78% |
| 8. P8 | 25 | 23 | 15 | 63/66% |
| 9. P9 | 23 | 27 | 15 | 65/68% |
| 10. P10 | 17 | 13 | 15 | 45/47% |
| 11. P11 | 23 | 21 | 14 | 58/60% |
| Mean | 24 | 23 | 16 | 63/66% |

CEFR = Common European Framework of Reference for Languages.

The evaluation of the end product consisted of three different scores given by native teachers. Table 5.6 illustrates the distribution of scores for each writer.

Table 5.6 shows, for instance, that P7 received the best total score in evaluation of the end product; nevertheless, the coherence of her text was evaluated as one of the lowest. For some reason, she did not seem to pay enough attention to this task, which affected the result; the evaluators commented that her text lacked textual organisation and inner coherence (e.g. the text was written in one paragraph). On the other hand, P6, who had average values in Table 5.5 illustrating text structure related quality, had the second highest total score (72/96, 75%) and highest coherence score (30/36). To answer the question of whether a relationship between fluency in writing and end product exists, correlations between different process-oriented (pause lengths, number of intra-lexical pauses, median transition times, total writing time, pause time in relation to total writing time, number of editions, number of deleted characters, length of initial writing phase, length of revision phase) and end product values (number of words, clauses and sentences, the average length of words and sentences, the number of characters and words in relation to total writing time, type/token ration, evaluations scores) were calculated. Only the significant correlations are shown in Table 5.7.

The total score significantly correlated with lexical and grammatical accuracy (0.860, $p \leq 0.01$), coherence (0.686, $p \leq 0.05$), CEFR (0.637, $p \leq 0.05$) and number of sentences and clauses (−0.756, $p \leq 0.01$), the last

**Table 5.7** Significant correlations

| Correlations in L2 French | Pearson (r) |
|---|---|
| A) General flow of processes | |
| Number of final characters vs number of words | 0.994 ($p \leq 0.01$) |
| Number of linear characters vs number of words | 0.784 ($p \leq 0.01$) |
| Total writing time vs pauses ($\geq 2$) | 0.803 ($p \leq 0.01$) |
| Total writing time vs pauses ($\geq 5$) | 0.860 ($p \leq 0.01$) |
| Total writing time vs intra-lexical pauses ($\geq 2$) | 0.622 ($p \leq 0.05$) |
| Total writing time vs intra-lexical pauses ($\geq 5$) | 0.647 ($p \leq 0.05$) |
| Total writing time vs editions | 0.632 ($p \leq 0.05$) |
| Total writing time vs deletions | 0.628 ($p \leq 0.05$) |
| Total writing time vs state 3 (reflective pauses) | 0.622 ($p \leq 0.05$) |
| Pauses ($\geq 2$) vs pauses ($\geq 5$) | 0.920 ($p \leq 0.01$) |
| Pauses ($\geq 2$) vs state 3 (reflective pauses) | 0.606 ($p \leq 0.05$) |
| Pauses ($\geq 2$) vs editions | 0.655 ($p \leq 0.05$) |
| Pauses ($\geq 2$) vs deletions | 0.613 ($p \leq 0.05$) |
| Pauses ($\geq 5$) vs state 3 (reflective pauses) | 0.754 ($p \leq 0.01$) |
| Editions vs deletions | 0.991 ($p \leq 0.01$) |
| B) Criteria of quality | |
| Number of words vs grammatical and lexical accuracy | 0.838 ($p \leq 0.01$) |
| Number of words vs CEFR evaluation | 0.715 ($p \leq 0.05$) |
| Total score vs grammatical and lexical accuracy | 0.860 ($p \leq 0.01$) |
| Total score vs coherence | 0.686 ($p \leq 0.05$) |
| Total score vs CEFR | 0.637 ($p \leq 0.05$) |
| Total score vs number of sentences and clauses | −0.756 ($p \leq 0.01$) |
| Number of words vs number of sentences | 0.687 ($p \leq 0.05$) |
| Number of words vs number of clauses | 0.949 ($p \leq 0.01$) |
| Number of sentences vs number of clauses | 0.754 ($p \leq 0.01$) |

CEFR = Common European Framework of Reference for Languages

being a negative correlation, that is a higher number of sentences and clauses resulted in a lower total score. The striking lack in Table 5.7 is the significant correlation between measures of the process and the end product. This means that the results indicated no significant correlations between the final scores of the text and the process-orientated fluency measures. In other words, the general flow of writing process did not have a direct impact on the success of the end product. This also means that the different writer profiles based on writing processes were not directly related to a good end result.

## Discussion

There has been a lack of studies on L2 writing fluency in which both process and product-oriented data are analysed. Therefore, in this study, these two perspectives were combined, the main focus being on writing processes and writer profiles created on the basis of different process-oriented measures. These were then compared to the evaluation of the end product, of which some parts, such as text coherence, are quite subjective criteria illustrating reader perception of a fluent end product. This was done to analyse the relationship between fluency in the writing process and in the end product, and to see how they were related to writer profiles.

The results show that there is no linear relationship between the measures studied as no significant correlations between the final scores of the text and the process-orientated fluency measures were found. The general flow of the writing process did not have a direct impact on the perceived quality of the end product; therefore, the different writer profiles based on writing processes did not predict a good end result in terms of evaluation. One could argue that cognitive fluency in writing processes shown as ease during writing (i.e. a non-stop writer profile) would result in a successful performance, but this was not shown in this experiment. The results should therefore be replicated with other populations with a different L2 and/or with a larger number of participants, and a more sophisticated statistical analysis such as regression analysis could be run. The writer profiles could also be defined according to a different categorisation (see e.g. Tillema *et al.*, 2011). Writer profiles are also related to strategic decisions during the process and more research needs to be conducted on the differences between expert and novice writers' processes (e.g. Roca de Larios *et al.*, 2016). For instance, verbalisations could also reveal some of their strategic choices (cf. Bowles, 2010; Gufoni, 1996; Mutta, 2007, 2017a; Olive, 2010; Turcotte & Cloutier, 2014). In future studies, participants' multilingualism and various proficiency levels in each language should also be taken into account when creating writer profiles. Furthermore, more longitudinal studies are needed to follow the changes in writer profiles related to increased expertise.

Writing on a computer differs from the handwriting process, but fluency can be studied partly with similar measures (e.g. Alves & Limpo, 2015; Olive, 2010, 2014): the rapid transition between keystrokes/letters or words per minute of the writing time (Kellogg, 1996; see also Chenoweth & Hayes, 2001; Ellis & Yuan, 2004). Even if these measures give an image of a certain type of fluency related to the speed of writing, and denoting the automaticity of some cognitive processes, they only provide a partial picture of the whole phenomenon. It is noteworthy that typing skills in general have supposedly changed due to technological development and the use of mobile devices, which should be taken into account in future studies among so-called digital natives and other writers (Gregg & Nelson, 2018: 88). Their writer profiles might diverge from profiles found in previous studies. Furthermore, instead of focusing on pausal behaviour in L2 writing, the study of bursts, which reflects the length of uninterrupted chunks of text between pauses, could yield new information on writing fluency (cf. Kowal, 2014; also Chenoweth & Hayes, 2001). The mean length of burst represents in Kowal's study continuity in the writing process and therefore fluent writing (e.g. Alves & Limpo, 2015).

On the other hand, in production-oriented studies, fluency is related to how coherent, logical, error-free and well-structured the text is (see e.g. Crossley *et al.*, 2016; Nation, 2009; Rose, 2018) and this could be studied in the CAF framework in the same way as oral production (Ellis & Yuan, 2004; Gunnarsson, 2012). In more recent speech fluency studies, the traditional fluency–disfluency distinction is seen as being more gradual than polar, and several disfluency characteristics, such as hesitation, false starts and repetition, can in fact in some contexts facilitate communication, making it more fluent (e.g. Peltonen & Lintunen, 2016). These can also be studied in writing as there are similarities in oral and written processes (e.g. Mutta & Suzanne, 2012).

## Conclusion

Fluency in writing, as in other language skills, can be approached from several perspectives. In this study, the general flow criteria were interpreted as revealing aspects of cognitive fluency during the writing process, whereas production (i.e. utterance) fluency was measured by the quality of the end product. Reader perception was related to perceived fluency, that is how logically and smoothly written the text is from the reader's perspective. In sum, fluency in writing combines all senses of fluency (Segalowitz, 2010, 2016) in different ways and exceeds the dichotomous boundaries of fluent and disfluent writing. By combining product- and process-oriented approaches and accompanying them with writers' verbalisations, research can reveal new information about the online management of writing processes and contribute to the field of L2 writing fluency.

## Notes

(1) Participants are considered multilingual as they all speak at least three languages. Finland is a multilingual society, as it is officially a bilingual, namely, Finnish-Swedish, Swedish being the minority language (roughly 5% of the population). English is the most studied L2 language in Finland.
(2) An HMM is a statistical model which describes the finite states of a phenomenon. HMMs are known for their application in temporal pattern recognition, such as speech and writing processes resembling to some extent speech processes (Ellis &

Yuan, 2004; Kowal, 2014; Olive, 2014). The model was used to represent the states of pauses, which reflect cognitive processes (Fayol, 1997; Olive, 2010). Emeritus Professor of Statistics at the University of Turku Esa Uusipaikka ran the calculations concerning the HMM model. We would like to thank him for making the experiment possible.

## References

Alves, R.A. and Limpo, T. (2015) Progress in written language bursts, pauses, transcription, and written composition across schooling. *Scientific Studies of Reading* 19 (5), 1–18.
Bowles, M.A. (2010) *The Think-aloud Controversy in Second Language Research*. New York: Routledge.
Chenoweth, N.A. and Hayes, J.R. (2001) Fluency in writing: Generating text in L1 and L2. *Written Communication* 18 (1), 80–98.
Council of Europe (2001) *Common European Framework of Reference for Languages. Learning, Teaching, Assessment*. Cambridge: Cambridge University Press. Retrieved from https://rm.coe.int/1680459f97.
Crossley, S.A., Kyle, K. and McNamara, D.S. (2016) The development and use of cohesive devices in L2 writing and their relations to judgments of essay quality. *Journal of Second Language Writing* 32, 1–16.
Ellis, R. and Yuan, F. (2004) The effects of planning on fluency, complexity, and accuracy in second language narrative writing. *Studies in Second Language Acquisition* 26 (1), 59–84.
Fayol, M. (1997) *Des idées au texte. Psychologie cognitive de la production verbale, orale et écrite*. [From ideas to texts. Cognitive psychology of verbal written and oral production]. Paris: Presses Universitaires de France.
Gaonac'h, D. and Larigauderie, P. (2000) *Mémoire et fonctionnement cognitif. La mémoire de travail*. [Memory and cognitive function. Working memory]. Paris: Armand Colin.
Gregg, N. and Nelson, J. (2018) Empirical studies on writing abilities of adolescent and adults with learning difficulties. In B. Miller, P. McCardle and V. Connelly (eds) *Writing Development in Struggling Learners. Understanding the Needs of Writers across the Lifecourse* (pp. 73–95). Leiden: Brill.
Gufoni, V. (1996) Les protocoles verbaux comme méthode d'étude de la production écrite: approche critique. [Verbal protocols as a method to study written production: critical approach]. *Étude de Linguistique Appliquée* 101, 20–32.
Gunnarsson, C. (2012) The development of complexity, accuracy and fluency in the written production of L2 French. In A. Housen, F. Kuiken and I. Vedder (eds) *Dimensions of L2 Performance and Proficiency. Complexity, Accuracy and Fluency in SLA* (pp. 247–276). Amsterdam: John Benjamins.
Hayes, J.R. and Flower, L.S. (1980) Identifying the organization of writing processes. In L.W. Gregg and E.R. Steinberg (eds) *Cognitive Processes in Writing* (pp. 3–30). Hillsdale, NJ: Lawrence Erlbaum.
Janssen, D., Van Waes, L. and Van den Bergh, H. (1996) Effects of thinking aloud on writing processes. In C.M. Levy and S. Ransdell (eds) *The Science of Writing: Theories, Methods, Individual Differences, and Applications* (pp. 233–250). Mahwah, NJ: Lawrence Erlbaum.
Kellogg, R.T. (1996) A model of working memory in writing. In C.M. Levy and S. Ransdell (eds) *The Science of Writing: Theories, Methods, Individual Differences, and Applications* (pp. 57–72). Mahwah, NJ: Lawrence Erlbaum.
Kowal, I. (2014) Fluency in second language writing: A developmental perspective. *Studia Linguistica Universitatis Iagellonicae Cracoviensis* 131, 229–246.

Lennon, P. (1990) Investigating fluency in EFL: A quantitative approach. *Language Learning* 40, 387–417.
Levelt, W.J.M., Roelofs, A. and Meyer, A.S. (1999) A theory of lexical access in speech production. *Behavioral and Brain Sciences* 22, 1–38.
Mutta, M. (2007) *Un processus cognitif peut en cacher un autre: étude de cas sur l'aisance rédactionnelle des scripteurs finnophones et francophones.* [A cognitive process can hide another. A case study of written fluency by Finnish and French writers]. Turku: University of Turku.
Mutta, M. (2017a) La conscience métapragmatique et l'attitude métacognitive épistémique des scripteurs universitaires: la révision de texte en temps réel. [Metapragmatic consciousness and epistemic stance of university writers: the case of online revision]. *Pratiques* 173–174.
Mutta, M. (2017b) Pausal behavior in the writing processes of foreign and native language writers: The importance of defining the individual pause length. In S. Plane *et al.* (eds) *Research on Writing: Multiple Perspectives* (pp. 511–529). International Exchanges on the Study of Writing. Fort Collins, Colorado: The WAC Clearinghouse and CREM.
Mutta, M. and Suzanne, V. (2012) Divergence et convergence dans les processus de production orale et écrite en FLE [Divergence and convergence in written and oral processes in L2 French]. In A. Kamber and C. Skupien Dekens (eds) *Recherches récentes en FLE* (pp. 123–145). Bern: Peter Lang.
Nation, I.S.P. (2009) *Teaching ESL/EFL. Reading and Writing.* New York: Routledge.
Olive, T. (2010) Methods, tools and techniques for the on-line study of the writing process. In N.L. Mertens (ed.) *Writing: Processes, Tools and Techniques* (pp. 1–18). New York: Nova Publishers.
Olive, T. (2014) Toward a parallel and cascading model of the writing system: A review of research on writing processes coordination. *Journal of Writing Research* 6 (2), 173–194.
Peltonen, P. and Lintunen, P. (2016) Integrating quantitative and qualitative approaches in L2 fluency analysis: A study of Finnish-speaking and Swedish-speaking learners of English at two school levels. *European Journal of Applied Linguistics* 4, 209–238.
Roca de Larios, J., Coyle, Y. and Nicolás-Conesa, F. (2016) Focus on writers: Processes and strategies. In R.M. Manchón and P.K. Matsuda (eds) *Handbook of Second and Foreign Language Writing* (pp. 267–286). Berlin: De Gruyter Mouton.
Roca de Larios, J., Manchón, R.M. and Murphy, L. (2006) Generating text in native and foreign language writing: A temporal analysis of problem-solving formulation processes. *The Modern Language Journal* 90, 100–114.
Roca de Larios, J., Manchón, R.M., Murphy, L. and Marín, J. (2008) The foreign language writer's strategic behaviour in the allocation of time to writing processes. *Journal of Second Language Writing* 17, 30–47.
Rose, D. (2018) Evaluating the task of language learning. In T. Muller, J. Adamson, P.S. Brown and S. Herder (eds) *Exploring EFL Fluency in Asia* (pp. 161–181). Basingstoke: Palgrave Macmillan.
Sasaki, M. (2004) A multiple-data analysis of the 3.5-year development of EFL student writers. *Language Learning* 54, 525–582.
Segalowitz, N. (2010) *The Cognitive Bases of Second Language Fluency.* New York: Routledge.
Segalowitz, N. (2016) Second language fluency and its underlying cognitive and social determinants. *International Review of Applied Linguistics in Language Teaching* 54 (2), 79–95.
Spelman Miller, K. (2000) Academic writers on-line: Investigating pausing in the production of text. *Language Teaching Research* 4 (2), 123–148.
Tillema, M., Van den Bergh H., Rijlaarsdam, G. and Sanders, T. (2011) Relating self reports of writing behaviour and online task execution using a temporal model. *Metacognition Learning* 6, 229–253.

Turcotte, C. and Cloutier, E. (2014) Le rappel stimulé pour mieux comprendre les stratégies de lecture d'élèves du primaire à risque et compétents. [Stimulated recall in strategic reading by elementary school pupils]. *Canadian Journal of Education/Revue canadienne de l'éducation* 37 (1), 72–95.

Van Waes, L. (1992) The influence of the computer on writer profiles. In H. Pander Maat and M. Steehouder (eds) *Studies of Functional Text Quality* (pp. 173–186). Amsterdam – Atlanta, GA: Editions Rodopi B.V.

Van Waes, L. and Schellens, P.J. (2003) Writing profiles: The effect of the writing mode on pausing and revision patterns of experiences writers. *Journal of Pragmatics* 35, 829–853.

Wengelin, Å. (2002) *Text Production in Adults with Reading and Writing Difficulties*. Gothenburg Monographs in Linguistics 20. Gothenburg: Department of Linguistics, Gothenburg University.

# 6 Fluency in English as a Lingua Franca Interaction

Niina Hynninen

## Introduction

Research on English as a lingua franca (ELF) is concerned with communication in English in settings where at least one of the speakers uses English as a second language (L2). ELF is sometimes taken to exclude native speakers of English and to apply only to speakers for whom English is not a first language (L1) (e.g. Firth, 1996; House, 1999), but the definition adopted here is one that accepts native speakers as part of the mix (e.g. Jenkins, 2007; Mauranen, 2012; Seidlhofer, 2004, 2011). Hence, I define ELF as 'a contact language between speakers or speaker groups when at least one of them uses it as a second language' (Mauranen, 2017: 8). A key term in understanding the definition is 'L2 use' (Mauranen, 2012). In ELF research, ELF communication is treated as perfectly normal language use, which takes place in settings where the speakers' primary goal is not to 'learn more English', but rather to communicate with their interlocutors (e.g. Ranta, 2009). An L2 speaker of English in an ELF setting is thus *a user*, rather than a learner, of English. ELF research explores communication between these L2 users of English, along with any L1 speakers of different varieties of English taking part in the interactions.

In addition, contrary to Second Language Acquisition (SLA) research, where the unit of analysis tends to be the individual L2 learner, the focus of much ELF research has been 'on a level above the individual' (Ranta, 2009: 88), and on wider patterns in the ways L2 users of English interact and make use of their linguistic resources in practice. The data are typically naturally occurring, rather than elicited samples. For instance, much research on ELF has explored spoken ELF interaction, and what speakers do to achieve mutual understanding in such interactions. While fluency has typically not been the main focus of ELF studies, much ELF research has duly been concerned with issues related to the smoothness, ease or effortlessness of communicating in ELF settings – all attributes typically associated with fluency. Particularly the focus of ELF research on communication, rather than on individuals, also raises a number of questions related to the concept of fluency and how fluency could be approached in studying L2 learning. This chapter reviews existing literature on ELF from the perspective of fluency and seeks connections between ELF and L2 fluency research. The chapter ends with a discussion of the implications of ELF research for studying L2 fluency.

## How Fluency has been Approached in ELF Research

Few studies have explicitly approached fluency in ELF. Hüttner's (2009) small-scale study on perceived fluency is one of the few where the concept has been defined and discussed in the light of ELF research. I start by presenting Hüttner's (2009) study because her suggestion to approach fluency as a descriptor of interactions rather than of individual speakers highlights the interactional focus of ELF research in general and provides a good starting point for our discussion of the implications of ELF research for studying L2 fluency.

Hüttner (2009: 275) proposes 'a dialogic conceptualisation of fluency, focusing on interactivity as a crucial characteristic of it, and fluency as an enactment of a speaker's language competence adjustable to contextual conditions'. In this conceptualisation, fluency is approached as an interactional, dialogic phenomenon where the key focus is on interaction and on fitting speech into context. Hüttner's (2009) proposition of fluency as an interactional phenomenon is supported by her analysis of two rated samples of ELF interactions. Interestingly, the raters described such ELF interactions as the most fluent where all participants contributed to the discussion and were involved in developing a coherent dialogue. In line with more interactionally oriented L2 fluency studies (e.g. McCarthy, 2010), the active involvement of participants in co-constructing the interaction thus seems to contribute to how fluent an interaction is perceived to be (Hüttner, 2009). One rater also commented that individual fluency levels could not be identified in one of the examples, which, Hüttner (2009) suggests, indicates that fluency could be viewed as a descriptor of interactions rather than of individual speakers.

While Hüttner's (2009) study is limited in its scope, her proposal is important in drawing attention to fluency not only as a characteristic of an individual speaker's production, but also and more importantly as a characteristic of the interaction the speaker is taking part in. This approach emphasises that speakers may appear more or less fluent depending on the person they are talking to or the situation in which they are interacting (e.g. Sato, 2014), which highlights the importance of considering speech in the interactional context in which it occurs (see also Bavelas *et al.*, 2000). Hüttner's (2009) proposition can thus be seen to have important implications for evaluating speaker performance (see below).

Another study which focuses on fluency in ELF is by Prodromou (2008). This book-length study links fluency to idiomaticity, which seems to be associated with the use of prefabricated language or formulaic sequences (cf. Wray, 2002). Prodromou (2008) observes that English native language (ENL) prefabrications enhance fluency in ELF interaction, but that they can also cause problems for intelligibility. These findings are in line with other ELF studies that have explored the use of ENL idioms in ELF interaction and which, importantly, also consider how new idioms may be created (e.g. Pitzl, 2012; Seidlhofer & Widdowson, 2009). Despite this attention to prefabrications, however, Prodromou's (2008) description of fluency takes pragmatic and sociocultural perspectives into account (see McCarthy, 2010). Similarly to Hüttner (2009), he leans towards a more interactional understanding of fluency, even though he does not go quite as far as proposing fluency as a characteristic of interaction; rather, Prodromou (2008: 69) describes fluency as an 'integrated ability to maintain smooth continuity in ongoing talk with pragmatic appropriateness of utterances'. While this definition seems to emphasise the individual speaker, it also sees this speaker as taking part in interactions.

Taken together, Hüttner's (2009) and Prodromou's (2008) work implies that L2 fluency research that explores interactional oral fluency (e.g. Peltonen, 2017; Sato, 2014) is the most relevant from an ELF perspective. In such L2 fluency research, features typically associated with the (dis)fluency of an individual speaker's production (e.g. pausing and repair) are re-examined in terms of their role in the interaction where the individual participates. To explain this connection between ELF research and interactional fluency studies in more detail, I now turn to ELF studies that have *not* focused on fluency as such but that can be reinterpreted in light of fluency research. I have structured the discussion around Segalowitz's (2010) three dimensions of fluency and thus examine ELF research findings in relation to (a) cognitive fluency, which refers to the speed and efficiency of speech production processing, (b) utterance fluency, which, following Skehan's (2003, 2009; Tavakoli & Skehan, 2005) classification, typically covers speed, pausing and repair and (c) perceived fluency, or the listener's fluency evaluations. At the same time, I seek connections to studies that adopt a more interactional perspective on fluency (e.g. McCarthy, 2010; Peltonen, 2017; Sato, 2014), where fluency relates to smooth turn-taking, for instance, and may therefore be viewed as 'a joint performance' (Sato, 2014: 88) between speakers.

## Cognitive fluency in ELF

Among the few studies within ELF research that can be seen to shed light on cognitive fluency in ELF, or the speed and efficiency of speech production processing (see e.g. Segalowitz, 2010), is Mauranen's (2012, see also 2007) corpus linguistic work on spoken academic ELF, and her focus on ELF phraseology in particular. Formulaic sequences, or chunks of language that are stored and accessed as whole units in one's memory, ease the cognitive load in language production (Wray, 2002). They have been found to make processing easier and more fluent, at least for L1 speakers (e.g. Pawley & Syder, 1983; Wray, 2002). Typically, formulaic sequences consist of lexical words and grammatical elements, with fixed and variable parts. Mauranen (2012: 141–161) shows that L2 users of English in ELF interaction may use such conventionalised, phraseological units in ways that do not entirely match the target form, that is, they resort to approximate forms of the language. She first provides a number of examples from the ELFA corpus of English as a lingua franca in academic settings that resemble formulaic sequences. These examples include expressions such as *take a closer look to the world*, *how to put the end on it* and *you said a lot of er good points*. Later she discusses special features of ELF phraseology in more detail, including the multi-word unit *some words about*, for instance.

As can be seen, non-standard articles and prepositions as well as lexis that is untypical in ENL occur in the examples. However, as Mauranen puts it, all of these sequences are 'recognisable as units of meaning in their contexts [...], these meanings match conventionalised phraseological units, because they seem to fall within an acceptable range of variability to be recognised and understood' (2012: 143–144). So, the examples provided above approximate to the following formulaic sequences: *take a closer look at*, *put an end to*, *make a point* and *a few words about*. The last example on the list was an interesting case of possible ELF-specific developments. In MICASE, a mainly ENL corpus of academic speaking (see Simpson *et al.*, 2002), *words about* only occurred in the cluster of *a few words about*, whereas there was more variation in ELFA, with *some words about* as the most common pattern (Mauranen, 2012: 153–154).

Mauranen's argument is that these kinds of examples are 'approximate versions of schematic wholes that to all intents look like being stored and processed as single wholes' (2012: 144). If this is true, it would mean that L2 users do not build every utterance from its smallest components (as suggested in Wray, 2002) but, similarly to L1 speakers, can rely on larger schematic units (see Vetchinnikova, 2014). In terms of cognitive fluency, this suggests that even though formulaic sequences in ELF may be malformed in relation to ENL, they may be accessed as prefabricated units and are thus quickly retrieved from memory, which can further be taken as evidence of normal processing and processing fluency.

What is more, Mauranen's (2012) findings illustrate that approximations rarely seemed to cause interactional disruption. Hence, it is possible that, similarly to speakers, listeners in ELF interaction may also rely on 'fuzzy processing' (Mauranen, 2017), and may not notice that there would be anything 'wrong' with the approximate forms used. In Mauranen's words, an approximate form, for example, may not be harder to understand than a precise form, because a typical hearer is not very precisely attuned to Standard English (or any particular variety of English), but is likely to rely on fairly fuzzy processing in making sense of the interlocutor's speech. (Mauranen, 2017: 18)

This engagement in fuzzy processing by both speakers and listeners in turn leads to acceptance of the approximations in interaction (Mauranen, 2012; 2017). In all, it could be argued that relying on this kind of fuzzy processing ensures the efficiency of speech production and reception in ELF.

## Utterance fluency in ELF

Out of the three components typically associated with utterance fluency, that is, speed (e.g. speech rate), breakdown (different aspects of pausing), and repair (false starts, repetitions and rephrasings), the last one has received the most attention in ELF research. Studies conducted on achieving mutual understanding in ELF interaction are a case in point (e.g. Jenkins, 2000; Kaur, 2009, 2011; Mauranen, 2006, 2007, 2012; Pietikäinen, 2018). Without drawing explicit links to fluency research, ELF research has approached repair (particularly repetitions and rephrasings) as they occur in interaction. Studies have examined the kinds of features that cause repair, and the functions that repairs serve in the interaction. This approach is similar to some L2 fluency studies, where repairs have been approached from an interactional, problem-solving perspective (e.g. Peltonen, 2017). The perspective is a response to previous fluency research that shows that many of the speed and (especially silent) pause measures differentiate between fluent and non-fluent speakers (e.g. Bosker *et al.*, 2013; Kormos & Dénes, 2004), whereas it appears that repairs are not straightforward markers of disfluency (e.g. Götz, 2013; Riggenbach, 1991). With its interactional focus, ELF research on repairs can contribute to the further characterisation of fluency in interactional settings.

Jenkins's (2000) seminal study on the phonology of ELF stemmed from recognising which pronunciation features caused misunderstandings in ELF interaction, and were consequently a potential cause for repair. This led her to suggest a set of pronunciation features (known as the Lingua Franca Core) that may be more central to achieving mutual understanding in ELF contexts compared to other pronunciation features. To avoid repair work to resolve non- or misunderstandings caused by these other features, Jenkins (2000) concluded that speakers need both receptive and productive accommodation skills (see also Cogo & Dewey, 2006). From an utterance fluency perspective, accommodation reduces the need for repair work; from a cognitive perspective, when speakers and listeners become more attuned to differences in pronunciation (and other) features, they become better at processing (see also Anckar & Veivo in the present volume).

Although accommodation is readily observable in ELF interaction (e.g. Cogo & Dewey, 2006; Hynninen, 2016), repair work is sometimes needed, and speakers have been found to draw on various means of preventing and resolving misunderstandings. These include the repetition of problematic items and (self-)rephrasing (see Pietikäinen, 2018 for a fuller list), which in L2 fluency research have often been treated as indicating disfluency (e.g. Skehan, 2009). What Mauranen (2007; 2012) suggests instead is that repetition and rephrasing in ELF may facilitate communication; that they may actually provide both speakers and listeners with 'breathing spaces' (Mauranen, 2012: 230) that afford them the opportunity to prepare for what is going to be said next. For instance, her findings show that

> repeats [i.e. single-word repetitions] that seem to indicate that the speaker is playing for time appear at various kinds of junctures in discourse – between chunk boundaries and clause boundaries, for instance. Thus they occur between elements that are principal message-bearing units and the most crucial contributors to the evolving shared understanding of content. In this way, the repeats, together with hesitations and filled pauses, facilitate processing for both speakers and hearers by dishing out the message in shortish chunks. (Mauranen, 2012: 230)

The so-called disfluency features mentioned in the above quote, repeats (as a special form of repetition), hesitations and pauses, along with other such features (e.g. rephrasing), are a normal part of speaking (see Rühlemann, 2007). While they may still be seen as making an individual's speech less fluent, both Mauranen's (2012) research on ELF and studies on L1 and L2 fluency (e.g. Carroll, 2000; Peltonen, 2017; Rühlemann *et al.*, 2011) suggest that they may serve important interactional functions and contribute to the fluency of the interaction (cf. Hüttner, 2009). For instance, Peltonen (2017) has shown how repetitions may function as fluency enhancing resources in interactions, rather than as markers of disfluency. In other words, what may seem to be a disfluency in an individual speaker's performance may actually benefit the interaction as a whole.

In terms of (self-)rephrasing, Mauranen's (2007) findings show that rephrasings typically concerned form and could thus be seen to work towards clarity and in helping to avoid misunderstandings. According to Mauranen (2007), rephrasings can be seen to increase the chances of being understood by listeners, as it is likely that at least one of the different formulations will get across to them. This is evident in one of Pietikäinen's (2018: 15–16) examples, where a speaker insisted on self-repairing until her interlocutor produced a satisfactory token of understanding (cf. Carroll, 2000). Similar findings are reported, for instance, by Kaur (2009), who concludes that speakers employed rephrasing when the listener was perceived to have difficulty in understanding them. Self-rephrasing may thus serve important interactional functions, even though the need to repair might also be related to the speaker's limited L2 competence.

As a result, it seems that both repetition and rephrasing in ELF serve important interactional or problem-solving functions in that they may increase the chances of mutual understanding. As also suggested in L2 fluency research, they are not straightforward markers of disfluency. The findings reported above can thus be seen to support approaching repair practices (i.e. repetition and rephrasing) in ELF as fluency-enhancing resources (cf. Peltonen, 2017), rather than simply as markers of disfluency in an individual's speech production, as well as considering the phenomenon not only by quantifying the features, but also from the perspective of the functions that the different forms of repair perform in the interaction. In all, the findings seem to be in line with Sato's (2014) suggestion that individual and interactional oral fluency may be two different constructs; that specific fluency features may be perceived differently when they occur in individual performance as opposed to during interaction. This direction is also evident in other L2 fluency studies where fluency is approached as an interactional phenomenon (e.g. Peltonen, 2017; Tavakoli, 2016).

In addition to repairs (as markers of repair fluency), utterance fluency studies have often focused on the amount and speed of speech (i.e. speed fluency) as well as the number, length and position of pauses (i.e. breakdown fluency) (see Skehan, 2003, 2009; Tavakoli & Skehan, 2005). The perspective has often been quantitative (however, see Peltonen & Lintunen, 2016), whereas in ELF studies, these aspects have received limited attention, and rather from a more qualitative perspective where, for instance, functions of the pauses in the interactive creation of meaning have been considered (e.g. Böhringer, 2007).

In L2 fluency studies, a higher speech rate with fewer discontinuities is often seen as an indication of more automatic language processing, and thus an indication of more fluent speech (see Segalowitz, 2010). This understanding is plausible from the perspective of an individual's speech production, but it seems that when the speed of delivery and pauses are considered as an interactional phenomenon, the situation becomes more complex. This interactional perspective has been adopted within some L2 fluency studies; for instance, drawing on his corpus analysis of interactional data, McCarthy (2010: 7) argues that fluency during interaction is a question of 'shared responsibility to fill silences and uncomfortably long pauses'. This kind of minimising of gaps and overlaps has actually been suggested as a universal feature of conversation (Stivers *et al.*, 2009). Sato (2014) similarly states that while pauses in monologic speech may be an indication of slow L2 processing, in interaction pauses relate to turn-taking and may be a sign of unwillingness to participate. He suggests that in interaction, 'pause phenomena could be conceptualised as worse turn-taking or higher levels of engagement, as opposed to the actual speed of producing L2' (Sato, 2014: 86).

In ELF research, the interactional focus has been particularly pronounced, and as discussed above in relation to repair fluency, considerable attention has been paid to how speakers jointly achieve mutual understanding. In terms of speed and breakdown fluency, Deterding's (2013: 173) study on misunderstandings in ELF suggests that fast speech delivery 'may have a negative impact on intelligibility and it can give rise to misunderstandings'. His conclusion is that participants in ELF interaction are best advised to slow down their speech if they want to increase their chances of being understood. Interestingly, Derwing and Munro's (2001) study on speech rates also shows that listeners preferred a somewhat slower speech rate when the accent of the speaker was other than their own, which tends to be the case in ELF interaction. The fluent speech of an individual – produced with a higher speech rate and fewer discontinuities – may thus not be productive in ELF interaction. Rather, it seems that what is called for is the ability of the speaker to adjust their speech rate and pause behaviour according to their interlocutors and the interactional situation, which further highlights the centrality of accommodation in ELF interaction (see Jenkins, 2000).

## Perceived fluency in ELF

In terms of perceived fluency, much L2 fluency research has focused on listener perceptions of an individual speaker's speech production. However, there seems to be no doubt that a speaker may be perceived as more or less fluent depending on the interactional situation and their co-interactants (see e.g. Fillmore, 1979; Tavakoli, 2016). For instance, Sato (2014: 88) concludes that 'oral fluency in an individual context is at best weakly indicative of performance in an interactional context', which leads him to distinguish between individual and interactional oral fluency. While individual fluency relates to the speaker's ability to produce fluent speech within their turn, interactional fluency relates to the shared responsibility of the participants to maintain fluency across turns (see McCarthy, 2010; Peltonen, 2017). Distinguishing between these two constructs may actually be key to also understanding the implications of ELF research for studying L2 fluency. As stated at the outset, the focus of ELF research has been on interaction, whereas much of L2 fluency research has dealt with monologic data. ELF research findings can thus shed light on what constitutes fluent conversation, as well as how individual fluency is manifested and perceived in interaction.

What, then, contributes to perceived fluency in an interactional rather than a monologic context? Hüttner (2009) found that the raters in her data did not pay attention to individual speech rate in ELF interactions, which led her to conclude that the speed of delivery may not be a decisive characteristic of fluency in ELF at all. In addition, she conjectures that interactional features such as backchannels and lack of pauses during the interaction possibly contributed to how the raters perceived the fluency of the samples. Similarly, Sato (2014) found that turn-taking, scaffolding and pauses during the interaction influenced how fluent a learner was perceived to be during peer interaction. The findings of these two studies, from ELF and L2 fluency research respectively, thus point in the same direction, namely that the level of co-construction in the interaction is likely to influence perceptions of individual fluency.

One important aspect related to perceived fluency that I have not yet touched upon is the question of who the raters used in evaluating L2 performance are. In L2 fluency studies, the raters tend to be L1 speakers of the target language, which means that the studies yield L1 speaker perceptions of L2 production, which also seems to be typical of studies that focus on interactional fluency, such as that of Sato (2014). However, from an ELF perspective, sole reliance on L1 raters is problematic because this appears to presume that L1 English speakers are automatically experts of ELF interaction and that L1 use of English is the production target. Quite the contrary, ELF research has shown that achieving mutual understanding requires adaptation on the part of all participants in the interaction – including L1 English speakers (e.g. Jenkins, 2000). ELF research thus questions measuring fluency against a 'native speaker' target or using only native speakers as raters. I will return to these issues in more detail below.

To sum up, research on ELF, with its focus on communication, can be seen to encourage the kind of fluency research that has considered how specific interactional features enhance the fluency of the interaction and the fluency of individuals as part of the interaction, that is, research that focuses on interactional oral fluency as a construct distinct from individual oral fluency (e.g. McCarthy, 2010; Peltonen, 2017; Sato, 2014).

## Implications of ELF Research for Studying and Assessing L2 Fluency

Based on the above discussion, ELF research seems to highlight three main issues that should be taken into account when approaching L2 fluency, particularly in ELF contexts. Firstly, fluency in ELF should be approached as an interactional phenomenon. In all three of Segalowitz's (2010) dimensions of fluency, the focus is on the individual. In terms of cognitive fluency, attention is paid to speed and effectiveness of speech processing and thus the limitations of an individual's cognitive capacities. Utterance fluency, which, following Skehan's (2003, 2009; Tavakoli & Skehan, 2005) classification, typically focuses on speed, breakdown and/or repair fluency, tends to be studied either by using monologic data or by considering an individual's speech as distinct from the interactional context. A similar focus on monologic performance is also true of most studies focusing on perceived fluency. However, more interactional perspectives on L2 fluency have also been suggested (McCarthy, 2010; Peltonen, 2017; Sato, 2014), and it is these studies that ELF research comes closest to. Hüttner (2009) goes as far as to say that fluency is a characteristic of the interaction, rather than of individual speakers, but I would suggest drawing on the distinction between the constructs of individual and interactional fluency as presented, for instance, in McCarthy (2010) and Sato (2014). While ELF research, because of its interactional focus, naturally seems to support approaching fluency in interaction, retaining this distinction makes it possible to consider not only how fluency is jointly achieved by participants in interaction (e.g. through smooth turn-taking), but also how an individual speaker may be more or less fluent in producing speech in more monologic stretches of language (e.g. by using more or fewer unfilled pauses).

Secondly, fluency in ELF interaction should not be evaluated against an L1 English model, or solely by L1 English speakers. Much fluency research seems to continue using monolingual L1 speech as a model to which L2 production is compared (e.g. Götz, 2013; Peltonen & Lintunen, 2016; however, see Chambers, 1997; House, 2002). Peltonen and Lintunen (2016) also point out that it is only in recent years that fluency researchers have tended to use an L1 speaker control group. In addition, in studies on perceived fluency, raters have typically been L1 speakers. From an ELF perspective, this sole reliance on L1 models is problematic. ELF interactions take place in situations that are essentially multilingual, and where there may not be any L1 English speakers present. It is therefore clear that using (often monolingual) L1 English speakers (typically from so-called 'inner circle' countries, see Kachru, 1996) or interactions between L1 English speakers as a model for ELF interaction makes little sense. It is true that much in ELF resembles ENL (Mauranen, 2012), but at the same time, norms related to ENL interaction may not be important – or may not even be familiar – to the participants in ELF interaction; rather, norms are negotiated without necessarily drawing on L1 norms at all (see Hynninen, 2016). This means that fluency in ELF should be viewed in its own right, without treating ENL interactions as a model, and furthermore, that perceptions of fluency in ELF interaction by L2 users are just as relevant, if not more relevant, than the perceptions of L1 speakers.

Thirdly, following from the discussion above, the construct of interactional fluency should be taken seriously in assessing L2 speech production. In addition, in order to cater for contextual factors, the construct should be developed by drawing on research on various kinds of interactions, including those conducted in ELF. It is striking that the *Common European Framework of Reference for Languages* (Council of Europe, 2001), for instance, seems to treat fluency very much as a characteristic of individual speech production. This is illustrated by the following extract from the descriptor for fluency at level B2:

> Can produce stretches of language with a fairly even tempo; although he/she can be hesitant as he/she searches for patterns and expressions, there are few noticeably long pauses. (Council of Europe, 2001: 129)

Fluency in the CEFR evidently seems to relate to speed, pausing and repair (see Skehan, 2003, 2009) in an individual speaker's production. Within SLA research, however, it has been suggested more generally that interactional aspects should be taken into account in assessment. For example, Lindemann's (2006) study on L1–L2 interactions revealed that the L2 speakers' performance in the interaction was influenced by the interactional behaviour of the L1 speaker (which in turn was influenced by speaker attitudes). Based on these findings, Lindemann (2006) argues that L2 speaker performance can be assessed in relation to what the listener does, since as she puts it, '[i]t takes (at least) two to converse' (Lindemann, 2006: 24). In a similar vein, Bavelas *et al.* (2000), who studied the role of the listener in the speaker's storytelling, argue that the relationship between speaker and listener is reciprocal and collaborative. Their findings show that 'the narrator elicits responses from the listener and the listener's responses affect the narrator' (Bavelas *et al.*, 2000: 951). Hence, the particular challenge for assessing L2 fluency seems to be that an individual speaker may appear more or less fluent depending on their co-interactant. This raises the question of the kind of fluency that the assessment should focus on: Should individual fluency be assessed in an interactional context or rather in monologic production only? Furthermore, if the focus is on interactional fluency, how can we incorporate a proficiency dimension into it, that is, distinguish between speakers who contribute to interactional fluency more than others?

## Some Open Questions

It was established above that ELF research suggests that fluency can be viewed as an interactional phenomenon, with the focus on the kind of language use that contributes to interactional fluency. The question which then arises is, what contributes to interactional fluency, namely what do speakers do to achieve it? Moreover, how do we distinguish, if indeed it is possible to do so (cf. Hüttner, 2009), between speakers who contribute to interactional fluency more than others? In what ways are these speakers fluent, or is it even possible to establish a connection between interactional fluency and the fluency of individual speakers taking part in the interaction?

ELF interaction has been found to require adaptation on the part of all participants (e.g. Jenkins, 2000). This observation raises the question of whether fluency is related to the flexibility of the participants to adapt their language and attune their ears according to the situation and their co-participants. Not much has been said about the issue in relation to fluency, but based on the discussion above it would appear that acting like this, combined with doing pre-emptive work to avoid non- and misunderstandings (e.g. Pietikäinen, 2018), for example, seems to move the interaction along. This in turn may be an indication of increased interactional fluency, resulting, for instance, in fewer or shorter pauses during interaction (see McCarthy, 2010). If this is true, a speaker who, say, self-repairs could be taking responsibility for the interaction and contributing to interactional fluency – even if the self-repairs may (or may not) be seen to decrease the speaker's individual fluency. In any case, there is a need to investigate further what kind of language use contributes to interactional fluency in ELF (and otherwise), and in what ways features associated with individual (dis)fluency may actually serve specific functions in interaction.

When it comes to who is likely to contribute to interactional fluency more than others, we may turn our attention to speakers who possess the capacity to function as an intermediary between speakers who, for whatever reason, do not seem to understand each other, or who run the risk of misunderstanding each other (see Hynninen, 2012, 2016). Interestingly, this intermediary role is also acknowledged in the CEFR Companion Volume (Council of Europe, 2018: 33–34; see also Council of Europe, 2001) where mediation is highlighted as one of the four communicative language strategies (the others being reception, production and interaction). The fact that intermediaries intervene in interaction is likely to reduce gaps in turn-taking, and thus the act itself can be seen to contribute to interactional fluency. Furthermore, the way intermediaries behave (e.g. by rephrasing a previous speaker's expression) can shed light on the interactional functions of specific (dis)-fluency features, such as repetitions and rephrasings.

## Conclusion

What this review of ELF research suggests is that both L2 fluency research and L2 assessment pay more attention to interaction and to how individuals' contributions are tied to the interactional situations in which they are communicating. Clearly, more work needs to be done to better understand the relationship between individual and interactional fluency, and the way in which the two constructs can be used when evaluating speaker performance in ELF interaction. In terms of assessing English, a further challenge is to empirically investigate what exactly constitutes fluent communication in ELF – and who can determine that. What kind of ELF interaction is perceived as fluent? Which features are typical of such interaction, and what do speakers do in such interaction? The aim of this review has been to provide some initial observations and a starting point for further research on these issues.

## References

Bavelas, J., Coates, L. and Johnson, T. (2000) Listeners as co-narrators. *Journal of Personality and Social Psychology* 79 (6), 941–952.

Böhringer, H. (2007) The sound of silence: Silent and filled pauses in English as a lingua franca business interaction. Unpublished MA thesis, University of Vienna.

Bosker, H.R., Pinget, A.-F., Quené, H., Sanders, T. and De Jong, N.H. (2013) What makes speech sound fluent? The contributions of pauses, speed and repairs. *Language Testing* 30, 159–175.

Carroll, D. (2000) Precision timing in novice-to-novice L2 conversations. *Issues in Applied Linguistics* 11 (1), 67–110.

Council of Europe (2001) *Common European Framework of Reference for Languages: Learning, Teaching, Assessment*. Cambrige: Cambridge University Press. Retrieved from https://rm.coe.int/1680459f97.

Council of Europe (2018) *Common European Framework of Reference for Languages: Learning, Teaching, Assessment. Companion Volume with New Descriptors.* Council of Europe. Retrieved from https://rm.coe.int/cefr-companion-volume-with-new-descriptors-2018/1680787989.

Chambers, F. (1997) What do we mean by fluency? *System* 25 (4), 535–44.

Cogo, A. and Dewey, M. (2006) Efficiency in ELF communication: From pragmatic motives to lexico-grammatical innovation. *Nordic Journal of English Studies* 5 (2), 59–93.

Derwing, T. and Munro, M. (2001) What speaking rates do nonnative listeners prefer? *Applied Linguistics* 22 (3), 324–337.

Deterding, D. (2013) *Misunderstandings in English as a Lingua Franca. An Analysis of ELF Interactions in South-East Asia*. Berlin: De Gruyter Mouton.

Fillmore, C.J. (1979) [2000] On fluency. In H. Riggenbach (ed.) *Perspectives on Fluency* (pp. 43–60). Ann Arbor, MI: University of Michigan Press.

Firth, A. (1996) The discursive accomplishment of normality: On 'lingua franca' English and conversation analysis. *Journal of Pragmatics* 26 (2), 237–259.

Götz, S. (2013) *Fluency in Native and Nonnative English Speech*. Amsterdam: John Benjamins.

House, J. (1999) Misunderstanding in intercultural communication: Interactions in English as lingua franca and the myth of mutual intelligibility. In C. Gnutzmann (ed.) *Teaching and Learning English as a Global Language* (pp. 73–89). Tübingen: Strauffenburg.

House, J. (2002) Developing pragmatic competence in English as a lingua franca. In K. Knapp and C. Meierkord (eds) *Lingua Franca Communication* (pp. 245–268). Frankfurt am Main: Peter Lang.

Hüttner, J. (2009) Fluent speakers – fluent interactions: On the creation of (co)-fluency in English as a lingua franca. In A. Mauranen and E. Ranta (eds) *English as a Lingua Franca: Studies and Findings* (pp. 274–297). Newcastle upon Tyne: Cambridge Scholars Publishing.

Hynninen, N. (2012) ICL at the micro level: L2 speakers taking on the role of language experts. *AILA Review* 25, 13–29.

Hynninen, N. (2016) *Language Regulation in English as a Lingua Franca: Focus on Academic Spoken Discourse*. Berlin: De Gruyter Mouton.

Jenkins, J. (2000) *The Phonology of English as an International Language*. Oxford: Oxford University Press.

Jenkins, J. (2007) *English as a Lingua Franca: Attitude and Identity*. Oxford: Oxford University Press.

Kachru, B.B. (1996) Opening borders with world Englishes: Theory in the classroom. In S. Cornwell, P. Rule and T. Sugino (eds) *On JALT96: Crossing Borders. The Proceedings of the 23rd Annual JALT International Conference on Language Teaching/Learning, Hiroshima, Japan, November 1996* (pp. 10–20). JALT, Tokyo.

Kaur, J. (2009) Pre-empting problems of understanding in English as a lingua franca. In A. Mauranen and E. Ranta (eds) *English as a Lingua Franca: Studies and Findings* (pp. 107–123). Newcastle upon Tyne: Cambridge Scholars Publishing.

Kaur, J. (2011) Raising explicitness through self-repair in English as a lingua franca. *Journal of Pragmatics* 43 (11), 2704–2715.

Kormos, J. and Dénes, M. (2004) Exploring measures and perceptions of fluency in the speech of second language learners. *System* 32, 145–164.

Lindemann, S. (2006) What the other half gives: The interlocutor's role in non-native speaker performance. In R. Hughes (ed.) *Spoken English, TESOL and Applied Linguistics: Challenges for Theory and Practice* (pp. 23–49). Basingstoke: Palgrave Macmillan.

Mauranen, A. (2006) Signaling and preventing misunderstanding in English as lingua franca communication. *International Journal of the Sociology of Language* 177, 123–150.

Mauranen, A. (2007) Hybrid voices: English as the lingua franca of academics. In K. Fløttum (ed.) *Language and Discipline Perspectives on Academic Discourse* (pp. 243–259). Newcastle upon Tyne: Cambridge Scholars Publishing.

Mauranen, A. (2012) *Exploring ELF. Academic English Shaped by Non-native Speakers.* Cambridge: Cambridge University Press.

Mauranen, A. (2017) Conceptualising ELF. In J. Jenkins, W. Baker and M. Dewey (eds) *The Routledge Handbook of English as a Lingua Franca* (pp. 7–24). New York: Routledge.

McCarthy, M. (2010) Spoken fluency revisited. *English Profile Journal* 1 (1), 1–15.

Pawley, A. and Syder, F. H. (1983) Two puzzles for linguistic theory: Nativelike selection and nativelike fluency. In J.C. Richards and R.W. Schmidt (eds) *Language and Communication* (pp. 191–225). London: Longman.

Peltonen, P. (2017) Temporal fluency and problem-solving in interaction: An exploratory study of fluency resources in L2 dialogue. *System* 70, 1–13.

Peltonen, P. and Lintunen, P. (2016) Integrating quantitative and qualitative approaches in L2 fluency analysis: A study of Finnish-speaking and Swedish-speaking learners of English at two school levels. *European Journal of Applied Linguistics* 4 (2), 209–238.

Pietikäinen, K.S. (2018) Misunderstandings and ensuring understanding in private ELF talk. *Applied Linguistics* 39 (2), 188–212.

Pitzl, M.-L. (2012) Creativity meets convention: Idiom variation and re-metaphorization in ELF. *Journal of English as a Lingua Franca* 1 (1), 27–55.

Prodromou, L. (2008) *English as a Lingua Franca. A Corpus-Based Analysis.* London: Continuum.

Ranta, E. (2009) Syntactic features in spoken ELF – Learner language or spoken grammar? In A. Mauranen and E. Ranta (eds) *English as a Lingua Franca: Studies and Findings* (pp. 84–106). Newcastle upon Tyne: Cambridge Scholars Publishing.

Riggenbach, H. (1991) Toward an understanding of fluency: A microanalysis of nonnative speaker conversations. *Discourse Processes* 14, 423–441.

Rühlemann, C. (2007) *Conversation in Context: A Corpus-driven Approach.* London: Continuum.

Rühlemann, C., Bagoutdinov, A. and O'Donnell, M.B. (2011) Windows on the mind: Pauses in conversational narrative. *International Journal of Corpus Linguistics* 16 (2), 198–230.

Sato, M. (2014) Exploring the construct of interactional oral fluency: Second language acquisition and language testing approaches. *System* 45, 79–91.

Segalowitz, N. (2010) *Cognitive Bases of Second Language Fluency.* New York: Routledge.

Seidlhofer, B. (2004) Research perspectives on teaching English as a lingua franca. *Annual Review of Applied Linguistics* 24, 209–239.

Seidlhofer, B. (2011) *Understanding English as a Lingua Franca.* Oxford: Oxford University Press.

Seidlhofer, B. and Widdowson, H. (2009) Conformity and creativity in ELF and learner English. In M. Albl-Mikasa, S. Braun and S. Kalina (eds) *Dimensionen der Zweitsprachenforschung. Dimensions of Second Language Research. (Festschrift for Kurt Kohn)* (pp. 93–107). Tübingen: Narr.

Simpson, R.C., Briggs, S.L., Ovens, J. and Swales, J.M. (2002) *The Michigan Corpus of Academic Spoken English*. Ann Arbor, MI: The Regents of the University of Michigan.

Skehan, P. (2003) Task-based instruction. *Language Teaching* 36 (1), 1–14.

Skehan, P. (2009) Modelling second language performance: Integrating complexity, accuracy, fluency, and lexis. *Applied Linguistics* 30 (4), 510–532.

Stivers, T., Enfield, N.J., Brown, P., Englert, C., Hayashi, M., Heinemann, T., Hoymanna, G., Rossano, F., de Ruiter, J.P., Yoon, K.-E. and Levinson, S.C. (2009) Universals and cultural variation in turn-taking in conversation. *PNAS (Proceedings of the National Academy of Sciences)* 106 (26), 10587–10592.

Tavakoli, P. (2016) Fluency in monologic and dialogic task performance: Challenges in defining and measuring L2 fluency. *International Review of Applied Linguistics in Language Teaching* 54, 133–150.

Tavakoli, P. and Skehan, P. (2005) Strategic planning, task structure, and performance testing. In R. Ellis (ed.) *Planning and Task Performance in a Second Language* (pp. 239–273). Amsterdam: John Benjamins.

Vetchinnikova, S. (2014) *Second Language Lexis and the Idiom Principle*. Helsinki: University of Helsinki.

Wray, A. (2002) *Formulaic Language and the Lexicon*. Cambridge: Cambridge University Press.

# 7 Fluency in Sign Language

Laura Kanto and Ulla-Maija Haapanen

## Introduction

Previous studies have mainly focused on the fluidity in speech produced and perceived in an auditory–oral modality and referring to the sequential vocal elements of speech that are produced smoothly and effortlessly in an oral mode (see e.g. Segalowitz *et al.*, 2017). However, recent studies have broadened the concept of fluency to include nonverbal aspects of fluency as well (see e.g. Götz, 2013). Yet in sign languages, fluency becomes visible in a visual–gestural modality, and it refers to both simultaneous and sequential manual and non-manual elements of signs produced smoothly and effortlessly (e.g. by means of hands, the head and torso) and perceived in a visual–gestural mode (see e.g. Puupponen *et al.*, 2015). As defined in more detail in the introductory chapter to this volume, in a broad sense, fluency in language production refers to the communicatively acceptable production that is underlined by efficient and fluid cognitive processes and perceived as being fluent (Götz, 2013; Segalowitz, 2016), but the question remains: what are the patterns of fluency in sign language, which is produced in a different modality than spoken languages? Thus, the aim of this chapter is to discuss the characteristics and patterns of fluency in sign language and how to operationalise fluency features in sign language. However, the previous research on fluency in sign language is still limited. For this reason, the chapter reviews the previous research literature on the conceptions of fluency in general in an attempt to combine those concepts with previous studies on the structure of sign languages as well as with those on learning and using sign language as an L2. The chapter seeks to create an opening for further discussion and to advance the field of research on fluency.

## Learning Sign Language as L2 and Heterogeneity of Native Sign Language Users

For many students, learning sign language as L2 in a visual–gestural modality means also learning a new language and an entirely new articulatory system in a new modality. Chen Pichler and Koulidobrova (2015) refer to these students as M2L2 learners, as they are learning their second language in a second modality. However, there are also students that have sign language as their L1 and are learning another sign language as their L2. They are referred to as M1L2 learners, as they are learning their second language in the same modality as their first language. Thus, these students already have knowledge of a visual–gestural language and may go through a different learning process than M2L2 learners. In previous research, the extent of modality effects has raised many questions regarding how L2 sign language learning proceeds in a different way between M2L2 and M1L2 learners and how previous knowledge of sign language affects learning outcomes (Frederiksen & Mayberry, 2019; Ortega & Morgan, 2015; Schlehofer & Tyler, 2016; Williams & Newman, 2016). However, these previous studies have mainly focused on describing the elements in sign language that might be especially difficult for M2L2 learners to learn due to the modality differences between their L1 and L2 languages.

The challenges M2L2 sign language learners have been documented to face have been related in particular with phonological parameters, the high degree of iconicity in signs, and the use of space as part of the grammar in reference tracking (Chen Pichler & Koulidobrova, 2015; Frederiksen & Mayberry, 2019; Ortega & Morgan, 2015; Schlehofer & Tyler, 2016; Williams & Newman, 2016). Hence, the features in phonological parameters, iconicity and the use of space produced by L2 signers can potentially cause disfluencies in L2 learners' signing. However, only a very limited number of studies have aimed to explain L2 (dis)fluency in sign language and there are not yet similar research trends on fluency in sign language compared to those on fluency in spoken languages (see e.g. Harrison, 2013; Notarrigo, 2017). In this chapter these features (phonological parameters, iconicity and the use of space) are discussed as possible features affecting the patterns of fluency of L2 signers.

M2L2 learners may also face different developmental patterns and (dis)fluency features in their L2 sign language which do not occur for M1L2 learners that already have the experience and knowledge on the phonological structure, iconicity and grammar of sign language. Additionally, there can be differences between these M1L2 and M2L2 sign language learners in terms of their L2 cognitive processing, which might also underlie the appearance of (dis)fluency in their L2 sign language production and in the ways how social context may contribute to their fluency attainment (Martinez & Singleton, 2018). However, as stated by Chen Pichler and Koulidobrova (2015), L2 sign language learners have varying language backgrounds with different early language experiences when acquiring L1, which may affect the L2 sign language learning process and outcomes in many ways.

Native sign language users are a highly heterogenous group. Children acquiring sign language show considerable differences in regard to both their level of hearing and access to language. Only the deaf children of deaf parents can be regarded as acquiring sign language naturally from their parents, representing typical native sign language acquisition (L1). However, most children of deaf parents are hearing and they simultaneously acquire both sign language and spoken language, achieving varying levels of bilingualism and sign language skills (Kanto, 2016; Mitchell & Karchmer, 2004). On the other hand, most deaf children (90%) are born to hearing parents who lack previous knowledge of sign language, which might delay the starting age of language acquisition (Mitchell & Karchmer, 2004). Thus, these children's early access to language and language exposure can consist of varying age of language acquisition and degrees of sign language, oral language and bilingual acquisition (Allen, 2015). As has been confirmed in many previous studies, there is a critical period for first language acquisition regardless of the modality of language acquired (Lenneberg, 1967; Mayberry & Eichen, 1991). Late acquisition of the first language among deaf children has been found to have long-lasting effects on, for example, cognitive processing and language production skills in sign language (Mayberry, 1993; Morford & Mayberry, 2000), which might also have effects on the different aspects of fluency (see e.g. Notarrigo, 2017). Furthermore, the acquisition of L1 has been documented to be the most important predictor in the acquisition of L2 in spoken language, and the fluency patterns between a person's L1 and L2 have been found to be strongly connected as well (Bosker *et al.*, 2014; Williams *et al.*, 2017). This connection between L1 and L2 also actualises among deaf and hearing L2 sign language learners (Williams *et al.*, 2017; Skotara *et al.*, 2012) and thus might have effects on some of their fluency features in L2 as well (see e.g. Notarrigo, 2017). As Notarrigo (2017) stated in her study, early experiences in sign language acquisition, depending on the age of sign language acquisition, clearly influenced the features of (dis)fluency in one's sign languages.

However, in investigations of L2 fluency, native speakers are often regarded as fluent by default. Thus, when describing the nature of (dis)fluency among L2 speakers, the differences between L2 speakers and native speakers are often highlighted (Kahng, 2014; Tavakoli, 2011). Due to the heterogeneity of L1 sign language users it is highly questionable to seek to highlight the differences in fluency between L2 signers and L1 sign language users. Thus, the comparison of fluency features among native and L2 sign language users should be made with caution. In order to understand how fluency operates in sign languages in general and acknowledging the challenges that fluency poses to L2 signers, it is important to study the L2 learning process of sign language as well as the patterns of (dis)fluency produced by both L2 signers and native sign language users. These studies can provide ways to overcome the challenges in fluency among L2 signers and support the development of fluency in L2 learners through educational practices.

## Fluency in the Signed Act

When narrowing the definition of fluency as the patterns in signed utterances, the movement of the signed act seems to play an important role. Unlike articulation movements in spoken languages, fluency in sign language is judged by the smoothness of visible articulators during the signing. Accordingly, during the sign articulation, the manual (e.g. handshape, orientation of palm and fingers, place of articulation and movement) and non-manual (e.g. head, mouth, eyebrows and torso) elements of the signs are synchronised simultaneously and then coordinated sequentially in time from the initial until the final location of the sign (Brentari, 1998; Jantunen, 2006; Puupponen et al., 2015). The manual movement of the sign can be classified as the path movement, when the elbow or shoulder joint articulates the movement, and the local movement, when the wrist or finger joints articulate the movement (Brentari, 1998). The complexity of the movements and the sign's phonological structure have been classified in previous studies on the basis of the involvement of both manual and non-manual movements, path and local movements, and the symmetry or independence of movement in two-handed signs (Brentari, 1998; Jantunen, 2006; Puupponen et al., 2015). Furthermore, during the transition between the final location of the previous signs and the initial location of the next sign, the manual and non-manual constructions are prepared for the articulation of the next coming sign (Jantunen, 2013).

As sign languages are produced by the different types of movements of different body parts, the fluency in sign languages also relates to global kinematics: the way in which these different articulators are moved. In this sense, fluency is referred to as the overall smoothness of these movements, which can be measured based on the combination of velocity and acceleration (Burger et al., 2013). According to Burger et al. (2013), in global kinematic, the movement is regarded as fluid when the velocity of the movement is high and acceleration low, whereas the combination of low velocity and high acceleration is regarded as a non-fluid movement. Thus, according to the global kinematic, signing that is produced with a relatively high but rather stable speed without high acceleration peaks could hypothetically be regarded as more fluent than signing that is produced with a relatively low speed, which includes a large number of rapid changes and high acceleration peaks. Jantunen (2013) studied the velocity and acceleration properties during the movements in signs and transitions among native signers by using motion capture data. The results showed that during signs, the speed is slower and contains more acceleration motion than movements during transitions. This finding suggests that during signs, movements are slower and more controlled in order to ensure that the important linguistic information will be received well by the addressee. Thus, in signing there are natural changes in the velocity and acceleration among native sign language users during the sign stream, which may also relate to the prosodic features of signing (e.g. intonation and stress) as well as ensuring the perception of important linguistic information for the addressee. Motion capture therefore provides an important methodological option to study the overall movements during the signing and offers specific information on both productive and perceptive fluency. It would be highly interesting to study L2 signers using motion capture to determine how this method can capture the possible patterns of (dis)fluency among L2 signers, how the movements might differ between native, M1L2 and M2L2 signers, and what features in motion capture data might correlate with the impression of fluency among receivers.

Consistent with this proposition, Hilger *et al.* (2015) found that the deaf native signers demonstrated a higher degree of consistency and stability in their produced movements during the production of individual sign tokens compared with the hearing M2L2 sign language learners. The researchers suggested that M2L2 sign language learners showed greater movement variability in their sign production due to the proximalisation of movements. This is in line with findings by Mirus *et al.* (2001) that, compared to native signers, L2 signers tend to proximalise their movements by using articulation joints closer to the torso instead of distal ones as native signers do. However, the findings of Cull (2014) did not support this proposition, since in her research she found that both native and M2L2 signers exhibited proximalisation when reproducing short signed utterances. Instead, the results showed that the duration of signed utterances, signs and transitional movements were longer among M2L2 signers than among native signers. According to these studies, the movements during the sign stream among M2L2 signers seem to be produced at a lower speed with high motion variability, which could be regarded as a feature of disfluency.

Regarding fluency in sign language, in addition to the speed and smoothness of the different manual and non-manual movements, these movements need to be also synchronised and rhythmically coordinated (Allen *et al.*, 1991; Hilger *et al.*, 2015). Thus, the fluency features of sign language are also related to the features of intonation and prosody, a rich system of rhythmic structures, and stress, as it has been noticed to play an important part in spoken language fluency (Götz, 2013: 51–55). Prosody in sign languages is produced by the modification of both manual and non-manual parameters (for example, by lengthening the duration of movement of the sign and the transition, holds of the hand in a particular shape and position, eye blinks and eyebrow movements, and changes in the position of the head and torso) (Ormel & Crasborn, 2012). By synchronising these movements of different parts of the body, signers create the prosody that is a constituent of both phonological and morphosyntactic structures and used to mark the clause-boundaries, connecting clauses together and creating the cohesion of the signed text (Jantunen *et al.*,

2016b; see the review of Ormel & Crasborn, 2012; Puupponen *et al.*, 2015; Sandler, 2010). As in previous research, it has been found that L2 signers often lack rhythm and other prosodic cues (e.g. side-to-side movement of the torso and eyebrow movements), compared with L1 signers (Allen *et al.*, 1991; Brentari *et al.*, 2012). Thus, the use of complex prosody in sign language may require a high level of sign language proficiency and fluency. However, considering the complexity and the initial stage of the research on prosody in sign language, a more detailed explanation of the prosodic structures in sign language is beyond the scope of this chapter. Yet, Götz (2013: 51–55) regarded intonation as one aspect of fluency in spoken language and considers that it relates to productive fluency but has communicative functions, and so includes it in perceived fluency as well. The connections between prosodic, foreign accent and fluency features in sign language demand further study.

It follows that one of the requirements for a fluent signed act is that especially M2L2 sign language learners, when compared with their native spoken language and with other L1 signers, must process and effectively control new motor plans in entirely new articulatory systems and perceive phonological parameters of signs in a different modality. According to previous studies, the movement parameters are highly diverse and the most sonorous element in a sign, but at the same time one of the most difficult and later acquired components to be perceived and produced accurately for L2 signers (Bochner *et al.*, 2011; Ortega & Morgan, 2015; Schlehofer & Tyler, 2016; Williams & Newman, 2016). Thus, the fluency of signed utterances may relate to the rapid and automatised process and control of the sequences of movement parameters, both inside the sign and transmission between signs. However, this topic requires further research, for which motion capture data could potentially offer new and important knowledge to deepen our understanding. Additionally, further study is needed to identify the prosodic cues used by L1 signers and the differences between L1 and L2 signers. This knowledge could offer important information for teaching sign language as L2 as well.

## Operationalising the Fluency Features in Sign Language

As sign language and spoken language are received and produced partly in different modalities, the recent research suggests that the linguistic processing in these languages is primarily governed by similar cognitive processes but also include modality-dependent mechanisms (e.g. in lexical access and organisation) (Carreiras, 2010; Caselli & Cohen-Goldberg, 2014; Hohenberger *et al.*, 2002; Marshall *et al.*, 2014; Williams *et al.*, 2017; Williams & Newman, 2017). The smoothness and effectiveness of different cognitive process are responsible for productive fluency in a speech act (see e.g. Olkkonen, 2017). Thus, regarding the previous research on the cognitive processes responsible for performing the fluency features in spoken utterances (Segalowitz, 2010, 2016), similar mechanisms might underlie the features of fluency in sign language utterances. However, future research is needed to broaden our understanding of the cognitive processing of L2 sign language fluency and to determine whether there is a modality-dependent process that underlies the fluidity of the signed act, especially among M2L2 signers. Additionally, it would be highly important to study how the less efficient linguistic processing (e.g. poor phonological encoding) among L2 signers underlies the aspects of disfluency (e.g. phonological errors) in signed utterances, since due to the visual-gestural modality, the (dis)fluency features of utterances might be somewhat different and show a unique pattern, compared with fluency features in spoken utterances (see e.g. Gutiérrez et al., 2012).

In previous research, operationalising and documenting the temporal features of speech fluency have been highly varied. For this reason, Segalowitz et al. (2017) have aimed to propose core fluency features of speech among L2 learners, in order to find a consensus to operationally define the features of L2 speech fluency for further research. Their proposed core fluency features are: (1) the number of syllables between silent pauses, (2) the number of seconds of phonation between silent pauses, (3) pruned articulated syllable duration and (4) mean silent pause duration (Segalowitz et al., 2017: 97). All these features correlated with each other, and L2 learners showed fluency gains according to these features after an immersion programme. Contrary to some previous research, Segalowitz et al. (2017) did not find correlations between filled pauses (e.g. *um, uh, er, euh, hmmm*) and other measured fluency features, and they did not regard filled pauses as core fluency features even though L2 speakers showed fluency gains in the filled pause duration. However, the researchers suggested that due to the communication function of the filled pauses, these pauses might reflect speech fluency in a different way than other core fluency features, and they proposed further research on this topic.

The operationalised fluency features in speech could be identified in a similar way in sign languages as well. However, for further study the question remains how the syllable rate and phonation used to operationalise speech fluency should be operationalised in signed languages. Thus, the definition of the syllable in sign language and the role of non-manual parameters when defining the fluency features from the signed stream need to be discussed (see e.g. Notarrigo & Meurant, 2014). As stated earlier in this chapter, the speed and the movement parameter of the sign seem to play an important role in the fluency of the signed act as stated also by Notarrigo (2017). Even though when skills are acquired relatively late, L2 signers have been documented to be able to gain native-like stability in their movement patterns (Hilger et al., 2015). For this reason, signing speed and movement may offer useful parameters when operationalising the fluency features in sign language. The previous studies have used the sign instead of the syllable as the unit when defining the signing rate and duration (see e.g. Jantunen *et al.*, 2016a; Wilbur, 2009). Regarding the speed of signing, the average sign rate has been documented in different sign languages to be two signs per second (Jantunen *et al.*, 2016a; Wilbur, 2009), which is somewhat slower than the produced word rate in speech. Cull (2014) found in her research that the duration of the utterances, signs and transition movement between the signs were longer among M2L2 signers, compared with native sign language users. In line with this finding, Sipronen (2018) found that the signing rate was clearly lower and the duration of signs was longer among three M2L2 signers, compared with two native signers. Thus, the rate of signing and the duration of sign and transition movements could be possible parameters of utterance fluency in sign language, and relatively high speed could be a sign of an efficient and automatised process and production of movements during the sign stream.

Filled and silent pauses, repetitions and different repair strategies, reformulations, false starts and replacements (e.g. the tips of the fingers and slips of the hands), which can be regarded as indicators of utterance (dis)fluency, have also been found in sign language expressions (Hohenberger *et al.*, 2002; Skehan *et al.*, 2016; Thompson *et al.*, 2005). However, in previous research signers have also established pauses, holds and lengthening of the final sign at the major syntactic boundaries (see e.g. Grosjean & Lane, 1977; Wilbur, 2009). Because these have been regarded as a natural part of the discourse, prosody and syntactic structure of sign language, the difficulty lies in determining when pauses, holds and lengthening are aspects of fluency and when of disfluency and caused by, for example, the cognitive mechanism that underlies the patterns of (dis)fluency (see e.g. Götz, 2013; Notarrigo, 2017). From the viewpoint of utterance fluency, random locations and a frequent emergence of pauses (e.g. within the signs and not at the end of the clause) might cause disfluency in signed utterances, as stated by Sipronen (2018). In her preliminary findings, Sipronen (2018) observed that during silent unfilled pauses, the signer removed his/her arms away from the signing space, which usually is on the front side of the signer. Alternatively, during filled pauses the signer held the hand in the signing space either by prolonging the sign or by producing points or repeated movements with fingers (e.g. wriggling of the fingers). Signers often produce non-lexical signs (e.g. PALM-UPs) during the sign stream for different purposes that can partly relate to, for example, discourse markers (Johnston, 2013), which makes it difficult to decide whether the feature is a natural part of the discourse or a marker of disfluency. M2L2 signers had clearly more silent and filled pauses during the signing, compared with native signers. However, Sipronen (2018) did not include, as did Notarrigo and Meurant (2014), the non-manual aspects (e.g. facial expressions, eyebrows or movements of head and torso) when classifying the pauses.

Sign language users have been shown to use fewer pauses, fillers, restarts and reformulations, and correct slips already within the sign, whereas spoken language users usually correct slips after the spoken word (Hohenberger et al., 2002). However, the findings of previous studies differ to some extent (see e.g. Meurant & Sinte, 2016). The explanation for the lower incidences of these disfluency features have been suggested to be related to the longer duration in the production time of signs, compared with spoken words. Thus, signers seem to catch occurring errors already within the signs, while spoken language users do this after the word production (Hohenberger et al., 2002). However, these are only preliminary findings and further study aimed at describing the patterns and use of these forms of disfluency in both native and L2 sign language users would provide highly interesting and important data on fluency in general. Thompson et al. (2005) reported the experiences of the tip of the fingers among native sign language users when a signer failed in the retrieval process of a sign; this is a similar phenomenon as the tip of the tongue among spoken language users. Signers were sometimes found to have partial access to a sign's phonological form; thus, they were able to recall handshape, location and orientation, but they were the least likely to recall the movement parameter of the sign.

### Broadening the Understanding of L2 Fluency in Sign Language

As stated by Segalowitz (2016) regarding the framework of L2 fluency in spoken languages, it is also important to broaden the conceptualisation of fluency with the ability to maintain fluent communication and discourse in sign language. This broader viewpoint on fluency is actualised especially when it comes to sign languages. Sign languages are highly dependent on the discourse; some signs are less conventionalised, having no status in the dictionary yet still being more likely to be produced and understood as part of the discourse (Johnston, 2013; Johnston & Ferrara, 2012). These units are called indexical units, non-conventionalised units and constructed action that are conventionalised at the level of form and meaning to some or all aspects, but the meaning is dependent on the components given from the discourse context (see e.g. Johnston, 2013; Johnston & Ferrara, 2012). Thus, in addition to the necessary linguistic knowledge on the particular sign language to establish effortless and smooth linguistic processing and production, L2 signers need to have knowledge of the visual discourse practices and pragmatic dimension of sign language (e.g. in order to establish cohesion, appropriate reference tracking, choice of register, spatial relationships and appropriate use of space and iconicity), which are somewhat different compared with discourse practices in spoken language (Ferrara & Nilsson, 2017; Ferrara & Johnston, 2014; Frederiksen & Mayberry, 2019). As stated by Segalowitz (2016: 88), '[p]oor knowledge on these aspects of the target language could compromise the ability to communicate fluently by leading to inefficient word searches and awkward attempts to produce appropriately structured utterances.' However, only a highly general overview of the very complex and multifaceted features of sign language can be made in this chapter. Still, as these features can be regarded as a core element of sign language and sign language discourse, they are an important part of fluency in sign language and worth mentioning.

Space is a multidimensional aspect of linguistic form and the discourse practices in sign language, attracting referents and creating cohesion within and between sentences and across the discourse (Ferrara & Nilsson, 2017; Ferrara & Johnston, 2014; Frederiksen & Mayberry, 2019). During the discourse, referents need to be introduced and then, regarding the language in use, appropriately referred back to as the story progresses. Across the discourse, the signer maps spatial relationships by assigning specific locations within the signing space called *buoys* for the characters and objects relevant for the discourse, consistently referring to this particular location as referring to the character or the object mentioned earlier in the discourse (see Liddell, 2003). Thus, during the production of a particular sign, a point can be placed in the locus in the signing space for marking the reference, and this place remains associated until the spatial setup is changed or the discourse ends.

Thus, space is used during the discourse for reference tracking, but it also functions as a gestural element in depicting signs (Johnston & Ferrara, 2012). Depicting signs can be modified spatially; the space (the place of the beginning and the end of the verb) is used to establish the agreement. Depicting signs are the core elements of expressive vocabulary in sign languages, but they do not have dictionary status. These signs, created during the discourse, are used in order to describe the movement, size and shape and location of an entity and how the entity is handled. L2 sign language learners face many challenges in the production and appropriate use of these signs and spatial relationships, as well as creating spatial setups. In previous studies, it has been reported that L2 signers use fewer depicting signs and are often found to rely more on conventional signs instead of depicting signs (Ferrara & Nilsson, 2017). L2 learners have also been found to struggle in the phonological parameters of these signs, especially when it comes to the use of appropriate orientation, handshape and movement, and coordinating signs within the signing space in relation to their own bodies (Ferrara & Nilsson, 2017; Frederiksen & Mayberry, 2019; Ortega & Morgan, 2015).

In sign language discourse and narrative, signers can both tell from a third-person or outsider's perspective and perform using a first-person perspective the action, thoughts or feeling attributed to the referent. From a third-person discourse, signers display and explain the scene from their own perspective (often, for example, by using depicting signs). However, in constructive action, a signer uses his or her body to illustrate the action, thoughts or feeling of the referent. Thus, it has been documented that constructive action functions as the core element of the clause (Ferrara &

Johnston, 2014) as well as a key part of the discourse, which is used to mark the referent (Cormier *et al.*, 2013). Thus, an appropriate use of constructed action is an essential part of fluent sign language discourse. Taub *et al.* (2008) found that L2 signers start to use depicting signs and construction action structures rather early during their L2 sign language studies. However, L2 signers had difficulties synchronising different elements (e.g. eye gaze and body posture). Frederiksen and Mayberry (2019) found that L2 signers had difficulties utilising the properties of reference tracking and discourse strategies in sign language, and they struggled in establishing the discourse structure, similar to native sign language users.

## Conclusion

The elements involved in fluency in sign language are highly multifaceted. In this chapter these features (phonological parameters, iconicity and the use of space) are discussed as possible features affecting the patterns of fluency of L2 signers. Due to the modality and structure of sign languages, it is essential that in future studies fluency in sign language is regarded as a broad framework including a combination of many different fluency features explained in this chapter (fluencemes called by Götz, 2013: 9): features in productive and perceptive fluency including non-manual elements of sign language interacting with cognitive processes responsible for performing the fluency features in L2 (Segalowitz, 2016). Because there are typical patterns of disfluency among all native language users, it is highly challenging to distinguish features of fluency and disfluency. Depending on the context, register, timing and frequency, the same feature might be regarded as a feature of fluency or disfluency (Götz, 2013; Notarrigo, 2017). According to previous studies, acquisition of the movement of sign language seems to be a necessary step towards more profound sign language proficiency and fluency in sign language. Generally fluent signing seems to depend on the integrity of the smoothness of different movements, which are rhythmically coordinated and synchronised, efficiency of the cognitive mechanism that underlies the patterns of L2 sign language fluency, and appropriate use of the visual discourse practices and the pragmatic dimension of sign language. However, operationalising the features of L2 fluency in sign language might be challenging but, in any case, a highly important task.

Defining which features of L2 fluency to examine is essential for the theoretical framework of fluency, but also for assessing and studying L2 sign language development and gains in fluency, learning experiences and educational practices. Still lacking is basic knowledge on how, by means of educational practices, teachers of sign language can support the development of fluency among L2 sign language learners. Additionally, in regard to the assessment of fluency in L2 sign language, it is necessary to gain knowledge of the patterns that affect fluency (e.g. language background) in sign language and how to measure fluency as part of language assessment. In further research, it would be interesting to study the fluency features among M1L2 and M2L2 sign language learners. In particular, studies should address whether there are differences between these learners. They could specifically ask whether the fluency features among M1L2 sign language learners resemble the features found in previous studies on spoken language among L2 speakers that are acquiring their L2 in the same modality and how the modality effect has an influence on the fluency features among M2L2 learners. Thus, knowledge of the fluency features in sign language is very important from both theoretical and educational perspectives, and it urgently demands further research. As found by Tavakoli *et al.* (2016), educational practices supporting the development of fluency focused on awareness-raising activities and fluency strategy training significantly increased students' fluency, even in a short four-week intervention. Thus, the awareness of the different aspects of sign language fluency and the strategies to increase fluency in a sign language discourse context would be an important new aspect for sign language education.

## References

Allen, T.E. (2015) The deaf community as a 'special linguistic demographic': Diversity rather than disability as a framework for conducting research with individuals who are deaf. In E. Orfanidou, B. Woll and G. Morgan (eds) *The Blackwell Guide to Research Methods in Sign Language Studies* (pp. 21–40). Hoboken, NJ: John Wiley.

Allen, G.D., Wilbur, R.B. and Schick, B.B. (1991) Aspects of rhythm in ASL. *Sign Language Studies* 72 (1), 297–320.

Bochner, J.H., Christie, K., Hauser, P.C. and Searls, J.M. (2011) When is a difference really different? Learners' discrimination of linguistic contrasts in American Sign Language. *Language Learning* 61, 1302–1327.

Bosker, H.R., Quené, H., Sanders, T. and De Jong, N.H. (2014) The perception of fluency in native and nonnative speech. *Language Learning* 64, 579–614.

Brentari, D. (1998) *A Prosodic Model of Sign Language Phonology*. Cambridge, MA & London: A Bradford Book.

Brentari, D., Nadolske, M.A. and Wolford, G. (2012) Can experience with co-speech gesture influence the prosody of a sign language? Sign language prosodic cues in bimodal bilinguals. *Bilingualism: Language and Cognition* 15, 402–412.

Burger, B., Saarikallio, S., Luck, G., Thompson, M.R. and Toiviainen, P. (2013) Relationships between perceived emotions in music and music-induced movement. *Music Perception: An Interdisciplinary Journal* 30, 517–533.

Carreiras, M. (2010) Sign language processing. *Language and Linguistics Compass* 4, 430–444.

Caselli, N.K. and Cohen-Goldberg, A.M. (2014) Lexical access in sign language: A computational model. *Frontiers in Psychology* 5, 1–11.

Chen Pichler, D. and Koulidobrova, E. (2015) Acquisition of sign language as a second language. In M. Marschark and P.E. Spencer (eds) *The Oxford Handbook of Deaf Studies in Language: Research, Policy, and Practice* (pp. 218–230). New York, NY: Oxford University Press.

Cormier, K., Smith, S. and Zwets, M. (2013) Framing constructed action in British Sign Language narratives. *Journal of Pragmatics* 55, 119–139.

Cull, A. (2014) Production of movement in users of American Sign Language and its influence on being identified as 'non-native'. PhD thesis, Gallaudet University.

Ferrara, L. and Nilsson, A.L. (2017) Describing spatial layouts as an L2M2 signed language learner. *Sign Language & Linguistics* 20, 1–26.

Ferrara, L. and Johnston, T. (2014) Elaborating who's what: A study of constructed action and clause structure in Auslan (Australian Sign Language). *Australian Journal of Linguistics* 34, 193–215.

Frederiksen, A.T. and Mayberry, R.I. (2019) Reference tracking in early stages of different modality L2 acquisition: Limited over-explicitness in novice ASL signers' referring expressions. *Second Language Research* 35 (2), 253–283.

Grosjean, F. and Lane, H. (1977) Pauses and syntax in American Sign Language. *Cognition* 5, 101–117.

Gutiérrez, E., Müller, O., Baus, C. and Carreiras, M. (2012) Electrophysiological evidence for phonological priming in Spanish Sign Language lexical access. *Neuropsychologia* 50, 1335–1346.

Götz, S. (2013) *Fluency in Native and Nonnative English Speech*. Amsterdam: John Benjamins.

Harrison, S. (2013) Visible bodily action in disfluencies when learning to sign. A classroom study of non-native sign language. *Todas as Letras-Revista de Língua e Literatura* 15, 51–61.

Hilger, A.I., Loucks, T.M., Quinto-Pozos, D. and Dye, M.W. (2015) Second language acquisition across modalities: Production variability in adult L2 learners of American Sign Language. *Second Language Research* 31, 375–388.

Hohenberger, A., Happ, D. and Leuninger, H. (2002) Modality dependent aspects of sign language production: Evidence from slips of the hands and their repairs in German Sign Language. In R.P. Meier, K. Cormier and D. Quinto-Pozos (eds) *Modality and Structure in Signed and Spoken Languages* (pp. 112–142). Cambridge: Cambridge University Press.

Jantunen, T. (2006) The complexity of lexical movements in FinSL. In M. Suominen, A. Arppe, A. Airola, O. Heinämäki, M. Miestamo, U. Määttä, J. Niemi, K.K. Pitkänen and K. Sinnemäki (eds) *A Man of Measure: Festschrift in Honour of Fred Karlsson on his 60th Birthday* [Special supplement to SKY Journal of Linguistics 19] (pp. 335–344). Turku: The Linguistic Association of Finland.

Jantunen, T. (2013) Signs and transitions: Do they differ phonetically and does it matter? *Sign Language Studies* 13, 211–237.

Jantunen, T., Mesch, J. and Puupponen, A. (2016a) Aspects of rhythm in Finnish and Swedish Sign Language, a paper to be presented in the *12th Conference on Theoretical Issues in Sign Language Research (TISLR 12)*. Melbourne, Australia, 4–7 January, 2016.

Jantunen, T., Mesch, J., Puupponen, A. and Laaksonen, J. (2016b) On the rhythm of head movements in Finnish and Swedish Sign Language sentences. In J. Barnes, A. Brugos, S. Shattuck-Hufnagel and N. Veilleux (eds) *Speech Prosody 2016: Proceedings of the 8th International Conference on Speech Prosody*, Boston University, USA, 31 May–3 June 2016 (pp. 850–853). Baixas: International Speech Communication Association.

Johnston, T. (2013) Towards a comparative semiotics of pointing actions in signed and spoken languages. *Gesture* 13, 109–142.

Johnston, T. and Ferrara L. (2012) Lexicalization in signed languages: When is an idiom not an idiom? *Proceedings of the 3rd UK Cognitive Linguistics Conference, University of Hertfordshire, 6–8 July 2010* (pp. 229–248). Hertfordshire: Cognitive Linguistics Association.

Kahng, J. (2014) Exploring utterance and cognitive fluency of L1 and L2 English speakers: Temporal measures and stimulated recall. *Language Learning* 64, 809–854.

Kanto, L. (2016) *Two Languages, Two Modalities: A Special Type of Early Bilingual Language Acquisition in Hearing Children of Deaf Parents*. Oulu: University of Oulu.

Lenneberg, E.H. (1967) *Biological Foundations of Language*. New York, NY: Wiley.

Liddell, S.K. (2003) *Grammar, Gesture and Meaning in American Sign Language*. Cambridge: Cambridge University Press.

Marshall, C., Rowley, K. and Atkinson, J. (2014) Modality-dependent and-independent factors in the organisation of the signed language lexicon: Insights from semantic and phonological fluency tasks in BSL. *Journal of Psycholinguistic Research* 43, 587–610.

Martinez, D. and Singleton, J. (2018) Predicting sign learning in hearing adults: The role of perceptual-motor (and phonological?) processes. *Applied Psycholinguistics,* 1–27.

Mayberry, R.I. (1993) First-language acquisition after childhood differs from second-language acquisition: The case of American Sign Language. *Journal of Speech, Language, and Hearing Research* 36, 1258–1270.

Mayberry, R.I. and Eichen, E.B. (1991) The long-lasting advantage of learning sign language in childhood: Another look at the critical period for language acquisition. *Journal of Memory and Language* 30, 486–512.

Meurant, L. and Sinte, A. (2016) La reformulation en langue des signes de Belgique francophone (LSFB): Analyse dans un corpus de trois types de discours: Narration, explication et conversation. [Reformulation in French Belgian Sign Language (LSFB): A corpus-based analysis of three discourse types: Narrative, explanation and conversation]. *Information Grammaticale* 149, 32–44.

Mirus, G., Rathmann, C. and Meier, R P. (2001) Proximalization and distalization of sign movement in adult learners. In V. Dively, M. Metzger, S. Taub and A.M. Baer (eds) *Signed languages: Discoveries from international research* (pp. 103–119). Washington, DC: Gallaudet University Press.

Mitchell, R.E. and Karchmer, M.A. (2004) Chasing the mythical ten percent: Parental hearing status of deaf and hard of hearing students in the United States. *Sign Language Studies* 4, 138–163.

Morford, J. and Mayberry, R. (2000) A reexamination of 'early exposure' and its implications for language acquisition by eye. In C. Chamberlain, J.P. Morford and R. Mayberry (eds) *Language Acquisition by Eye* (pp. 111–128). Mahwah, NJ: Lawrence Erlbaum Publishers.

Notarrigo, I. (2017) *Marqueurs de (dis)fluence en langue des signes de Belgique francophone.* [Markers of (dis)fluency in French Belgian Sign Language]. PhD thesis, University of Namur.

Notarrigo, I. and Meurant, L. (2014) Nonmanuals and markers of (dis)fluency in French Belgian Sign Language (LSFB). In O. Crasborn, E. Efthimiou, E. Fotinea, T. Hanke, J. Hochgesang, J. Kristoffersen and J. Mesch (eds) *Proceedings of the 6th Workshop on the Representation and Processing of Sign Languages: Beyond the Manual Channel,* (organized as a part of the Language Resources and Evaluation Conference (LREC) at Reykjavik, Iceland May 31, 2014) (pp. 135–142). Paris: ELRA.

Olkkonen, S. (2017) *Second and Foreign Language Fluency from Cognitive Perspective: Inefficiency and Control of Attention in Lexical Access*. Jyväskylä Studies in Humanities 314. Jyväskylä: University of Jyväskylä.

Ormel, E. and Crasborn, O. (2012) Prosodic correlates of sentences in signed languages: A literature review and suggestions for new types of studies. *Sign Language Studies* 12, 279–315.

Ortega, G. and Morgan, G. (2015) Phonological development in hearing learners of a sign language: The influence of phonological parameters, sign complexity, and iconicity. *Language Learning* 65, 660–688.

Puupponen, A., Wainio, T., Burger, B. and Jantunen, T. (2015) Head movements in Finnish Sign Language on the basis of Motion Capture data. A study of the form and

function of nods, nodding, head thursts, and head pulls. *Sign Language & Linguistics* 18, 41–89.
Sandler, W. (2010) Prosody and syntax in sign languages. *Transactions of the Philological Society* 108, 298–328.
Schlehofer, D. and Tyler, I.J. (2016) Errors in second language learners' production of phonological contrasts in American Sign Language. *International Journal of Language and Linguistics* 3, 30–38.
Segalowitz, N. (2010) *Cognitive Bases of Second Language Fluency*. New York: Routledge.
Segalowitz, N. (2016) Second language fluency and its underlying cognitive and social determinants. *International Review of Applied Linguistics in Language Teaching* 54, 79–95.
Segalowitz, N., French, L. and Guay, J.D. (2017) What features best characterize adult second language utterance fluency and what do they reveal about fluency gains in short-term immersion? *Canadian Journal of Applied Linguistics/Revue canadienne de linguistique appliquée* 20, 90–116.
Sipronen, S. (2018) Vauhti- ja taukosujuvuus suomalaisessa viittomakielessä. [Speed fluency and breakdown fluency in Finnish Sign Language]. Unpublished MA thesis, University of Jyväskylä.
Skehan, P., Foster, P. and Shum, S. (2016) Ladders and snakes in second language fluency. *International Review of Applied Linguistics in Language Teaching* 54, 97–111.
Skotara, N., Salden, U., Kügow, M., Hänel-Faulhaber, B. and Röder, B. (2012) The influence of language deprivation in early childhood on L2 processing: An ERP comparison of deaf native signers and deaf signers with a delayed language acquisition. *BMC neuroscience* 13, 1–14.
Taub, S., Galvan, D., Piñar, P. and Mather, S. (2008) Gesture and ASL L2 acquisition. *Signlanguages: Spinning and unravelling the past, present and future*. Petrópolis: Arara Azul.
Tavakoli, P. (2011) Pausing patterns: Differences between L2 learners and native speakers. *ELT Journal* 65, 71–79.
Tavakoli, P., Campbell, C. and McCormack, J. (2016) Development of speech fluency over a short period of time: Effects of pedagogic intervention. *TESOL Quarterly* 50, 447–471.
Thompson, R., Emmorey, K. and Gollan, T.H. (2005) 'Tip of the fingers' experiences by deaf signers: Insights into the organization of a sign-based lexicon. *Psychological Science* 16, 856–860.
Wilbur, R.B. (2009) Effects of varying rate of signing on ASL manual signs and non-manual markers. *Language and speech* 52, 245–285.
Williams, J.T., Darcy, I. and Newman, S.D. (2017) The beneficial role of L1 spoken language skills on initial L2 sign language learning: Cognitive and Linguistic Predictors of M2L2 Acquisition. *Studies in Second Language Acquisition* 39, 833–850.
Williams, J. and Newman, S. (2016) Phonological substitution errors in L2 ASL sentence processing by hearing M2L2 learners. *Second Language Research* 32, 347–366.
Williams, J.T. and Newman, S.D. (2017) Spoken language activation alters subsequent sign language activation in L2 learners of American Sign Language. *Journal of Psycholinguistic Research* 46, 211–225.

# 8 Gestures as Fluency-enhancing Resources in L2 Interaction: A Case Study on Multimodal Fluency

Pauliina Peltonen

## Introduction

Second language (L2) fluency has generally been analysed from audio-recorded monologue speech. The analyses have thus focused on the verbal output, while non-verbal conduct, such as gestures or gaze, have usually not been examined. Furthermore, L2 speech fluency has often been examined with a relatively narrow, temporal approach, while different means to maintain fluency have been studied less. However, in real communicative situations, to maintain fluency and to overcome problems in interaction, learners employ both verbal resources and non-verbal resources, such as compensatory gestures. Focusing on the use of gestures, the aim of this chapter is to explore how non-verbal fluency resources are used to maintain fluency in addition to so-called verbal fluency resources (e.g. communication strategies, such as paraphrases, and stalling mechanisms, such as repetitions and filler words; Peltonen, 2017a). In other words, by exploring the links between non-verbal and verbal fluency resources, this study examines to what extent learners rely on gestures during problem-solving (see also Gullberg, 1998). Furthermore, from the perspective of L2 fluency research, the study shows how a video-based, multimodal analysis can provide new insights into the study of L2 speech fluency by offering a broader perspective of communicative fluency.

For this exploratory case study, four Finnish learners of English from two school levels (ninth grade of compulsory education, 15-year-olds, and upper secondary school, 17-year-olds) were chosen from a larger pool of participants (see Peltonen, 2017a). In the analysis, the participants' use of gestures during a problem-solving task was examined. The gestures' co-occurrence with verbal resources, including stalling mechanisms and communication strategies, was also examined. The analysis thus focused on examining how gestures facilitated maintaining fluency, either when being used instead of verbal resources or when complementing verbal content. The objectives of the study were thus to examine (1) how learners use gestures to maintain fluency during a problem-solving task and (2) how the use of gestures relates to the use of verbal resources.

## L2 Speech Fluency, Gestures and Fluency Resources

Traditionally, L2 speech fluency has been understood as smoothness and effortlessness of speech (e.g. Chambers, 1997) composed of three main dimensions: speed fluency, breakdown fluency and repair fluency (Skehan, 2009). The measures associated with these main aspects of L2 speech fluency, for example speech rate, the number or length of pauses, and the number of different types of corrections, are all indicators of utterance fluency and can be viewed as providing insights into the learners' underlying cognitive fluency (see Segalowitz, 2010). Along with other aspects of L2 proficiency, including accuracy and complexity, the measures characterise one dimension of learners' L2 oral proficiency (on the CAF-framework, see e.g. Housen *et al.*, 2012). In the current chapter, however, fluency is approached from a broader, problem-solving perspective, which links L2 fluency to strategic language use (*The Fluency Resources Framework,* Peltonen, 2017a; see below).

Overall, L2 speech fluency research, with the focus chiefly on temporal aspects of monologue speech, can be regarded as relatively narrow in its scope (see also Wright & Tavakoli, 2016; cf. Lennon's 1990 notion of narrow and broad senses of fluency). First, as studies of interactional data are rare (for recent exceptions, see e.g. Peltonen, 2017a; Tavakoli, 2016), fluency has mainly been approached as an individual's property, whereas collaborative aspects of fluency have received less attention (but see McCarthy's concept 'confluence', 2010; Peltonen, 2017b). Second, fluency has mostly been analysed quantitatively with temporal measures, while qualitative analyses focusing on the functions or contexts of fluency-related features are rare. For instance, some hesitation phenomena, such as filled pauses and repetitions, have mostly been considered indicators of disfluency and not from a functional perspective as potentially fluency-enhancing features (i.e. as stalling mechanisms, which can contribute to keeping the flow of talk going during speech planning). Third, L2 speech fluency studies have focused on verbal fluency and not incorporated analyses of non-verbal means for maintaining fluency (but for a theoretical approach, see Götz, 2013), potentially due to the main research materials consisting of audio-recorded monologue speech. Video data may not always be available, and participants gesture more in (especially face-to-face) dialogue than in monologue (e.g. Bavelas *et al.*, 2008). However, multimodal aspects of L2 interaction, including gestures, have been widely studied from other perspectives besides fluency: for instance, in studies of L2 interactional competence drawing on conversation analysis (CA-SLA/CA-for-SLA, see e.g. Kasper & Wagner, 2011), non-verbal resources are commonly analysed along with verbal resources. The present study addresses these three gaps in L2 speech fluency research and aims to broaden the scope of fluency analysis by examining interactional L2 data, using video-recorded data that enable a multimodal fluency analysis, and approaching fluency from the perspective of fluency resources.

According to *The Fluency Resources Framework*, which links L2 fluency analysis to a broader problem-solving perspective (Dörnyei & Kormos, 1998), communication strategies and stalling mechanisms can facilitate the maintenance of fluency and compensation for local disfluencies (Peltonen, 2017a). Communication strategies, for example paraphrases, are used to solve mainly lexical problems, and stalling mechanisms, for example filled pauses and (self-)repetitions, are used to minimise time spent in silence and for keeping the flow of talk going while planning (Dörnyei & Kormos, 1998). In interaction, filled pauses in particular can also have additional functions, such as keeping the floor and indicating engagement in a word search to the interlocutor (e.g. Clark & Fox Tree, 2002; see also Goodwin & Goodwin, 1986). While the role of these two types of problem-solving mechanisms has previously been examined from the perspective of speech fluency, non-verbal means, too, can be used as problem-solving mechanisms. For instance, in Dörnyei and Scott's (1997: 190) inventory of L2 communication strategies, 'mime (non-linguistic/paralinguistic strategies)' is included as one of the 33 strategy types and characterised as '[d]escribing whole concepts nonverbally, or accompanying a verbal strategy with a visual illustration'. Thus, according to Dörnyei and Scott's characterisation, gestures can either be used *instead of* verbal strategies or *along with* verbal strategies to overcome problems in communication. Similarly, Gullberg (1998) regards strategic gestures as either substitutive (used during silences) or complementary (co-occurring with speech; superimposed on speech or oral strategies).

In other words, despite the common assumption, not all learners' gestures are used during silence to compensate for lexical gaps. Gullberg's (1998) pioneering study of gestures as communication strategies among adult L2 speakers showed that while some gestures were used in the expected way, to compensate for lexical items and to solve lexis-related problems, gestures could also be used to overcome grammar or discourse-related difficulties and to provide metalinguistic comments, such as marking word searches. Gullberg (1998: 222–224) thus notes that making clear distinctions between strategic and non-strategic gestures can be challenging, and strategic gesture use could rather be viewed as a continuum from simply helpful gestures (the least conscious) to compensatory gestures and finally to strategic gestures (prototypical, mainly lexical strategies; the most conscious). In the present chapter, compensatory and strategic gestures are not distinguished and will be referred to as compensatory gestures. Furthermore, the majority (175/212; 82.5%) of the strategic gestures in Gullberg's study did not occur as substitutive strategies replacing speech but as complementary strategies during speech. Combinations of oral and gestural strategies were also relatively common, especially among low proficiency participants. It should be noted, however, that the balance between the use of verbal and non-verbal resources in problem-solving can be influenced by multiple factors, including task type, the participants' proficiency, and the participants' individual differences (e.g. Gullberg, 1998, 2011).

Several other studies have also suggested that gestures in general co-occur mainly with (fluent) speech rather than silence (or other disfluencies) in both L1 and L2 speech (e.g. Kosmala & Morgenstern, 2017; McNeill, 1985), although the tendency seems to be stronger for L1 speech (Graziano & Gullberg, 2018). Representational gestures (expressing semantic content) in particular tend to co-occur with speech, while other, pragmatic, gestures may also occur during silences (e.g. McNeill, 1985; see also Graziano & Gullberg, 2018). Similarly to verbal stalling mechanisms, such as filled pauses, pragmatic gestures can be viewed as commenting on the ongoing speech processing (see e.g. Gullberg, 2011). Furthermore, ongoing gestures tend to be suspended during disfluencies in L1 and L2 (Graziano & Gullberg, 2018), which provides further support for the notion that speech and gesture are tightly coordinated (see also Mayberry *et al.*, 1998). The differences found in the timing and location of gesture suspensions between fluent and disfluent speech also suggest that gestures are sensitive to disfluencies (Seyfeddinipur, 2006). In the context of the present study, the question of whether gestures occur during speech or silence is particularly interesting from the perspective of compensation: to what extent do the participants' gestures occur as replacements to speech and to what extent as complementing speech?

## Data and Methods

The data for the study are a part of a larger project examining Finnish learners' fluency in English at different school levels (e.g. Peltonen, 2017a). From the data set, two L2 English dialogues containing relatively frequent gesturing and instances of problem-solving were chosen for the analysis. The participants were two ninth graders (participants A and B; 15-year-olds) and two upper secondary school students (participants C and D; 17-year-olds). The ninth graders had studied English for six years and the upper secondary school students for eight years. According to the vocabulary test scores assessing the participants' general proficiency in English (LexTALE; Lemhöfer & Broersma, 2012), the ninth grade participants represented proficiency level B1 or lower in the *Common European Framework of Reference for Languages* (participant A's score = 57.50%, participant B's score = 55.00%; ninth grade M = 59%) and the upper secondary school participants represented levels B2 (participant C's score 72.50%) and C1–C2 (participant D's score 97.50%; upper secondary school M = 73%). Note that the ninth-grade participants' proficiency levels are similar, while the proficiency levels of the upper secondary school participants are less symmetrical. The upper secondary school pair's interaction has been analysed from the perspective of other-repetitions and collaborative completions in a previous study of (verbal) interactional L2 fluency (see Peltonen, 2017b), and the group level tendencies for the ninth grade and the upper secondary school participants' temporal fluency and verbal fluency resources have been reported in Peltonen (2017a).

The participants' task was to discuss 16 items in English and to rank them in the order of their potential usefulness for survival on a desert island. The task was designed to encourage collaboration between the participants and to elicit communication strategies: in addition to objects that were likely to be well known to the participants in English (e.g. umbrella), the task also included objects they were less likely to be able to name in English (e.g. flares). The participants had two minutes of individual preparation time before the task, and the time for task completion was six minutes. The pairs also attended a stimulated recall session one day after the task. During the session, they watched the video from their interaction and were asked to recall what they had thought during the task. The comments from the sessions were used to facilitate the identification of communication strategies from the dialogues and are reported in the findings where relevant.

The analysis focused on examining how gestures (hand/arm movements, excluding so-called self-adaptors, e.g. hair touching; following Gullberg, 1998: 43) contributed to maintaining fluency. Gestures that could be considered compensatory were of particular interest; that is, gestures that occurred in conjunction with instances of problem-solving, such as word searches. During problem-solving, the relationship between non-verbal resources (i.e. compensatory gestures) and verbal resources (i.e. stalling mechanisms and communication strategies) was also examined. While the focus of the analysis was on gestures, the direction of gaze was included in the analyses where relevant, especially to distinguish solitary word searches from collaborative ones (Goodwin & Goodwin, 1986). Gestures were counted as separate when the hands returned to the rest position between gestures (i.e. when the hands were placed in one's lap); holds in the air (local rest) were not considered as separating gestures (following McNeill, 1992).

In addition to examining whether the gestures occurred in conjunction with problem-solving (as compensatory gestures) or not, the gestures' relation to speech (substitutive vs complementary gestures) as well as their types (based on McNeill's 1992 categorisation) were examined. These categories, with definitions, are compiled in Table 8.1.

McNeill's (1992) categorisation has been widely used in gesture studies and enables the examination of whether particular gesture types,

**Table 8.1** Gesture categories with definitions

| Gestures' relation to speech | |
|---|---|
| Substitutive gestures | Replace speech/verbal resources |
| Complementary gestures | Co-occur with speech/verbal resources |

| Gesture types | |
|---|---|
| Iconic gestures | Closely linked to the semantic content of speech, often depicting concrete objects or actions |
| Metaphoric gestures | |
| – Referential metaphorics | Comparable to iconic gestures but depicting abstract concepts rather than concrete objects or actions |
| – Attitudinal metaphorics | Involving metalinguistic commentaries, e.g. marking word searches |
| Deictic gestures | Pointing; concrete or abstract |
| Beat gestures | Short and quick rhythmic gestures that punctuate speech but do not convey information |

*Note:* Both categories and definitions are based on Gullberg (1998); gesture types originally McNeill (1992).

particularly non-representational gestures, such as attitudinal metaphorics or beats, occur more often during silence than representational, such as iconic, gestures (see discussion in the previous section).

## Findings

Before the findings related to the use of gestures are discussed, basic information about the participants' samples along with selected verbal fluency measures are provided in Table 8.2.

As can be seen from Table 8.2, for the ninth-grade pair, the discussion lasted for almost four minutes, and they produced 240 syllables during the interaction (participant A 32% of them). The discussion for the upper secondary school pair was somewhat shorter (approximately three minutes), but they produced almost three times as many syllables during the interaction (674; participant C 59% of them). As indicated by the individual articulation rates, the ninth graders spoke slower than the upper secondary school participants, participant A's articulation rate being particularly slow. Participant A's pauses within turns were also quite long compared to participant B's and especially to the upper secondary school participants' within-turn pauses. The difference in between-turn pauses across the pairs further demonstrates that the upper secondary school participants' interaction was fast-paced, while the ninth graders' interaction contained relatively lengthy pauses between turns. Against this background, the findings related to the ninth-grade pair are discussed first, followed by discussion of the findings for the upper secondary school pair.

**Table 8.2** Basic information about the participants' samples (duration, syllables) and selected verbal fluency measures (articulation rate, pause duration)

| Measure | Ninth grade pair | | Upper secondary school pair | |
| --- | --- | --- | --- | --- |
| | A | B | C | D |
| Dialogue duration (in seconds) | 227.01 | | 173.79 | |
| Number of syllables (total) | 240 | | 674 | |
| Number of syllables (individual) | 77 | 163 | 397 | 277 |
| Articulation rate (syllables per minute of speaking time, excluding all pauses) | 121.23 | 157.31 | 248.38 | 243.72 |
| Mean length of within-turn pauses (in seconds) | 1.41 | 0.70 | 0.46 | 0.43 |
| Mean length of between-turn pauses (in seconds) | 1.72 | | 0.44 | |

## The ninth-grade pair: Facilitating communication with compensatory gestures despite verbal difficulties

Despite both participants producing relatively little speech, their collaboration during the interaction worked well, and they discussed 14 of the total 16 items. While participant A in particular struggled with communicating the meanings of the items verbally, as evidenced by his scarce and overall disfluent verbal output as well as the use of verbal communication strategies, he actively attempted to overcome his lexical problems with non-verbal resources. In particular, participant A frequently complemented his short and simple verbal communication strategies (the majority being approximations, e.g. *fire* for matches) with gestures to convey the meanings of the items. The nine gestures produced by participant A (participant B did not produce any) can all be considered compensatory gestures, since they were used during problem-solving in conjunction with word searches. However, in contrast to what could be expected of compensatory gestures, the gestures did not solely occur during silence: while some seemed to replace speech and occurred during silence, others overlapped with speech. Furthermore, while eight gestures were iconic, seven of them also contained some other element, either a pragmatic/metalinguistic element (5/7 cases) or a deictic element (2/7 cases).

The first example illustrates participant A's use of compensatory gestures during silences.

### Example 1

```
3    A:   and (2.21) fire (1.47)
4                    * HANDS RAISED FROM REST POSITION; ROTATES RIGHT HAND SLIGHTLY AND
5                      WIGGLES LEFT INDEX FINGER (FIG. 1A)
6                  * RAISES GAZE, DIRECTED TOWARDS PARTICIPANT B; B MEETS GAZE BRIEFLY
7    A:   um
8         * MOVEMENT STOPS
9         (1.49)
```

```
10          * MOVES LEFT AND RIGHT INDEX FINGERS BACK AND FORTH QUICKLY (FIG. 1B)
11     B:   fire sticks?
12          * MOVEMENT STOPS
13          (1.72)
14     A:   $_joo eiku s-_$
15          * HANDS RETURN TO REST POSITION
16          (1.24)
17     B:   we: (.) can make of them a (.) fire (0.63)
18          it's very good (0.34) idea
```

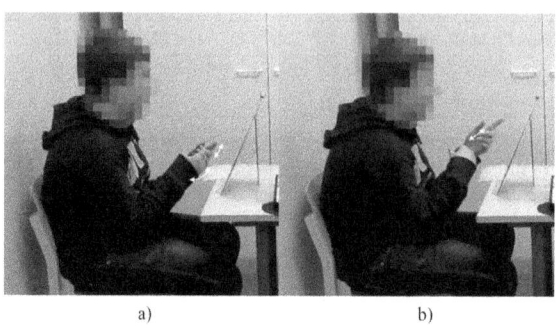

**Figure 8.1** Gestures during silence (*fire sticks*)

In Example 1, participant A is searching for the word *matches*. First, he uses a verbal communication strategy, an approximation *fire* (line 3), which is followed by hesitations (relatively long silent pauses and a filled pause *um*; lines 3, 7, 9). During the first, 1.47 second pause, the participant uses a compensatory gesture to indicate word search (lines 4–5, Figure 8.1a). This gesture can be labelled as an attitudinal metaphoric gesture following Gullberg's (1998) terminology, as it signals that the participant is trying to solve the lexical problem. Combined with the gaze directed at B (line 6), it also functions as a non-verbal request for the interlocutor to participate in the word search. However, B gazes at A only briefly and does not respond right away, giving participant A space to continue the word search by himself. Interestingly, during participant A's subsequent filled pause, the gesture is stopped (lines 7–8); thus, there seems to be a relatively clear pattern of gesture movement occurring during silence and the movement stopping during speech (in this case a filled pause). From the perspective of fluency, the gesture and the filled pause can both be viewed as stalling mechanisms filling the silence and demonstrating ongoing processing to the interlocutor (see also Gullberg, 2011: 144–145).

When the gesture movement resumes during the second pause, a subtle change towards a more iconic form can be observed (potentially due to participant B's lack of verbal response): the index fingers appear to indicate the length and shape of the matches (lines 9–10, Figure 8.1b). This compensatory gesture replacing speech provides the interlocutor with further information about the intended item, which results in the interlocutor providing a try-marked (uttered with a rising intonation) suggestion for the lexical item (*fire sticks*, line 11). Participant A accepts this suggestion: he stops the gesture movement (line 12), nods, and confirms acceptance of the lexical item also verbally (*yes* in Finnish, line 14).[1] Participant B then takes the floor and gives a justification for choosing the item (lines 17–18). Another example of a similar sequence occurred when participant A tried to communicate *fishing gears*: he provided the word *fishing* verbally and continued with an iconic gesture referring to the rod's shape, stopping the gesture movement when B took the turn and confirmed understanding. This pattern of participant A first suggesting an item with a combination of non-verbal and verbal resources, followed by participant B's explicit confirmation of understanding (with *yes* or, more rarely, providing the target lexical item, as in Example 1) and an elaboration justifying the item's usefulness, was common in the interaction (see also Gullberg, 1998).

While in Example 1 the gestural movement occurred during silence, Example 2 illustrates that the division between gesture and speech was not always clear in participant A's turns. In Example 2, participant A attempts to communicate the meaning of the magnifying glass.

*Example 2*

```
90    A:   and uh (1.53)
91         that uh (3.02)
92              * RIGHT HAND RAISED FROM REST POSITION TO A ROUND, HOLDING SHAPE (FIG. 2A)
93                 * LEFT HAND RAISED TO THE SIDE, WIGGLES LEFT INDEX FINGER
94                      (FIG. 2B)
95    A:   bigger (.) *heh* $eh$
96              * HANDS RAISED, MOVE IN THE AIR BACK AND FORTH, CIRCLING MOTION (FIG. 2C)
97                      * HANDS RETURN TO REST POSITION
98    B:   *heh*
99    A:   *heh*
100        (3.66)
```

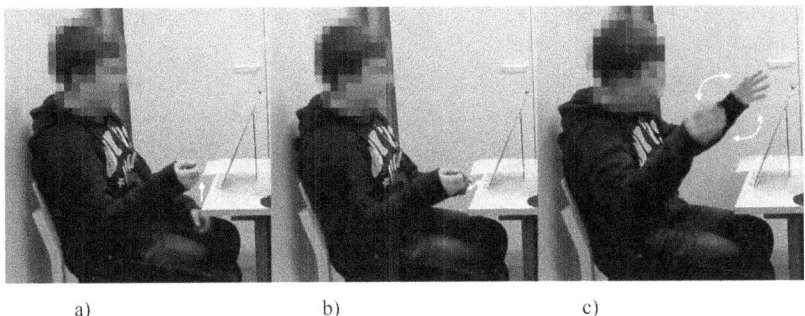

a)          b)          c)

**Figure 8.2** The three parts of the *magnifying glass* gesture

Before the gesture (lines 90–91), participant A's verbal production is scarce, as he only uses the deictic *that* to refer to the item; a strategy he uses when referring to some of the other more difficult items towards the end of the interaction as well. Furthermore, the beginning of the turn can be considered disfluent: despite the use of two filled pauses to keep the floor and to indicate a word search to the interlocutor, participant A's speech is quite fragmentary due to the two lengthy silent pauses. The gesture starts during a relatively long silence with participant A making a round shape with his right hand as if holding a magnifying glass (line 92, Figure 8.2a). After this more iconic part of the gesture, there is a subtle non-verbal indication of a word search when the participant's left index finger briefly moves back and forth (lines 93–94, Figure 8.2b). After the pause, the gesture continues during speech (lines 95–96), now complementing the word *bigger* with hands moving in the air back and forth in a circling motion (Figure 8.2c). The sequence is followed by both participants' laughter, and participant A seems to give up as the interlocutor does not indicate understanding. After the sequence depicted in Example 2, participant A engages in a second attempt to convey *magnifying glass* with the same holding gesture, combined with a deictic gesture (pointing at the table). However, this strategy is not successful either, and ends with the participants' laughter and B changing the topic and suggesting a different item. In contrast to the previous example, where communication was maintained successfully, this example illustrates the only part of the interaction where the communication was not successful. The main obstacle seemed to be the lack of sufficient verbal context for interpreting the gestures (see also Gullberg, 1998: 174–177).

Together, the examples of the ninth-grade participants' interaction demonstrate that while all of participant A's gestures can be regarded as compensatory, since they occurred during problem-solving (word searches), they did not only occur during silence as substitutive gestures, as might be expected of compensatory strategies. Instead, the gestures were used along with, albeit relatively simple and non-specific, verbal communication strategies and in some cases contained parts that overlapped with speech, as in Example 2. Of the total nine gestures, four occurred clearly during silence (one being an attitudinal metaphoric gesture indicating word search), while the other gestures could be regarded as complementary, as they overlapped with speech at least to some extent. For instance, when talking about the rope, A suggests that it can be used as a *trapper (1.16) thing*, gesturing during the word *trapper* and continuing the gesture during silence. Furthermore, the gestures had multiple functions: in addition to communicating referential meanings with iconic gestures, most gestures also included an element of metalinguistic commentary. These metalinguistic commentaries, involving superimposed back and forth movements of hands and/or index fingers, indicated word searches and were potentially also aimed at eliciting assistance from the interlocutor.

## The upper secondary school pair: Complementing verbal content with gestures

Compared to the ninth-grade pair, the upper secondary school pair's interaction was very fast-paced. Both the interaction and the participants' individual contributions were fluent, and the participants talked about all the objects during the interaction in a collaborative manner. During the interaction, the participants produced a total of 12 gestures (participant C three gestures: two iconic, one deictic; participant D nine gestures: seven iconic, one beat, and one deictic with a superimposed beat). Unlike in the ninth graders' interaction, few of the gestures occurred during problem-solving (2/3 for participant C, 2/9 for participant D), and the majority of the gestures were therefore not compensatory in nature. Rather, the majority of the gestures supported the spoken content.

Example 3 illustrates how participant D used iconic gestures to support and complement the meaning conveyed with speech.

*Example 3*
```
76   C:   [but-]
77   D:   [°or°] (.) kill boars [with it *heh*]
78                      * HANDS RAISED FROM REST POSITION
79                        * HANDS IN A FIST, RIGHT HAND MAKES A 'STRIKING' MOVEMENT
80                          PAST THE LEFT HAND (FIG. 3)
81                            * HANDS RETURN TO REST POSITION
82   C:                       [*ahahahah*  ] yes
```

**Figure 8.3** Gesture accompanying speech (*kill boars*)

In Example 8.3, the manner of *killing boars* is demonstrated nonverbally with an iconic co-speech gesture (lines 78–81, Figure 8.3). Although the stimulated recall sessions revealed that the participant used a verbal strategy *boars* (covert self-correction from the word *bears*), the speech production is fluent, as it does not contain silent pauses or other hesitations, just a brief micropause. That is, even when participant D used gestures during problem-solving, the gestures themselves were not compensatory but supported the verbal content. In fact, the majority of the gestures in the upper secondary school participants' interaction occurred during speech (except for one superimposed beat gesture, which occurred partly during silence, and the stroke part of the *flute* gesture, discussed below), as illustrated in Example 3. Some of participant D's gestures were even stopped during silence and seemed to be synchronised with speech in this way. For instance, before Example 3, the participant used another iconic gesture demonstrating the manner of *gutting the fish*, where the stroke of the gesture was closely matched with the verb *gut*. Overall, participant D's gestures can thus be viewed as mostly complementary rather than compensatory.

However, the upper secondary school participants' interaction did also include two gestures that can be regarded as compensatory. Example 4 illustrates participant C's use of a non-verbal communication strategy to communicate the meaning of *binoculars*.

*Example 4*

```
169   C:   (m)uhh (0.32) uh (.) but mm-maybe the (.)
170   C:   what (.) are these called
171        * HANDS RAISED FROM REST POSITION TO EYE LEVEL
172                  * MAKES TWO ROUND SHAPES AND SLIGHTLY ROTATES HANDS (FIG. 4A)
173                  * RAISES GAZE, DIRECTED TOWARDS PARTICIPANT D; D MEETS GAZE
174   C:   (.) the [(black) things]
175        * HANDS RETURN TO REST POSITION
176   D:          [ uh the bino  ]culars
177                  * HANDS RAISED FROM REST POSITION TO EYE LEVEL
178                       * MAKES TWO ROUND SHAPES (FIG. 4B)
179                            * HANDS RETURN TO REST POSITION
180   C:   yeah yes $binoculars$ (0.46)
```

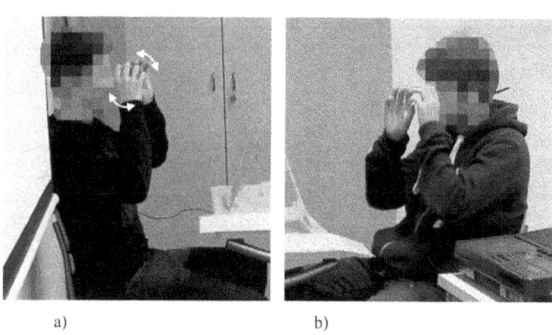

**Figure 8.4** Compensatory gesture and gestural mimicry (*binoculars*)

Participant C starts his turn with a word search (lines 169–170). While the beginning of the turn (line 169) can be viewed as somewhat hesitant, the flow of speech is only slightly interrupted: in particular, the filled pauses (*uh*) contribute to maintaining fluency by reducing time spent in silence (the turn contains only one silent pause, the rest being micropauses of less than 0.25 seconds in duration). Furthermore, the filled pauses have an interactional function: they help participant C to keep the floor while demonstrating to the interlocutor that he is engaged in a word search. On line 170, participant C invites the interlocutor to collaborate in the word search by explicitly appealing for help with a wh-question and by directing his gaze towards participant D (line 173). During the question, participant C raises his hands to eye level, makes two round shapes, and slightly rotates his hands to communicate the meaning of *binoculars* with an iconic gesture and to clarify the referent for *these* (lines 171–172, Figure 8.4a). He continues to specify the meaning also verbally with an approximation (*the black things*, line 174). However, this turn overlaps with participant D already providing the target word *binoculars* (line 176) and repeating participant C's gesture (lines 177–179, Figure 8.4b). After this, participant C accepts participant D's suggestion and repeats the target word on line 180. Example 4 thus illustrates how the participants' collaboration is not only apparent in their verbal communication, but also in their non-verbal conduct: by adopting participant C's gesture, participant D displays understanding and reinforces the link between the meaning of the gesture and the target word. This repetition of gesture, or *gestural mimicry* (Kimbara, 2006), functions similarly to a verbal repetition (see Peltonen, 2017b): it conveys acknowledgement of the interlocutor's contribution and helps to build mutual understanding (see also Gullberg, 2011: 139–141).

Furthermore, Example 4 illustrates how the participants employ multiple verbal and nonverbal resources during problem-solving: verbally, participant C uses stalling mechanisms (filled pauses) during the word search, potentially first attempting to retrieve the target word by himself, followed by an appeal for help and an approximation (*the black thing*). Non-verbally, the direction of the gaze indicates invitation for the interlocutor to participate in the word search (Goodwin & Goodwin, 1986), and the gesture communicates the meaning of the intended concept *binoculars* successfully, as the interlocutor repeats the gesture and provides the target lexical item. With the use of these multiple resources, the problem-solving is efficient and fast. Another instance where participant C uses a multimodal communication strategy occurs when he refers to the item *recorder* verbally with a communication strategy, the approximation *flute*, but specifies the meaning by demonstrating how to hold (upright position) and play (fingers moving) the flute with an iconic gesture. The meaning is thus communicated partly verbally and partly non-verbally.

## Discussion

The purpose of the analysis was to examine how learners used gestures to maintain fluency during a problem-solving task and how the use of gestures related to the use of verbal resources. Overall, in both pairs' interactions, gestures supported the communication but differed in the extent to which they were compensatory. In the ninth-grade pair's interaction, participant A's gestures occurred during problem-solving and were mostly compensatory, often used alongside verbal strategies, whereas most of the gestures in the upper secondary school's interaction did not occur during problem-solving and were not compensatory in nature. Furthermore, while the upper secondary school participants communicated most of the content verbally, gestures playing a minor, supporting role, participant A of the ninth-grade pair relied on iconic gestures to communicate the intended items and to complement the relatively simple and non-specific verbal content. Occasionally, it even seemed that participant A communicated the majority of the content gesturally, not orally; as McNeill (1985: 354) has aptly described gesturing during silence, '[s]peaking was temporarily transferred to the person's gestures'. Similarly, Gullberg (1998: 227) has suggested that gestural cues may receive more weight in communication particularly when oral cues are 'incomplete or less than optimal'.

The findings related to the reliance on compensatory gestures have implications regarding the nature and role of compensatory gestures in L2 communication. Despite the overall tendency of participant A of the ninth grade pair to use more (iconic) gestures to compensate for relatively weak spoken English skills in conjunction with problem-solving, not all of his gestures occurred solely during silence (see also Gullberg, 1998). While it has been assumed that low proficiency learners in particular rely on gestures to communicate meanings instead of speech, 56% of the ninth-grade participant A's gestures overlapped with speech at least to some extent (cf. 82.5% in Gullberg's study). Furthermore, the majority of participant A's gestures were not purely iconic; that is, they did not only communicate referential content, but also contained pragmatic elements to indicate word searches (e.g. wiggling of left index finger in Examples 1 and 2). That is, even if mainly compensating for lexical items, participant A's gestures can be considered rather complex and were used to convey a variety of meanings (see also Gullberg, 1998). On the other hand, while the use of compensatory gestures was rare in the upper secondary school participants' interaction, participant C used two compensatory gestures alongside verbal communication strategies to facilitate problem-solving. Gestures that compensate for verbal content can thus also occur in relatively advanced learners' interaction.

While the analysis presented in this chapter has demonstrated tendencies in how gestures can be used to maintain fluency during a problem-solving task, the findings should be considered preliminary and not necessarily generalisable to larger populations, as they are based on a case study analysis of only two pairs and a small set of gestures. However, the findings can be used as basis for further analyses with larger data sets. For instance, to further examine the links between non-verbal and verbal fluency, the issue of whether gestures occur mostly during speech rather than silence could be explored further with more specifically targeted research questions. While clear differences regarding certain gesture types occurring during silence could not be found in the present study (cf. e.g.

McNeill, 1985), potentially due to the small sample and the task type eliciting mostly iconic gestures (cf. Gullberg's 1998 narrative task eliciting a broader range of different types), the connection between compensatory gestures and silence warrants further study. While some of participant A's compensatory gestures overlapped with silence, participant D's non-compensatory gestures were more clearly aligned with speech (and also seemed to be sensitive to disfluencies; see Graziano & Gullberg, 2018; Seyfeddinipur, 2006). Furthermore, the differences in the participants' gesture frequencies, participants A and D producing more gestures than participants B and C, point to individual differences in the participants' general communication styles that could be studied further. As Gullberg (1998, 2011) has noted, some people are more inclined to gesture regardless of whether they are speaking their first or second language. Therefore, ideally, L1 data from the participants would serve as the point of comparison for individual patterns in gesturing.

In addition to the implications for the analysis of gestures in L2 communication, the findings have implications for L2 (speech) fluency research. In particular, the holistic, multimodal approach to L2 fluency employed in the present study demonstrated that examining non-verbal resources in addition to verbal resources during problem-solving provides a more comprehensive account of learners' fluency resources than a purely speech-focused L2 fluency analysis. A modified fluency resources framework (see Peltonen, 2017a), including non-verbal stalling mechanisms and communication strategies along with verbal resources, thus seems a viable starting point for conducting multimodal L2 fluency analysis. The analysis demonstrated that non-verbal and verbal resources may be used for similar purposes: for instance, in addition to verbal stalling mechanisms (e.g. filled pauses and repetitions), metalinguistic gestures (rapid hand or finger movements) can have a stalling function from the speaker's perspective, alleviating processing time pressure and providing more planning time, while simultaneously indicating a word search to the interlocutor from an interactional perspective. Similarly, multimodal strategies, involving non-verbal and verbal components, were relatively commonly used to communicate concepts for 'missing' or temporarily forgotten lexical items (see also Gullberg, 1998). Thus, when examining what types of resources learners can use for maintaining fluency, non-verbal stalling mechanisms and communication strategies should be considered alongside verbal resources.

## Conclusion

This chapter has presented an exploratory multimodal L2 fluency analysis and highlighted the role of gestures in maintaining fluency during problem-solving. The findings, based on a case study of two pairs' interactions, suggested that while gestures were used in addition to verbal resources in both interactions, the pairs relied on compensatory gestures to a different extent. That is, the flow of interaction was maintained multimodally by both pairs, albeit with different emphases: while participant A of the ninth-grade pair seemed to use more gestures to compensate for lexical gaps, the upper secondary school participants relied less on compensatory gestures. Yet the findings also showed that participant A's gestures were not solely used for communicating meanings of lexical items but also involved metalinguistic elements, and, on the other hand, the upper secondary school participants' interaction, too, included some non-verbal compensatory strategies. From the perspective of (communicative) fluency, the extent of reliance on verbal and non-verbal resources can thus be viewed as forming a continuum, where the balance between what is communicated verbally and what non-verbally can vary.

This chapter has further shown that when L2 fluency is considered from a broader perspective of communication, rather than solely from the perspective of temporal speech fluency (see also Wright & Tavakoli, 2016), gestures have an important role in contributing to how well the interaction is maintained. As Gullberg (2011: 145) has noted, multimodal solutions during problem-solving can be viewed as 'interactional glue that helps sustain interaction'. Analyses based on video-recorded data can reveal, for instance, what happens during silences, which provides important insights into learners' non-verbal means for maintaining fluency and thus contributes to achieving a comprehensive picture of fluency resources in L2 interaction. Whether the participants can be seen or just heard can also affect L2 oral proficiency assessment: participants usually receive higher scores if the assessment is based on video, including non-verbal conduct, as opposed to audio only (e.g. Gullberg, 1998). Therefore, gestures have, at least in theory, the potential to influence assessments of perceived fluency (Segalowitz, 2010). The influence of non-verbal elements on L2 fluency ratings, along with speech rate, pausing and other temporal aspects, would be an interesting topic for future L2 fluency research. This chapter, with its multimodal L2 fluency analysis, has sought to highlight some of the benefits in using video data to analyse non-verbal fluency and to provide ideas for how to explore the links between non-verbal and verbal fluency further in future studies.

### Note

(1) This is followed by a cut-off *eiku siis*, roughly translatable to *or I mean*, which is unrelated to the confirmation but rather a comment acknowledging the (most likely) accidental use of Finnish in the middle of the English production.

### References

Bavelas, J., Gerwing, J., Sutton, C. and Prevost, D. (2008) Gesturing on the telephone: Independent effects of dialogue and visibility. *Journal of Memory and Language* 58, 495–520.

Chambers, F. (1997) What do we mean by fluency? *System* 25, 535–544.
Clark, H.H. and Fox Tree, J.E. (2002) Using uh and um in spontaneous speaking. *Cognition* 84, 73–111.
Dörnyei, Z. and Kormos, J. (1998) Problem-solving mechanisms in L2 communication: A psycholinguistic perspective. *Studies in Second Language Acquisition* 20, 349–385.
Dörnyei, Z. and Scott, M.L. (1997) Communication strategies in a second language: Definitions and taxonomies. *Language Learning* 47, 173–210.
Goodwin, M.H. and Goodwin, C. (1986) Gesture and coparticipation in the activity of searching for a word. *Semiotica* 62, 51–76.
Götz, S. (2013) *Fluency in Native and Nonnative English Speech*. Amsterdam: John Benjamins.
Graziano, M. and Gullberg, M. (2018) When speech stops, gesture stops: Evidence from developmental and crosslinguistic comparisons. *Frontiers in Psychology* 9, 1–17.
Gullberg, M. (1998) *Gesture as a Communication Strategy in Second Language Discourse: A Study of Learners of French and Swedish*. Lund: Lund University Press.
Gullberg, M. (2011) Multilingual multimodality: Communicative difficulties and their solutions in second-language use. In J. Streeck, C. Goodwin and C. LeBaron (eds) *Embodied Interaction: Language and Body in the Material World* (pp. 137–151). Cambridge: Cambridge University Press.
Housen, A., Kuiken, F. and Vedder, I. (eds) (2012) *Dimensions of L2 Performance and Proficiency: Complexity, Accuracy and Fluency in SLA*. Amsterdam: John Benjamins.
Kasper, G. and Wagner, J. (2011) A conversation-analytic approach to second language acquisition. In D. Atkinson (ed.) *Alternative Approaches to Second Language Acquisition* (pp. 117–142). New York: Routledge.
Kimbara, I. (2006) On gestural mimicry. *Gesture* 6, 39–61.
Kosmala, L. and Morgenstern, A. (2017) A preliminary study of hesitation phenomena in L1 and L2 productions: A multimodal approach. In R. Eklund and R. Rose (eds) *Proceedings of DiSS 2017: The 8th Workshop on Disfluency in Spontaneous Speech* (pp. 37–40). Stockholm: Royal Institute of Technology (KTH).
Lemhöfer, K. and Broersma, M. (2012) Introducing LexTALE: A quick and valid lexical test for advanced learners of English. *Behavior Research Methods* 44, 325–343.
Lennon, P. (1990) Investigating fluency in EFL: A quantitative approach. *Language Learning* 40, 387–417.
Mayberry, R.I., Jacques J. and DeDe, G. (1998) What stuttering reveals about the development of the gesture–speech relationship. *New Directions for Child Development* 79, 77–87.
McCarthy, M. (2010) Spoken fluency revisited. *English Profile Journal* 1 (1), 1–15.
McNeill, D. (1985) So you think gestures are nonverbal? *Psychological Review* 92, 350–371.
McNeill, D. (1992) *Hand and Mind: What Gestures Reveal About Thought*. Chicago: The University of Chicago Press.
Peltonen, P. (2017a) Temporal fluency and problem-solving in interaction: An exploratory study of fluency resources in L2 dialogue. *System* 70, 1–13.
Peltonen, P. (2017b) L2 fluency in spoken interaction: A case study on the use of other-repetitions and collaborative completions. In M. Kuronen, P. Lintunen and T. Nieminen (eds) *Näkökulmia toisen kielen puheeseen – Insights into Second Language Speech*. AFinLA-e: Soveltavan kielitieteen tutkimuksia 10. Jyväskylä: Finnish Association of Applied Linguistics AFinLA, 118–138.
Segalowitz, N. (2010) *Cognitive Bases of Second Language Fluency*. New York: Routledge.
Seyfeddinipur, M. (2006) *Disfluency: Interrupting Speech and Gesture*. PhD thesis, Radboud University.
Skehan, P. (2009) Modelling second language performance: Integrating complexity, accuracy, fluency, and lexis. *Applied Linguistics* 30, 510–532.

Tavakoli, P. (2016) Fluency in monologic and dialogic task performance: Challenges in defining and measuring L2 fluency. *International Review of Applied Linguistics in Language Teaching* 54, 133–150.

Wright, C. and Tavakoli, P. (2016) New directions and developments in defining, analyzing and measuring L2 speech fluency. *International Review of Applied Linguistics in Language Teaching* 54, 73–77.

## Appendix: Transcription conventions

| | | |
|---|---|---|
| :: :: ::: | Colon(s) | Extended or stretched sound, syllable, or word. |
| _tota_ | Underlining | Code-switching to Finnish. |
| (.) | Micropause | A brief pause of less than 0.25 seconds. |
| (0.67) | Timed pause | A pause of 0.25 seconds or longer. |
| um | Filled pause | Non-lexical filled pauses. |
| ( ) | Single parentheses | Transcriptionist doubt. |
| ? | Question mark | Rising vocal pitch. |
| - | Hyphen | Halting, abrupt cut off of sound or word. |
| *hah* | Laugh syllable | A separate laugh syllable (cf. chuckling talk below). |
| $ | Smile voice | Laughing/chuckling talk between markers. |
| [ ] | Brackets | Speech overlap. |
| * | Asterisk | The starting point for non-verbal activity. |
| POINTS | Small caps | Descriptions of gesturing/gaze. |

# 9 Fluency in Language Assessment

Ari Huhta, Heini Kallio, Sari Ohranen and Riikka Ullakonoja

## Introduction

Fluency is one of the most commonly used dimensions of proficiency in the assessment of foreign and second language (L2) oral skills. However, as is the case with many other concepts in applied linguistics, there is no consensus about its exact meaning. The main purpose of this chapter is to give an overview of how oral fluency has been conceptualised in L2 assessment through an analysis of (1) research studies carried out in the field of language assessment and (2) practical language assessment instruments. Research that can shed light on fluency in L2 assessment comes in two forms: one type of study specifically aims at increasing language testers' understanding of constructs such as fluency, the other simply uses measures of fluency as a way to obtain information about L2 learners' oral skills. A scrutiny of language assessment instruments, for its part, is useful for our analysis because in order to assess fluency, examination bodies have to create detailed rating scales for their raters or scoring algorithms for their computerised systems. An analysis of such scales and algorithms enables us to see what fluency means in practical L2 assessment. In addition to the analysis of the definitions of fluency in L2 assessment, this chapter reviews research on the role of fluency in oral skills assessment compared with other dimensions (criteria) of proficiency and research on the features in speech that influence fluency ratings.

The only previous surveys of fluency in L2 assessment appear to be those by Huhta (1993) and De Jong (2016), but their coverage was limited to a small number of tests. This chapter provides a more comprehensive picture of fluency in L2 assessment; it analyses major trends and differences in defining fluency, and discusses possible reasons for the findings. While we attempt to link our analysis to the more general discussions of fluency in applied linguistics, there are serious limitations in this due to the nature of information available. Our key data are the rating scales and descriptions of the scoring algorithms and although they allow us to see how different tests define fluency, the organisations responsible for their design almost never publish details about the design and the reasons for defining fluency in a particular way. Therefore, it is difficult to know if certain developments in related fields on defining fluency have influenced specific fluency scales or algorithms. It is very likely that each language examination – or a researcher assessing fluency – is affected by the more general views on fluency to a very different degree, depending on how knowledgeable the test designers (or researchers) happen to be of such developments. Therefore, the key takeaway from this chapter, particularly for readers outside the field of language assessment, is an increased awareness of the considerable variation in what fluency means in L2 assessment and research. The exact meaning of fluency should be checked whenever one encounters that term.

## Definitions of Fluency in Language Assessment Literature

Early literature on L2 assessment does not discuss concepts such as fluency in detail. Rather, they are assumed to be understood by language teachers, testers and researchers. Interestingly, however, this lack of explicit definitions is often accompanied in the publications by operational definitions of fluency in the form of rating scales. For example, Valette (1967/1977), whose book *Modern Language Testing* was among the first extensive expositions of L2 assessment, does not define fluency but provides practical examples of fluency, and other, scales. These include the well-known scales designed by the US Foreign Service Institute (FSI) for assessing L2 learners' speaking skills in a structured oral interview.

The situation has changed to some extent in the past two decades. The more recent assessment studies usually define fluency in some way although often quite briefly, leaving room for interpretation (see the studies listed in Table 9.2, p. 136). This change relates to an increasing interest among language testers in better definitions of the constructs that are assessed. Therefore, several testing researchers have investigated such key dimensions of oral proficiency as fluency by using different methodologies. One approach relies on detailed qualitative analyses of learners' speaking performances to identify features that could be used for assessment purposes (e.g. Fulcher, 1996; Hasselgreen, 2004). Another approach focuses on acoustic analyses of learners' speech, and studies which of the features extracted in the analyses correlate with human ratings of fluency (e.g. Bosker *et al.*, 2012; Pinget *et al.*, 2014).

Work on fluency in other areas of applied linguistics has undoubtedly influenced language testers' views even if in most cases it is not possible to tell exactly what underlies particular operationalisations of fluency, as was mentioned above. Influential intermediaries in this respect include researchers such as Peter Skehan, whose empirical and theoretical work encompasses language testing, second language acquisition and task-based teaching (Skehan & Foster, 1999; Skehan, 2009). Skehan (2009) has, for example, promoted the view that fluency can be divided into breakdown, speed and repair fluency. Speed fluency concerns the rate and density of speech delivery; breakdown fluency relates to interruptions in the continuous speech signal; and repair fluency refers to the number of corrections and repetitions. Many fluency scales cover these types of fluency (see Table 9.1, p. 135) but the similarity between them and definitions by researchers does not imply a clear causal relationship. In fact, the FSI scales were developed already in the 1950s, which means that certain ideas about the nature of fluency have a long pedigree in language testing and applied linguistics.

Another prominent researcher, Glenn Fulcher, should also be mentioned here, as his 1996 investigation was a pioneering study on fluency in L2 oral assessment. His view of fluency is clearly broader than Skehan's, which is probably explained by the fact that Fulcher studied performances in oral interaction tasks. Hence, his definition of fluency includes systematic references to the interaction between an interviewer and a candidate (test-taker). The following extracts from level three in Fulcher's six-point fluency scale illustrate this:

> A candidate ... will hardly ever misunderstand a question or be unable to respond to a question ... when it does happen ... candidate will almost always ask for clarification from the interviewer ... candidate ... often pauses to think about the word which has been used, or to select another... The candidate may even question the interviewer overtly regarding the appropriacy of the word ... Often candidates ... will give examples, counterexamples or reasons to support their point of view ... there is an increasing tendency for candidates to use 'back-channelling' - the use of 'hm' or 'yeah' - when the interviewer is talking, giving the interview a greater sense of normal conversation ... (Fulcher, 1996: 236–237)

There is no official definition of terms like fluency in language assessment. However, it is worth consulting how the only dictionary on L2 assessment that has an entry for fluency summarised its meaning at the turn of the 20th century:

> Fluency may include any or all of the following:
> - the speed of utterance;
> - a lack of hesitation, repetition, self-correction and other false starts;
> - appropriate stress, rhythm and intonation; or
> - a general ability to communicate ideas effectively.
>
> ... More generally, the term 'fluent' is used to describe a speaker who has a very good overall command of a foreign or a second language. (Davies *et al.*, 1999: 64)

Davies *et al.*'s summary is particularly interesting as it clearly states that the meanings of fluency in L2 assessment have ranged from speed and hesitations to prosodic features and even to overall oral or general L2 proficiency. Huhta's (1993) analysis of L2 rating criteria also concluded that definitions of fluency varied more than the other criteria and often included aspects of oral proficiency that go well beyond the core temporal phenomena of speed and pausing. Before surveying current fluency scales and scoring algorithms to see how fluency is defined in current L2 assessments, we investigate what is known about the contribution of fluency to overall ratings of L2 oral proficiency and what acoustic characteristics of speech underlie fluency ratings.

## Relative Importance of Fluency in L2 Oral Proficiency Assessments

As was mentioned earlier, fluency is very often included in the rating of L2 speaking. An interesting question is how it compares with the other dimensions such as pronunciation or vocabulary in raters' overall evaluations of learners' oral proficiency. How important is fluency and do different kinds of raters value it differently?

A small number of studies have compared fluency with other rating criteria and concluded that fluency is a very important feature in the evaluation of L2 speakers' proficiency. Overall, research suggests that both trained and untrained raters can assess fluency rather consistently (e.g. Cucchiriani *et al.*, 2002; Derwing *et al.*, 2004; Rossiter, 2009). However, trained, professional raters and non-professionals appear to value fluency somewhat differently, as was found by Duijm *et al.* (2018). They had raters assess Dutch L2 speech samples which were manipulated for fluency and/or accuracy. The findings showed that the improvement of either fluency or accuracy led to higher ratings in both professional and non-professional rater groups, indicating that both are important features of speaking. However, the non-professionals gave more points to the fluency-improved samples, whereas the professional raters awarded more points to accuracy-improved samples, which suggests that untrained persons value fluency even more than specialist raters.

Other studies support Duijm *et al.*'s finding that professional raters find fluency an important criterion, even if they might also value other criteria. Iwashita *et al.* (2008) compared the relative contribution of fluency, linguistic resources (i.e. grammar and vocabulary) and phonology (i.e. pronunciation, intonation and rhythm) on overall TOEFL iBT ratings. They found that the two features that had the biggest impact on the overall ratings were fluency (particularly speech rate) and vocabulary (particularly the number of words spoken by the learner). An ongoing study of the raters working for the Finnish National Certificates of Language Proficiency also points towards the importance of fluency. Preliminary findings based on ratings of Finnish L2 speaking performances suggest that fluency ratings were among the strongest correlates of the overall ratings (see www.jyu.fi/broken-finnish).

Research thus indicates that fluency is a key aspect in the assessment of L2 oral proficiency and it may be particularly important for listeners who are not specialists in language assessment.

## Features Underlying Fluency Assessments

Research on the correlates of rated fluency has focused on acoustic features of speech, since it is relatively easy to measure certain fluency-related features from speech. This ease with which such features can be operationalised in practice must partly explain why fluency is included in practically all automatic assessments of speaking. We will next review findings from studies on the relationship between acoustically measured features in learner's speech and human ratings of fluency.

Bosker *et al*. (2012) studied L2 Dutch speakers' fluency by using the three fluency aspects discussed by Skehan (2009). They operationalised speed fluency as mean length of syllables; breakdown fluency as number of silent and filled pauses, and mean length of silent pauses; and repair fluency as number of repetitions and corrections. Overall, acoustic fluency features explained 84% of the variance in fluency ratings. Breakdown fluency was the best predictor (59% of explained variance), followed by speed fluency (54%) and repair fluency (16%). The two acoustic features of breakdown fluency that best predicted ratings were duration and number of silent pauses. In another study on L2 French, Préfontaine *et al*. (2016) found mean length of run and articulation rate to be the best predictors of fluency ratings. However, deviating from previous research, the frequency of pauses turned out to be a rather weak predictor, and even more surprisingly, the length of unfilled pauses was related positively with fluency ratings. In their study of TOEFL raters, Iwashita *et al*. (2008) found that speed rate was more important for fluency ratings than filled or unfilled pauses, repairs, total pausing time, or mean length of run.

Although the results of individual studies can vary, the temporal features of speech shown to relate to fluency ratings include speech and articulation rate, mean length of runs, phonation-time-ratio, number of stressed syllables as well as number of disfluencies (Bosker *et al*., 2012; Cucchiarini *et al*., 2002; Derwing *et al*., 2004; Kallio *et al*., 2017; Kormos & Dénes, 2004; Trofimovich & Baker, 2007; Ullakonoja, 2011). There are, thus, two clusters of temporal variables that underlie typical fluency ratings: one promoting fluency and related to the speed of delivery, and another that interferes with fluency (disfluencies) and includes pauses, self-corrections, repetitions and false starts.

Research on correlates of fluency ratings has been limited to the acoustic and temporal aspects of fluency and excluded the more interactionist features discussed by Fulcher (1996). This is because most studies focus on monologue speech in which interaction is nonexistent. A recent study by Peltonen (2017) can pave way for research on the interactionist aspects of fluency. In her study, Peltonen linked temporal fluency analysis to a broader problem-solving perspective in a dialogue setting, and proposed a new framework for studying L2 fluency.

## Definitions of Fluency in Rating Scales

Oral fluency scales offer a window into how L2 examination bodies and language testing researchers define this construct. We next scrutinise such scales to see how language testers operationalise fluency in practice. Table 9.1 presents a systematic content analysis of the fluency scales used in language examinations and Table 9.2 does the same for studies published in the journals *Language Testing* and *Language Assessment Quarterly* and in books reporting on research on language assessment. The fluency scales reviewed in Table 9.1 represent established – and, thus, influential – international and some national L2 examination that have published their scales; most examinations concern only English but some (as well as the CEFR) are multilingual. For Table 9.2, studies were included if they involved fluency and provided some formal or operational definition of fluency; with one exception, only studies published after 2000 were included.

First, it is apparent in Table 9.1 that some examinations do not have a scale titled 'fluency'. However, a closer examination of the scales used in such examinations reveals that they often cover at least some of the components of oral fluency included in Davies *et al.*'s (1999), Skehan's (2009) and Fulcher's (1996) definitions. Examples include *fluency and coherence* (IELTS), *discourse management* (Cambridge English examinations), *delivery* (TOEFL iBT), *size and discourse management* (CET) and *clarity and naturalness of speech* (BIFIE; see also examples of definitions in Table 9.3). However, some examinations just use a scale titled *fluency* (e.g. TEEP, ICAO, OET, Finnish National Certificates) or *oral fluency* (PTE Academic). Similarly, the influential *Common European Framework of Reference for Languages* (CEFR) contains two scales titled *fluency* and *spoken fluency*.

Another pattern can be seen by comparing Tables 9.1 and 9.2: the operational definitions of fluency in research studies are narrower than in most language examinations. Scales used for research are usually called simply *fluency* and they refer to pauses, speed, self-corrections and hesitations. Language examinations appear to operationalise fluency in more varied ways, and they also often combine fluency with other aspects of proficiency (e.g. coherence; see also De Jong, 2016). However, the same 'core' fluency features as those included in research studies also appear in many examination scales. Particularly hesitation is very frequent, although it can be referred to as halting or fragmented speech, or searching or groping for words. Interestingly, the other typical element in the examination scales concerns the length of expressions that learners can say without pausing; this is rather similar to 'mean length of run' which is an often-used aspect of fluency in more general fluency research, and could be seen as a combination of Skehan's speed and breakdown fluency.

Fluency in Language Assessment 135

Table 9.1 Fluency in L2 examinations and frameworks

| Examinations | Name of the criterion | Pauses/ silent pauses | Hesitation | Speed | Pace/ tempo/ rhythm/ (un) evenness | Repetition | Self-correction/ circumlocution/ false starts | (Un)Naturalness | Fillers | Ease/ flow/ smoothness/ effort | Spontaneity/ automatisation | Coherence | Cohesion/ linking words | Topic familiarity/ nature of topic | Length of expressions | Pronunciation | Prosody/ intonation | Communication/ interaction | Listener effect/ strain | Intelligibility/ clarity | Fluency (general) |
|---|---|---|---|---|---|---|---|---|---|---|---|---|---|---|---|---|---|---|---|---|---|
| IELTS | Fluency and Coherence | ■ | ■ |  |  | ■ | ■ |  |  |  |  |  | ■ |  |  |  |  |  |  |  |  |
| Cambridge English: Preliminary (B1) | Discourse management |  |  |  |  |  |  |  |  |  |  | ■ | ■ |  |  |  |  |  |  |  |  |
| TOEFL iBT | Delivery |  |  |  | ■ |  |  |  |  | ■ |  |  |  |  |  |  | ■ |  |  | ■ |  |
| TEEP | Fluency |  |  |  |  |  |  |  |  | ■ |  |  |  |  |  |  |  |  |  |  |  |
| PTE Academic | Oral fluency |  |  |  | ■ | ■ |  |  |  | ■ |  |  |  |  |  |  |  |  |  |  |  |
| OET | Fluency |  |  |  |  |  |  |  |  |  |  |  |  |  |  |  |  |  |  |  |  |
| CET | Size and discourse management |  |  |  |  |  |  |  |  | ■ |  |  |  | ■ |  |  |  | ■ |  |  |  |
| FSI | Fluency |  |  |  |  |  |  |  |  | ■ |  |  |  |  |  |  |  | ■ |  |  |  |
| EDEXCEL GCSE | Content and response |  |  |  |  |  |  |  |  |  |  |  |  |  |  |  |  |  |  |  |  |
| ICAO | Fluency |  |  |  |  |  |  |  |  | ■ |  |  |  |  |  |  |  |  |  |  |  |
| Finnish National Certificates | Fluency |  |  |  |  |  |  |  |  | ■ | ■ |  |  |  |  |  |  | ■ |  |  | ■ |
| BIFIE | Clarity & Naturalness of speech |  |  |  |  |  |  |  |  |  |  |  |  |  |  | ■ |  |  | ■ | ■ |  |
| *FRAMEWORKS* | | | | | | | | | | | | | | | | | | | | | |
| CEFR 2017 | Spoken fluency |  |  |  |  |  |  | ■ |  |  |  |  |  |  |  |  |  |  |  |  | ■ |
| | Fluency |  |  |  |  |  |  |  |  |  |  |  |  |  |  |  |  |  |  |  |  |
| WIDA 2017 | Language control |  | ■ |  |  |  |  |  |  |  |  |  |  |  |  |  |  |  |  |  | ■ |

BIFIE (Bundesinstitut für Bildungsforschung, Innovation und Entwicklung des Bildungswesens – Austria); CET (College English Test – China) EDEXCEL (a multinational education and examination body owned by Pearson); ICAO (International Civil Aviation Organization); OET (Occupational English Test); TEEP (Test of English for Educational Purposes – UK); WIDA (an educational consortium of state departments of education covering almost 40 states in the USA)

136  Fluency in L2 Learning and Use

**Table 9.2** Fluency in language assessment research

| Study | Name of the criterion | Pauses/ silent pauses | Hesitation | Speed | Pace/ tempo/ rhythm/ (un)evenness | Repetition | Self-correction/ circumlocution/ false starts | (Un)Naturalness | Fillers | Ease/ flow/ smoothness/ effort | Spontaneity/ automatisation | Coherence | Cohesion/ linking words | Topic familiarity/ nature of topic | Length of expressions | Pronunciation | Prosody/ intonation | Communication/ interaction | Listener effect/ strain | Intelligibility/ clarity | Fluency (general) |
|---|---|---|---|---|---|---|---|---|---|---|---|---|---|---|---|---|---|---|---|---|---|
| Isaacs et al., 2018 | Fluency | ● | | | | | | | | | | | | | ● | | | | | ● | |
| Duijm et al., 2018 | Fluency | | | | | | | | | | | | | | | | | | | | ● |
| Han, 2016 | Fluency of delivery | ● | | ● | | | | | | | | | | | | | | | | | |
| Ockey et al., 2013, 2015 | Fluency | | | | ● | | | | | ● | ● | | | | | | | ● | ● | | |
| Leaper and Riazi, 2013 | Fluency | ● | ● | | | | | | | | | | | | | | | | | | |
| Hirai and Koizumi, 2013 | Communicative efficiency | | | | | | | | | | | ● | | | | | | | | | |
| Kang, 2012 | Suprasegmental fluency measures | | | | | | | | | | | | | | | | ● | | | | |
| Kiddle and Kormos, 2011 | Fluency and delivery | ● | | ● | ● | | | | | | | | | | | | | | ● | | ● |
| Zhang and Elder, 2010 | Fluency | | | | | | | | | | | | | | | | | | | | |
| Butler and Lee, 2010 | Fluency (self-assessed) | | | | | | | | | | | | | | | | | | | | |
| Wigglesworth and Elder, 2010 | Fluency | | | | | | ● | | | | | | | | | | | ● | | | |
| Davis, 2009 | Fluency | | | | | | | | | | | | | | | | | ● | | | ● |
| Hasselgreen, 2004 | Fluency | | | ● | | | | | | ● | | | | | | | | | | | |
| Elder et al., 2002 | Fluency | | | | | | | | | | | | | | | | | | | | |
| Bonk and Ockey, 2003 | Fluency | ● | | | ● | | | | | ● | | | | ● | | | | ● | | | ● |
| O'Loughlin, 2001 | Fluency 1 / Fluency 2 | | | ● | | | | | | | | | | | | | | | | | |
| Fulcher, 1996 | Fluency | | | | | | | | | ● | | | | | ● | | | | | | |

**Table 9.3** Fluency scales: Examples of definitions of lower vs higher levels of fluency

| Examination; title of the fluency scale; number of scale points | Lower / limited fluency | Higher / more advanced fluency |
| --- | --- | --- |
| IELTS (International English Language Testing System) *Fluency and coherence* (9-point scale) | 4 Cannot respond without noticeable pauses and may speak slowly, with frequent repetition and self-correction. Links basic sentence but with repetitious use of simple connectives and some breakdowns in coherence. | 8 Speaks fluently with only occasional repetition of self-correction; hesitation is usually content-related and only rarely to search for language. Develops topics coherently and appropriately. |
| TOEFL iBT (Test of English as a Foreign Language Internet Based Test; ETS, 2014), *Delivery* (4-point scale) | 1 Consistent pronunciation, stress and intonation difficulties cause considerable listener effort; delivery is choppy, fragmented, or telegraphic; frequent pauses and hesitations. | 4 Generally well-paced flow (fluid expression). Speech is clear. It may include minor lapses, or minor difficulties with pronunciation or intonation patterns, which do not affect overall intelligibility. |
| FSI (Foreign Service Institute), *Fluency* (6-point scale; Valette 1977: 159) | 2 Speed is very slow and uneven except for short or routine sentences. | 5 Speech is effortless and smooth, but perceptibly non-native in speed and evenness. |
| BIFIE (Austrian school leaving examination), *Clarity & Naturalness of Speech* (7-point scale) | 3 Noticeable pauses, hesitation or false starts, sometimes causing breakdown of communication. Short contribution and exchanges linked with some simple connectors. Intelligible pronunciation, foreign accent or mispronunciations which sometimes impair understanding. | 7 Fluent and spontaneous at a fairly even tempo with natural pauses. Longer stretches of language. Clear, natural pronunciation and intonation. |

Certain fluency scales contain somewhat uncommon features, for example, the native speaker as a point of reference. This is rather common in the older fluency scales such as the FSI scale (but also in Bonk & Ockey, 2003; Elder *et al*., 2002). It has, however, disappeared from the more current scales (and also from the new companion volume to the original CEFR; Council of Europe, 2001, 2018). This is probably due to the criticisms of using native speakers as a reference point because of variation in their L1 skills (e.g. Bachman, 1990). Some fluency scales refer to intelligibility (e.g. CEFR; TOEFL iBT; see also Isaacs *et al*., 2018), which is natural since intelligibility depends on both segmental and suprasegmental (prosodic) features of speech, and listeners' familiarity with particular varieties of L2 speech affects how intelligible and fluent a speaker is considered (Brown & Fulcher, 2017).

Apart from considering the content of different fluency scales, it is useful to note that a scale, in fact, contains more than one definition of the phenomenon it depicts. This is because assessment means evaluating the degree of fluency in learners' speech, which is typically done by using a rating scale. Each level point is, thus, a definition of fluency *at that level* of proficiency. In other words, fluency scales are in fact a rank-order series of definitions of fluency. Therefore, to get a more nuanced understanding of how rating scales define fluency, we present examples of definitions of two levels in Table 9.3, one representing a modest degree of fluency and the other more advanced fluency. The scales come from the examinations listed in Table 9.1, and they also illustrate variation in how fluency is defined and how it can be combined with other dimensions of proficiency. Of the examples, the FSI scales illustrates a narrow definition of fluency that focuses on speed and evenness of delivery. The other three exemplify scales in which fluency is merged, in the rating at least, with coherence and sometimes also with pronunciation and prosody.

The examples illustrate how lower levels of fluency are typically described in terms of the number and length of pauses and false starts. References to slow speed and uneven or hesitating delivery are also usual. Such disfluencies cause listener effort and even breakdowns in communication. In contrast, higher fluency is characterised by fewer pauses, hesitations and false starts, as well as smooth or even delivery at a higher speed. The scales that combine fluency and coherence define low coherence with reference to breakdowns in coherence and limited use of (simple) connectors, whereas more advanced coherence is characterised by coherent topic development and, presumably, by more varied connectors.

To conclude our review of how fluency is defined in L2 rating scales, we briefly discuss the relationship between language assessment and other fields of applied linguistics. In this context, the key point of interest is whether the design of fluency scales is informed by relevant developments in other fields. However, as mentioned in the introduction, as examination bodies seldom report how their rating scales were developed, we rarely know to what extent empirical and theoretical work on fluency has influenced their scales. An exception to this is the development of the computer-based TOEFL iBT, which has been documented quite extensively. Jamieson and Poonpon (2013) discuss the three scoring criteria for speaking used in that examination, namely delivery, language use and topic development. Their report reveals that the development of the delivery scale, which includes fluency, was based on an extensive analysis of research on speaking; Jamieson and Poonpon refer, for example, not only to the previously mentioned studies by Fulcher (1996) and Skehan (2009) but also to more general work on fluency (e.g. Lennon, 1990; Koponen & Riggenbach, 2000). They do not explicate why fluency is not rated separately, as an independent criterion, but practical considerations probably played a significant role. Despite being computer-delivered,

TOEFL iBT is not fully automated; speaking is assessed by human raters who can use only a limited number of criteria. Scale developers apparently wanted to cover a range of dimension of speaking but to limit the number of rating scales; therefore, they placed fluency in the same scale with certain other dimensions of speaking. Jamieson and Poonpon (2013: 9) state that 'the description of delivery includes the conceptually overlapping qualities of fluency (i.e. fluidity), pronunciation, intonation, and intelligibility', which indicates that Educational Testing Service (the organisation responsible for TOEFL iBT) considered these aspects of speaking be close enough to be rated together.

We lack detailed information for other L2 examinations about their reasons for defining fluency in a particular way or for combining it with other aspects of speaking in the rating scales. Furthermore, as far as individual research studies are concerned, only some researchers provide reasons for their definition of fluency or for the choice of a particular fluency scale. In general, such justifications are absent from the articles reporting on investigations in which learners' oral fluency has been assessed. Exceptions to this include Bosker *et al.* (2012), whose study was covered earlier and who designed their fluency measures with reference to the tripartition of fluency into speed, repair and breakdown fluency.

## Definition of Fluency in Automated Speaking Assessments

Automated assessment of L2 oral skills provides us with another window into how fluency is defined in language assessment. Rating scales detail what human raters should focus on when they rate L2 learners' fluency; scoring algorithms do the same for computers. Thus, an analysis of what scoring algorithms have been programmed to do when evaluating fluency informs us about how fluency is operationalised in automated assessment. Studies have shown high correlations between human and computer ratings (e.g. Johnson *et al.*, 2016; Ordinate, 2004; Pearson, 2011; Ullakonoja & van Moere, in progress), which means that it is possible to design automated rating systems that simulate human ratings very closely. Automatic assessment of fluency is based on automatic speech recognition (ASR) that detects certain acoustic features from speech signal. Assessment algorithms are trained with human ratings and with extensive speech data to achieve close agreement with human ratings (see Cheng *et al.*, 2014; Pearson, 2017, for details).

Although automatic speech recognition has developed considerably in the past decades, the systems still perform best for tasks that restrict variability, such as short reading or repeating tasks. This is due to considerable acoustic variation in the speech signal. Since non-native speech contains even more variation than native speech, ASR training data with different L2 accents is essential in assessment systems that do not use native speakers as a reference. It must be noted, however, that the limitations in the speaking tasks of ASR-based assessment systems can deteriorate the ecological validity of the assessment.

The operationalisations of fluency can vary depending on the technology at hand and purpose of assessment. One of the first widely used automatic systems, PhonePass, assessed such constructs as reading fluency and repeat fluency (Townshend et al., 1998: 181) and employed only two task types (reading a text and repeating sentences). Apart from mentioning pace, Townshend et al. do not provide details of how fluency was operationalised. However, in the successor to the PhonePass, the SET-10 (Spoken English Test), fluency 'reflects the rhythm, phrasing and timing evident in constructing, reading, and repeating sentences' (Ordinate, 2004: 9). The more recent Versant tests use exactly the same definition of fluency as the SET-10 did (Pearson, 2011: 11). Bernstein et al. (2010: 262) elaborate that in Versant, fluency is based on the duration of various events such as 'response latency, words per time, segments per articulation time, inter-word times'.

The operationalisation of fluency in the fully automated examination PTE Academic, used for entry into higher education, is presumably the same as in the Versant tests. The score guide (Pearson, 2017: 6) defines oral fluency as '[s]mooth, effortless and natural-paced delivery of speech'. Extracts from the 6-point oral fluency scale elaborate on this definition (Pearson, 2017: 24–25):

---

5 Native-like

...

4 Advanced

Speech has an acceptable rhythm with appropriate phrasing and word emphasis. There is no more than one hesitation, one repetition or a false start. There are no significant non-native phonological simplifications.

3 Good

...

2 Intermediate

Speech may be uneven or staccato. Speech (if >= 6 words) has at least one smooth three-word run, and no more than two or three hesitations, repetitions or false starts. There may be one long pause, but not two or more

1 Limited

...

0 Disfluent

Speech is slow and labored with little discernible phrase grouping, multiple hesitations, pauses, false starts, and/or major phonological simplifications. Most words are isolated, and there may be more than one long pause

Two points in PTA Academic's descriptions are worth noting: using native-speakers as a yardstick, which differs from the trend in the rating scales that human raters use, and the mention of (non-native) phonological simplification. The latter is a unique feature among the scales reviewed for this chapter but, unfortunately, Pearson's publications do not provide details on what the precise nature of such simplification might be.

In SpeechRater by Educational Testing Service (ETS), fluency is part of delivery, the other two parts being pronunciation and prosody. Fluency refers to the number of interruption points of repair/repeat, disfluencies per clause, number of silences and long silences per word, number of repetitions per word, proportion of long within-clause silences to all within-clause silences, average duration of all within-clause silences, average chunk length in words, and number of words per second (Zechner *et al.*, 2015: 16). The exact combination of fluency features varies depending on the test for which the SpeechRater is adapted. For example, for testing teenage learners of English as a foreign language, only speech rate, words per chunk, number of pauses and long pauses were selected (Evanini & Wang, 2014). Unlike the Pearson/Versant technologies, SpeechRater is intended to work with more open-ended speech samples and require less task-specific training.

Although there are some differences in the constructs and operationalisations of fluency in automatic assessment systems, all of them rely on acoustic measurements of speech; more specifically the temporal features previous research has proven to be important cues in assessing L2 oral fluency. Phonological features such as sound production, intonation and temporal features of speech are acoustically measurable and thus easy to detect automatically. Therefore, it is not surprising that these features are integrated into the fluency concepts of automated rating systems. However, what exactly is automatically scored depends on the test provider and the purpose of the assessment. Given the limitations and complexity of automatic assessments, it can be expected that designs combining human and automated assessment become more common (see Luo *et al.*, 2016). For example, the DigiTala project is developing such a system for the final school leaving examination in Finland (Karhila *et al.*, 2016; Rouhe *et al.*, 2017). The system is expected to focus on features that relate to pronunciation and fluency and let the human raters concentrate on the more complex aspects of oral proficiency.

## Conclusion

Fluency is a common assessment criterion in L2 oral assessments, and it contributes significantly to overall ratings of oral proficiency. Our analyses of fluency scales indicate that the meaning of fluency in L2 assessments varies, often considerably. Some examinations combine it with other aspects of oral proficiency (e.g. coherence) while others focus on the prototypical fluency features of speed, pausing and hesitation. In contrast to language examinations, individual research studies appear to define fluency more narrowly and focus on pausing, hesitations and speed. Automated rating of speaking is the third area in which dimensions of speaking, including fluency, have to be clearly defined. Our review of automated assessments indicates that they operationalise fluency relatively narrowly as speed, pauses and repetitions. This is not surprising because, in general, automated systems are limited in what they can analyse.

It is important to be aware that definitions of fluency in rating scales are one thing and how human raters use the scale and how they value different components of fluency in their ratings of fluency is another. Research that we reported earlier on the aspects of fluency that determine fluency ratings is useful in understanding raters' behaviour and because it can be used in rater training. Language testing differs from most other fields of applied linguistics in that testing often has serious consequences to the test-takers. Therefore, whatever their personal views of fluency, raters working for high-stakes examinations should adhere to the definition of fluency used in their examination so that test-takers' marks would not be based on raters' possibly idiosyncratic views on that construct. Unlike human raters, automated scoring systems do not make personal interpretations but process speech in exactly the same way across test-takers. The problems with computerised scoring of speaking lie in the accuracy of speech recognition: the more errors it makes, the less reliable the scoring system. If the analysis of test-takers' speed is based, for example, on counting the number of syllables they produce per second, wrongly identified syllables will distort the calculations and, thus, fluency estimates of the test-takers.

We conclude with a general issue in fluency assessments, namely variation in learners' first language fluency. Speakers' L1 and L2 fluency are often correlated (e.g. De Jong *et al.*, 2015) implying that learners' L2 fluency ratings are influenced by their L1 fluency. Variation in L1 fluency is partly individual – some persons simply speak faster than others, for instance – and partly due to different L1 interaction norms. For example, in some languages (e.g. French) fluent conversation is characterised by filled pauses, whereas in others (e.g. Finnish; Toivola *et al.*, 2009) silent pauses are normal. It has been suggested, therefore, that test takers' L1 fluency could be taken into account in their L2 fluency assessments (e.g. De Jong *et al.*, 2015). This is not only a practical challenge (how to find out about one's L1 fluency without administering a separate L1 speaking test) but also a theoretical problem. Assessments usually happen with reference to some norms, and the fundamental question here is whether L2 fluency should be judged only against L2 norms or whether learners' background such as their first language should also be considered in some way.

In this chapter, we have analysed how fluency is conceptualised in L2 assessment and demonstrated that while certain features such as pauses and hesitation appear in most fluency scales, considerable variation exists.

Particularly examinations with human raters appear to use quite broad and varied definitions of fluency, whereas tests with an automated assessment system as well as individual research studies operationalise fluency more narrowly. Users of assessment results should, thus, carefully check what fluency actually means in the particular context as no commonly agreed on definition exists in L2 assessment.

### References

Bachman, L. (1990) *Fundamental Considerations in Language Testing.* Oxford: Oxford University Press.

Bernstein, J., van Moere, A. and Cheng, J. (2010) Validating automated speaking tests. *Language Testing* 27 (3), 355–377.

Bonk, W. and Ockey, G. (2003) A many-facet Rasch analysis of the second language group oral discussion task. *Language Testing* 20 (1), 89–110.

Bosker, H., Pinget, A., Quené, H., Sanders, T. and De Jong, N. (2012) What makes speech sound fluent? The contributions of pauses, speed and repairs. *Language Testing* 30 (2), 159–175.

Brown, K. and Fulcher, G. (2017) Pronunciation and intelligibility in assessing spoken fluency. In T. Isaacs and P. Trofimovich (eds) *Second Language Pronunciation Assessment: Interdisciplinary Perspectives* (pp. 37–53). Bristol: Multilingual Matters.

Butler, Y. and Lee, J. (2010) The effects of self-assessment among young learners of English. *Language Testing* 27 (1), 5–31.

Cheng, J., D'Antilio, Y., Chen, X. and Bernstein, J. (2014) Automatic assessment of the speech of young English learners. *Proceedings of the Ninth Workshop on Innovative Use of NLP for Building Educational Applications*, 12–21.

Council of Europe (2001) *Common European Framework of Reference for Languages: Learning, Teaching, Assessment.* Cambridge: Cambridge University Press. Retrieved from https://rm.coe.int/1680459f97.

Council of Europe (2018) *Common European Framework of Reference for Languages: Learning, Teaching, Assessment. Companion Volume with New Descriptors.* Council of Europe. Retrieved from https://rm.coe.int/cefr-companion-volume-with-new-descriptors-2018/1680787989.

Cucchiarini, C., Strik, H. and Boves, L. (2002) Quantitative assessment of second language learners' fluency: Comparisons between read and spontaneous speech. *The Journal of the Acoustical Society of America* 111 (6), 2862–2873.

Davies, A., Brown, A., Elder, C., Hill, K., Lumley, T. and McNamara, T. (1999) *Dictionary of Language Testing.* Cambridge: Cambridge University Press.

Davis, L. (2009) The influence of interlocutor proficiency in a paired oral assessment. *Language Testing* 26 (3), 367–396.

De Jong, N., Groenhout, R., Schoonen, R. and Hulstijn, J. (2015) Second language fluency: Speaking style or proficiency? Correcting measures of second language fluency for first language behavior. *Applied Psycholinguistics* 36 (2), 223–243.

De Jong, N. (2016) Fluency in second language assessment. In D. Tsagari and J. Banerjee (eds) *Handbook of Second Language Assessment* (pp. 203–218). Berlin: De Gruyter Mouton.

Derwing, T., Rossiter, M., Munro, M. and Thomson, R. (2004) Second language fluency: Judgments on different tasks. *Language Learning* 54 (4), 655–679.

Duijm, K., Schoonen, R. and Hulstijn, J. (2018) Professional and non-professional raters' responsiveness to fluency and accuracy in L2 speech: An experimental approach. *Language Testing* 35 (4), 501–527.

Elder, C., Iwashita, N. and McNamara, T. (2002) Estimating the difficulty of oral proficiency tasks: what does the test-taker have to offer? *Language Testing* 19 (4), 347–368.

ETS (2014) *TOEFL iBT Speaking Section Scoring Guide*. Princeton, NJ: Educational Testing Service. https://www.ets.org/toefl/ibt/scores/understand/, accessed 11 March 2018.

Evanini, K. and Wang, X. (2013) Automated speech scoring for non-native Middle School students with multiple task types. *Proceedings of Interspeech* 2013, 2435–2439.

Fulcher, G. (1996) Does thick description lead to smart tests? A data-based approach to rating scale construction. *Language Testing* 13 (2), 208–238.

Han, C. (2016) Investigating score dependability in English/Chinese interpreter certification performance testing: A generalizability theory approach. *Language Assessment Quarterly* 13 (3), 186–201.

Hasselgreen, A. (2004) *Testing the Spoken English of Young Norwegians: A Study of Test Validity and the Role of 'Smallwords' in Contributing to Pupils' Fluency*. Cambridge: Cambridge University Press.

Hirai, A. and Koizumi, R. (2013) Validation of empirically derived rating scales for a story retelling speaking test. *Language Assessment Quarterly* 10 (4), 398–422.

Huhta, A. (1993) Suullisen kielitaidon arviointi. [Assessment of oral proficiency]. In S. Takala (ed.) *Suullinen kielitaito ja sen arviointi*. [Oral proficiency and its assessment]. (pp. 143–225). Jyväskylä: University of Jyväskylä.

Isaacs, T., Trofimovich, P. and Foote, J. (2018) Developing a user-oriented second language comprehensibility scale for English-medium universities. *Language Testing* 35 (2), 193–216.

Iwashita, N., Brown, A., McNamara, T. and O'Hagan, S. (2008) Assessed levels of second language speaking proficiency: How distinct? *Applied Linguistics* 29 (1), 24–49.

Jamieson, J. and Poonpon, K. (2013) *Developing Analytic Rating Guides for TOEFL iBT Integrated Speaking Tasks*. TOEF iBT Research Report RR-20. Princeton, NJ: Educational Testing Service.

Johnson, D.O., Kang, O. and Ghanem, R. (2016) Improved automatic English proficiency rating of unconstrained speech with multiple corpora. *International Journal of Speech Technology* 19 (4), 755–768.

Kallio, H., Šimko, J., Huhta, A., Karhila, R., Vainio, M., Lindroos, E., Hilden, R. and Kurimo, M. (2017) Towards the phonetic basis of spoken second language assessment: Temporal features as indicators of perceived proficiency level. In M. Kuronen, P. Lintunen and T. Nieminen (eds) *Näkökulmia toisen kielen puheeseen – Insights into Second Language Speech. AFinLA-e: Soveltavan kielitieteen tutkimuksia 10*. Jyväskylä: Finnish Association of Applied Linguistics AFinLA, 193–213.

Kang, O. (2012) Impact of rater characteristics and prosodic features of speaker accentedness on ratings of international teaching assistants' oral performance. *Language Assessment Quarterly* 9 (3), 249–269.

Karhila, R., Rouhe, A., Smit, P., Mansikkaniemi, A., Kallio, H., Lindroos, E., Hildén, R., Vainio, M. and Kurimo, M. (2016) Digitala: An augmented test and review process prototype for high-stakes spoken foreign language examination. *Proceedings of Interspeech* 2016, 784–785.

Kiddle, T. and Kormos, J. (2011) The effect of mode of response on a semidirect test of oral proficiency. *Language Assessment Quarterly* 8 (4), 342–360.

Koponen, M. and Riggenbach, H. (2000) Overview: Varying perspectives on fluency. In H. Riggenbach (ed.) *Perspectives on Fluency* (pp. 5–24). Ann Arbor: University of Michigan Press.

Kormos, J. and Dénes, M. (2004) Exploring measures and perceptions of fluency in the speech of second language learners. *System* 32 (2), 145–164.

Leaper, D. and Riazi, M. (2013) The influence of prompt on group oral tests. *Language Testing* 31 (2), 177–204.

Lennon, P. (1990) Investigating fluency in EFL: A quantitative approach. *Language Learning* 40, 387–417.

Luo, D., Gu, W., Luo, R. and Wang, L. (2016) Investigation of the effects of automatic scoring technology on human raters' performances in L2 speech proficiency assessment. *Chinese Spoken Language Processing (ISCSLP) 2016*, 1–5.

Ockey, G., Koyama, D. and Setoguchi, E. (2013) Stakeholder input and test design: A case study on changing the interlocutor familiarity facet of the group oral discussion test. *Language Assessment Quarterly* 10 (3), 292–308.

Ockey, G.J., Koyama, D., Setoguchi, E. and Sun, A. (2015) The extent to which TOEFL iBT speaking scores are associated with performance on oral language tasks and oral ability components for Japanese university students. *Language Testing* 32 (1), 39–62.

O'Loughlin, K. (2001) *The Equivalence of Direct and Semi-direct Speaking Tests*. Cambridge: Cambridge University Press.

Ordinate (2004) *SET-10 Test Description & Validation Summary*. Menlo Park, CA: Ordinate Corporation: http://www.7act.net/7ACT_files/set10.pdf, accessed 11 March 2018.

Pearson (2011) *Versant English Test. Test Description and Validation Summary*. Pearson Education, http://www.versanttest.com/technology/VersantEnglishTestValidation.pdf, accessed 11 March 2018.

Pearson (2017) *PTE Academic Score Guide*. Pearson Education. https://pearsonpte.com/wp-content/uploads/2017/08/Score-Guide.pdf, accessed 11 March 2018.

Peltonen, P. (2017) Temporal fluency and problem-solving in interaction: An exploratory study of fluency resources in L2 dialogue. *System* 70, 1–13.

Pinget, A., Bosker, H., Quené, H. and De Jong, N. (2014) Native speakers' perceptions of fluency and accent in L2 speech. *Language Testing* 31 (3), 349–365.

Préfontaine, Y., Kormos, J. and Johnson, D. (2016) How do utterance measures predict raters' perceptions of fluency in French as a second language? *Language Testing* 33 (1), 53–73.

Rossiter, M. (2009) Perceptions of L2 fluency by native and non-native speakers of English. *Canadian Modern Language Review* 65 (3), 395–412.

Rouhe, A., Karhila, R., Smit, P. and Kurimo, M. (2017) Reading validation for pronunciation evaluation in the Digitala project. *Proceedings of Interspeech 2017*, 2050–2051.

Skehan, P. (2009) Modelling second language performance: Integrating complexity, accuracy, fluency, and lexis. *Applied Linguistics* 30, 510–532.

Skehan, P. and Foster, P. (1999) The influence of task structure and processing conditions on narrative retellings. *Language Learning* 49 (1), 93–120.

Toivola, M., Lennes, M. and Aho, E. (2009) Speech rate and pauses in non-native Finnish. *Proceedings of Interspeech 2009*, 1707–1710.

Townshend, P., Bernstein, J., Todic, O. and Warren, E. (1998) Estimation of spoken language proficiency. *Proceedings of ESCA Workshop on Speech Technology in Language Learning (StiLL 98)*, 179–182. http://www.isca-speech.org/archive_open/archive_papers/still98/stl8_179.pdf, accessed 11 March 2018.

Trofimovich, P. and Baker, W. (2007) Learning prosody and fluency characteristics of second language speech: The effect of experience on child learners' acquisition of five suprasegmentals. *Applied Psycholinguistics* 28 (2), 251–276.

Ullakonoja, R. (2011) *Da. Eto vopros! Prosodic Development of Finnish Students' Readaloud Russian during Study in Russia*. Jyväskylä: University of Jyväskylä. http://urn.fi/URN:ISBN:978-951-39-4209-0

Ullakonoja, R. and van Moere, A. (in progress) Young Finnish EFL learners' reading fluency in extensive reading.

Valette, R. (1967/1977) *Modern Language Testing*. New York: Harcourt.

Wigglesworth, G. and Elder, C. (2010) An investigation of the effectiveness and validity of planning time in speaking test tasks. *Language Assessment Quarterly* 7 (1), 1–24.

Zechner, K., Chen, L., Davis, L., Evanini, K., Lee, C., Leong, C., Wang, X. and Yoon, S.-Y. (2015) *Automated Scoring of Speaking Tasks in the Test of English-for-Teaching (TEFT)*. ETS Research Report RR-15–31. Princeton, NJ: Educational Testing Service.

Zhang, Y. and Elder, C. (2010) Judgments of oral proficiency by non-native and native English speaking teacher raters: Competing or complementary constructs? *Language Testing* 28 (1), 31–50.

# 10 Fluency in Evaluating and Assessing Translations

Leena Salmi

## Introduction

This chapter approaches the concept of fluency from the viewpoint of Translation Studies and of professional translation, where fluency is seen as one of the two main criteria, along with accuracy/adequacy, in assessing the output of translators, interpreters or Machine Translation (MT) engines. The focus is on language use in professional contexts of translating and interpreting, rather than on language learning or the use of second language (L2) specifically, and on fluency as an assessment criterion. The starting point for writing this chapter was terminological: how fluency is considered in Translation Studies. The chapter thus presents a review of how the concept of fluency is understood and how the term is used in connection with translating (and interpreting) in professional contexts. The emphasis is on the assessment of (written) translations.

The use of the terms accuracy and fluency in assessing translations differs from that of the current Complexity-Accuracy-Fluency (CAF) framework used to describe L2 proficiency and L2 production (Housen *et al.*, 2012) in that there is always a need to compare the product to another, already existing product, that is, the text that has been translated (the source text). In Translation Studies, accuracy and adequacy are the (synonymous) terms used to describe this comparison: if a translation is accurate, it conveys the message and the content of the source text. In contrast, fluency relates to the textual and linguistic aspects of the translation, its adherence to linguistic and grammatical norms. In terms of Segalowitz' (2010) three senses of fluency (cognitive fluency, perceived fluency and utterance fluency), the fluency discussed in this chapter relates to perceived fluency: how fluency is perceived when (written) translations or (oral) interpreting are assessed. From the Translation Studies point of view, perception is at the core, as the audience is an essential element in translating. As pointed out since the 1980s by the functionalist translation theorists, translation is seen as a purposeful activity and intercultural communication, and the aim, function and target audience determine how translations should be produced and evaluated (for an overview of the theories, see Nord, 2016).

The chapter is organised as follows: after a definition of terms related to translating, the chapter presents the use of the concept of fluency within Translation Studies and discusses translation assessment practices on a general level. Fluency as it appears in translation assessment criteria and methods, along with accuracy, is discussed in the rest of the chapter, with examples from a selection of assessment grids.

## Definitions of Concepts Related to Translating

Translation is a means of intercultural communication. A basic definition of translating is transferring content expressed in one language into another language, or 'meaning transfer', as Koby and Champe (2013: 157) put it. It should be noted that the notions of translation may vary from a narrow consideration that defines translation as transferring 'a written source text into a written target text of roughly equivalent length' (Melby *et al.*, 2014: 397) to a broader view where translation is 'the creation of target content that corresponds to source content according to agreed-upon specifications' (Melby *et al.*, 2014: 395). 'Content' may vary from audiovisual material such as a film or a web site to a comics album, or from a publicity slogan to legislation. This broader definition of translation is used also for the purposes of this chapter.

Translation Studies is defined by Munday (2016) as 'the discipline that studies phenomena associated with translation in its many forms'. Although translations and translating are age-old phenomena, their study as an independent discipline only began to emerge in the second half of the 20th century. Having its roots in literary studies, modern languages and linguistics, the objects of study of Translation Studies today encompass a variety of phenomena. Along with Translation Studies, Interpreting Studies is 'the academic discipline that has interpreting as its object of study' and can be considered as a (sub)discipline of Translation Studies (Pöchhacker, 2011). As for the research topics within the discipline, the more text-related ones include, for example, linguistic features of translated texts (Tirkkonen-Condit, 2004) or literature retranslated several times (see Koskinen & Paloposki, 2016), both being examples of studies related to the hypothesis of translation universals: the idea that there are some universal features common to translations or translated language (Mauranen & Kujamäki, 2004). In the case of the first example, the hypothesis is that translated language contains linguistic features different from those of non-translated text, and in the second, that a second translation in time of a given (literary) text is 'closer' to the original than the first one (Koskinen & Paloposki, 2016). Forming another area of translation research are empirical studies into the cognitive processes of translating – research on the translation process has been conducted since the 1980s (e.g. Lörscher, 1986; Krings, 1987), first by using think-aloud methods (see Jääskeläinen & Tirkkonen-Condit, 2000) and, since the mid-1990s, using keylogging software to record the process, combined more recently with eye-tracking equipment (see, for example, Göpferich *et al.*, 2008, 2009, or Mees *et al.*, 2011). The same methods are used in studying the writing process (see Mutta in this volume).

As for the concepts of *translating* and *interpreting*, the first refers to written communication and the second to oral. Within the theoretical framework of functionalist translation theories, developed in the 1980s by German scholars Hans Vermeer, Katharina Reiss and Justa Holz-Mänttäri, translation is seen 'as a purposeful activity intended to mediate between members of different culture communities' (Nord, 2016). The purpose of the translation is agreed upon by the translator and the client (or whatever instance that orders the translation) in a specification, also referred to as the translator's brief, that includes information about the aim, function and audience of the translation. These determine how the text is to be translated for the specified audience, in order to function in that given communicative situation, in the target culture. According to Nord (2016), it is this functionality that sets the standard for evaluating the translation, not its 'correspondence' or 'equivalence' with the source text.

Both in research and practice, the languages from and into which translating or interpreting takes place are referred to as the source language (the language in which the text to be translated is written) and target language (the language in which the translation is written). Translation process may refer to two separate things: either the cognitive process taking place in the translator's mind, or the production process of translations, from the request for a translation by a client to the delivery of the product. The former is a topic in Translation Studies research (examples mentioned above) and the latter is part of the translation industry practice, defined, for example, in the international standard ISO 17100 that describes the requirements for the processes and resources related to translation service provision.

Translators and interpreters work with (at least) two languages, which may be either a first language (L1) or second language (L2) for them; in fact, translation studies and translator and interpreter education tend to use the terms A language, B language and C language, referring to the order of fluency in those languages (meant here in the sense of broad or higher-order fluency given by Lennon, 1990, or in the sense of very broad fluency given by Tavakoli & Hunter, 2018). An A language is most often the L1 of the translator or interpreter, that is, the language in which they have native proficiency. A B language is 'a language in which the interpreter has fully functional proficiency in speaking and listening' (Translator/Interpreter Handbook, 2014: 14) or a 'language other than the interpreter's native language, of which she or he has a perfect command and into which she or he works from one or more of her or his other languages' (AIIC, 2018). A C language is defined as a 'language that a translator or interpreter can read and understand well enough to translate out of, but cannot write or speak well enough to translate or interpret into' (trans-k, 2018). Ideally, translating and interpreting should both be done only into the translator's or interpreter's A language, but with languages of small or limited diffusion, such as Finnish or the Baltic languages, with 5 million or fewer speakers, translating often takes place into the B language(s) as well.

The following section presents the concept of fluency as it is used within Translation Studies.

## Fluency as a concept within Translation Studies

Within Translation Studies and translator education, the concept of fluency usually emerges in connection with evaluating or assessing translations or translators (i.e. professional translators or translator students). Translations are traditionally assessed with two aspects in mind: whether their content corresponds to that of the source text and whether they adhere to the norms and conventions of the target language. Table 10.1 presents the different aspects of both concepts.

As can be seen from Table 10.1, accuracy is related to the relationship between the source and the target texts, whereas fluency is related to the linguistic properties or 'well-formedness' of the text. In their definition of fluency, taken from the Multi-Dimensional Quality Metrics (MQM) framework, Lommel *et al.* (2015a) extend the concept of fluency to any text. This is related to the context in which the definition is presented, the framework for assessing translation quality (see the section 'Fluency as a criterion in translation assessment'). Assessing accuracy thus means assessing the content of the translation, by comparing the content of

**Table 10.1** Accuracy and fluency

|  | Accuracy | Fluency |
|---|---|---|
| Synonymous terms | - equivalence (of content)<br>- adequacy (Toury, 2012: 79) | acceptability (Toury, 2012: 79) |
| Definitions | - 'a bilingual notion referring to the correspondence between the source and target text' (Koby *et al.*, 2014: 415)<br>- 'extent to which the informational content conveyed by a target text matches that of the source text' (Lommel *et al.*, 2015a: Section 2) | - 'a monolingual notion referring to properties of the target text such as grammar, spelling, and cohesion' (Koby *et al.*, 2014: 415)<br>- 'Fluency includes those issues about the linguistic 'well-formedness' of the text that can be assessed without regard to whether the text is a translation or not.' (Lommel *et al.*, 2015a: Section 5.1.2) |
| Object of assessment | source text and target text | (target) text |
| Scope of assessment | comparing the content of source and target texts | linguistic and textual features of the target text |

translation to that of the source text and by considering whether all the essential and necessary elements are rendered, whereas assessing fluency means assessing the linguistic and textual expression of the translation. Accuracy and fluency are thus separate concepts used for assessing the two main aspects of a translation, and accuracy is not used in defining fluency; basically, accuracy relates to *what* is expressed and fluency to *how* it is expressed. In other words, the fluency of a text (any text) can be considered without referring to the source text, but when considering accuracy, a comparison of the two is needed. Following the expressions used by Lommel *et al*. (2015a) for accuracy, fluency could be defined as the extent to which the linguistic and textual expression of the target text matches the linguistic norms and conventions of the target language (grammar, spelling, cohesion, etc.) and the textual requirements of the purpose of the translation (style, genre etc.). In terms of Segalowitz' (2010) three senses of fluency, the fluency of a translation is related to the text's fluency as perceived by the target readers.

In interpreting, definitions of fluency relate to oral language production. According to the *Routledge Encyclopedia of Interpreting Studies* (Pradas Macías, 2015: 221–222), fluency can be considered, broadly, as expressional fluency, defined as 'a speaker's oral (or signed) proficiency in a given language', an essential goal both in public speaking and in foreign language acquisition, and more specifically as delivery, which means 'the physical characteristics of the acoustic signal produced by the speaker', with speech rate and pauses as its central parameters. This division is, in fact, identical to Lennon's (1990) definitions of broad or higher-order vs narrow or lower-order fluency, and delivery corresponds to Segalowitz' (2010) utterance fluency.

## Assessment and Translating

The perspective towards fluency chosen in this chapter is to focus on how fluency and accuracy are assessed in translations. For this reason, we start by considering the different purposes of translation assessment in general. As Brunette (2000: 169) puts it, people have tried, since the time of Cicero, to define what a good translation is like and to establish means of measuring the quality. Today, assessing or evaluating translations is important in the areas of translator education, professional translation (the translation industry), and research. Colina (2011) points out that in Translation Studies, the two terms are often used interchangeably, although she suggests that assessment 'refers to a process by which information is collected relative to some known objective or goal', such as tests or students' homework, whereas evaluation 'has a subjective component; when we evaluate, we judge, classifying according to some defined criteria'. In educational sciences, Hattie and Brown (2010) distinguish the two terms as follows:

Assessment relates to the identification of characteristics of a trait, and evaluation relates to the establishment of value and worth of a product, process, person, policy or program. (Hattie & Brown, 2010: 103)

In the remaining parts of this chapter, the terms *assess* and *assessment* are used, as this chapter deals with fluency as a characteristic or trait of an assessed translation (for a discussion of fluency in language assessment, see Huhta *et al.* in this volume).

Brunette (2000) discusses the many areas where assessment of translations is used. In translator education, it is used for giving students feedback on their translations in order to improve their skills, or for assessing their performance and skills at the end of a course. Within the translation industry, test translations by candidates for a translator position may be assessed to make the selection, translations outsourced to freelancers may be assessed to monitor the quality of the work, and the output of translators employed in a translation agency may be assessed in order to measure their productivity (Brunette, 2000). An example of assessing translations for research purposes is the assessment of the output of MT engines to define the quality of the engine and to make improvements to its functionality.

Assessment procedures vary according to the aim and the purpose of the assessment, which can range from training contexts to administrative purposes. Brunette (2000: 170–173) distinguishes between five different procedures: Quality Assessment, Didactic Revision, Pragmatic Revision, Quality Control and Fresh Look. She describes the procedures according to different parameters. The status of the target text may be final (as in Quality Assessment when selecting a candidate or in measuring a translator's productivity) or non-final (as in Didactic or Pragmatic Revision, for giving feedback to a translator student or in checking the translation before it is delivered to a client). The translation may be assessed in its entirety (as in Didactic or Pragmatic Revision) or from a sample (as in Quality Control that 'can range from a partial monolingual reading to a bilingual revision of samples') (Brunette, 2000: 173), the source and target texts may be compared or not (as in Fresh Look, where the idea is to consider the translated text as an independent text and determine how it will be received by the target culture), an evaluation grid may be used (as in Quality Control) or not, a grade given (as in translation courses within translator education) or not, and feedback given to the translator always (as for didactic purposes), upon request or not at all.

## Translation Assessment in Practice

After the brief description of translation assessment purposes in general, this section discusses the practical approaches of assessing translations. The discussion is restricted to the assessment of translations, that is, written texts, and the translation process – neither the cognitive nor the production process is discussed here as criteria for assessment.

Translation assessment is an area in which relatively little agreement exists among translation scholars on how it should be done in practice, even though a large amount of work has been done on it (Marais, 2013). It is, however, a practice that takes place every day both within translator education and the translation industry. The methods of translation assessment can be divided into two basic types: error-based and criterion-based assessment. Error-based assessment is usually done in the form of an error analysis, where problematic passages in the translation are marked and classified according to a predefined error classification. In criterion-based assessment, the translation is compared against predefined criteria that describe either what the translation should be like or the translation skills it should demonstrate (Angelelli, 2009: 40–41; Turner *et al.*, 2010). Both methods have a means (error categories or criteria descriptors) for assessing both accuracy – the correspondence in content between the source and target texts – and fluency – the adherence of the target text to the target language norms.

### Error analysis and criterion-based assessment

Error analysis is the traditional method, with (minus) points given according to the type and severity of the error, while criterion-based (also known as rubric-based) assessment methods are a more recent means of assessing translations (Hale *et al.*, 2012: 53). Error analysis is widely used within the translation industry: according to the study by Sharon O'Brien (2012) that compared 11 translation quality assessment models either publicly available or in use in 'companies engaged in translation as clients' (O'Brien, 2012: 56), 10 out of 11 used an error-based method. Error analysis is used in many translator certification examinations (cf. Hale *et al.*, 2012: 58), although some certification examinations also use criterion-based assessment, such as the one in use in the state of Bavaria in Germany (Kivilehto & Salmi, 2017: 64), or a combination of both.

Error analysis consists of marking errors in a translation and then classifying them into error types. The number of error types may vary, for instance, from the two used by the Canadian Translators, Terminologists and Interpreters Council (CTTIC, 2018) to the 23 used by the American Translators' Association (ATA, 2017). The criterion-based approach consists of defining criteria that need to be met, defining descriptors of performance at various levels of performance in translating the text, and comparing the translation to the descriptors to award a level (Hale *et al.*, 2012: 53). The criterion-based assessment grid usually consists of a table containing descriptions of criteria according to different performance levels. For example, an assessment grid for assessing translations within translator education, described in the interactive wiki Database for Teaching Methods in Translation and Interpreting created by and for Finnish translation teachers, has three criteria: Content, Language and

Adherence to the translator's brief – in other words accuracy, fluency and functionality (or appropriateness) of the translation. The performance levels for the grades from 1 to 5 and failed are described according to each criterion. For example, the description for grade 5 in the criterion Language reads as follows: '[The student] is able to produce a grammatically correct, idiomatic and fluent translation that follows the conventions of the textual genre' (my translation). Another form of criterion-based assessment is a check-list of criteria that the translation needs to meet (e.g. Marais, 2013; Suojanen *et al.*, 2015: 89–91; described below).

Both error-based and criterion-based methods have a means (error categories or criteria descriptors) for assessing both accuracy – the correspondence in content between the source and target texts – and fluency – the adherence of the target text to the target language norms. Studies comparing the two methods show that criterion-based assessment can be as trustworthy as error-based assessment (Turner *et al.*, 2010). Examples of assessment grids are discussed below.

## Automatic assessment of machine translations

In addition to the assessment methods discussed above, performed by humans to translations produced by human translators, automated assessment methods have been developed to assess machine-translated texts. These are based on comparing an MT of a given source text to a human translation of the same source text, known as a reference translation (Han, 2018; Snover *et al.*, 2006). Several different formulas exist to compute the differences between the MT and the reference translation, such as BLEU (abbreviated from Bilingual Evaluation Understudy), WER (Word Edit Rate), TER (Translation Edit Rate) or METEOR (Metric for Evaluation of Translation with Explicit ORdering); they all are metrics that compare the MT and the reference using different methods, and rank the MT according to its closeness to the reference translation (Banerjee & Lavie, 2005; Snover *et al.*, 2006). They have the advantage of being fast and able to assess large amounts of data (contrary to human assessment), but as the comparison is a mechanical, sentence-by-sentence comparison of the words contained in the translation, and the basis for comparison is often only one reference translation, they do not take into account the natural and acceptable variation that exists between translations of a same source text that can be different in expression but convey the same meaning (Koehn, 2010).

Han (2018) presents an overview of the development of MT evaluation research, in which fluency has been used as a criterion since the 1990s, in MT evaluation campaigns where human evaluators have been asked to determine, on a sentence-by-sentence basis, 'whether the translation reads like good English' (Han, 2018: 196). In the early days, the evaluators did not have a reference translation, and therefore were not able to assess the accuracy of the content, and the task was 'to determine whether each sentence is well-formed and fluent in context' (Han, 2018: 196). Bojar *et al.* (2016a) discuss the development of such campaigns from 2006 onwards: the campaigns are organised yearly to compare MT engines from different developers in order to find the best technology. The same source text is translated by the engines participating in the campaign, and the output is evaluated both automatically (comparing the engine's translation to a reference translation done by a human translator) and by human evaluators. For the human evaluation, different methods are in use, such as ranking the accuracy and fluency of each sentence on a five-point scale, or ranking the output from several engines from best to worse. The accuracy/fluency assessment has at times been abandoned, because it has proved to be 'inconsistent and hard to normalize' (Bojar *et al.*, 2016a: 28), but has recently been experimented with again in the 2016 WMT evaluation campaign (Bojar *et al.*, 2016b: 140, 145–146). Several methods have thus been used and the ranking method, with the output presented with the source text and a reference translation, has been the primary method from 2009 to 2016 (Bojar *et al.*, 2016a).

After this description of the three types of translation assessment method, a selection of (human) assessment systems is presented in the following section.

### Fluency as a Criterion in Translation Assessment

This section presents some of the publicly available assessment systems and their ways of defining fluency. Only translations, that is written texts, are discussed, and fluency, again, refers to the perceived fluency. According to the definitions of accuracy and fluency discussed above (Table 10.1), accuracy relates to the content of the target text, in correspondence with the source text content, and fluency to the linguistic and textual expression of the target language. Fluency is usually present in some form in the assessment of translations, both in error typologies as well as in criterion-based assessment.

The systems were selected on the basis that they were publicly available and include both error-based (the first four in the list below) and criterion-based methods (the last two). The error-based systems are widely used in the translation industry (MQM) or present in some translator certification systems that the author is familiar with. The systems selected are those of the following bodies or authors:

- Multidimensional Quality Metrics (MQM) (Lommel *et al.*, 2015a, 2015b; Mariana *et al.*, 2015)
- Authorized Translator's Examination in Finland (EDUFI, 2017)
- Canadian Translators, Terminologists and Interpreters Council (CTTIC, 2005)

- American Translators Association (ATA, 2017)
- Assessment instrument for translator education (Marais, 2013)
- Heuristic check-list for translations (Suojanen *et al.*, 2015; Suojanen & Tuominen, 2015).

The Multidimensional Quality Metrics (MQM) method is a 'framework for describing and defining quality metrics used to assess the quality of translated texts and to identify specific issues in those texts', based on textual features (Lommel *et al.*, 2015a). It is designed to be a flexible framework, within which users may define subsets of the core for their needs. It is recommended that a typology 'contain at least the issue types accuracy and fluency' (Lommel *et al.*, 2015a, Section 5.2). The MQM terminology makes a distinction between *issue* and *error*: the former is a potential error that can be detected automatically (such as a term appearing in a source text but for which the equivalent in the target language does not appear in the target text), and the latter 'an instance of an issue that has been verified to be incorrect' by a human assessor (Lommel *et al.*, 2015a: Section 2).

The framework contains eight high-level categories, or branches, for issues that can be found in translations: accuracy, fluency, design, internationalisation, locale convention, style, terminology and verity. Each category contains a varying number of subcategories. As mentioned in Table 10.1, fluency issues are defined as 'issues about the linguistic "well-formedness" of the text' (Lommel *et al.*, 2015a: Section 5.1.2). The following list (from Lommel *et al.*, 2015a: Section 5.2) shows the hierarchy of the eight high-level categories and the main subcategories within them:

- accuracy (addition, mistranslation, omission of content or untranslated item);
- fluency (grammar, grammatical register, inconsistency, spelling, typography or unintelligible passages);
- design;
- internationalisation;
- locale convention;
- style;
- terminology;
- verity (completeness, legal requirements or locale-specific content);
- other.

As can be seen from the list, fluency includes the subcategories grammar, grammatical register (for example, the use of informal instead of formal pronouns or verb forms), inconsistency (the information contained in the text is inconsistent, for instance, between an image and the text referring to it), spelling, typography, and unintelligible passages in the text – defined by Mariana *et al.* (2015: 140) as 'the text makes no sense, but the error does not fall into another category'. As mentioned in Table 10.1, fluency issues can be applied equally to source and target texts, since some of the subcategories, such as inconsistency or unintelligible passages, may be problems in either the source or the target text. However, as the detailed description of the MQM issue types (Lommel *et al.*, 2015b, Section 1.2) notes, '[i]f an issue can be detected *only* by comparing the source and target, it MUST NOT be categorised as fluency or any of its children' (emphasis as in the original). For the complete list of possible issues grouped under fluency by Lommel *et al.* (2015b: Section 1.1.4), see Appendix 1.

In MQM, a large proportion of the issues relate to the technical format of the translation (such as character encoding or problems with hyperlinks) or to the layout of the translation (such as typography) and not to the grammatical or textual features of the text. These are, however, problems in the translated text if they appear in a translation that will be published, such as the interface of a computer program, and can thus be listed under fluency. As mentioned above, the list is intended to be a collection of options to choose from, and the items relevant for software localisation, for example, can be omitted when assessing translations in a certification examination.

In Finland, error-based assessment is used in the Authorized Translator's Examination. The examination grants a translator the right to translate official documents, or documents 'required by any official institution, for whatever reason (academic enrolments, applications for visa, passports, etc.)' (Pym *et al.*, 2012: 23). The grid used in classifying errors was recently reviewed and modified by reducing the number of error types from 14 to 7. The new grid (see EDUFI, 2019) has the main division into Accuracy and Fluency (dubbed 'equivalence of content' and 'acceptability and readability of text') that already existed in the earlier grid (for details of the earlier grid, see Kivilehto & Salmi, 2017), but, in addition, the renewed grid contains a third category, errors related to the Task Accomplishment (EDUFI, 2019; Salmi & Kivilehto, 2018). This reflects the functionalist-theoretical thinking according to which the function of the translation is a key issue and a basis for evaluation. The third category also refers to issues specific to this type of translating of official documents issued from another culture. In the examination grid, the Fluency category is divided into two subcategories; (1) with issues relating to 'syntax, morphology, style, register or idiomaticity', and (2) with issues relating to 'spelling or orthography' (EDUFI, 2019; Salmi & Kivilehto, 2018).

The Canadian Translators, Terminologists and Interpreters Council (CTTIC) and the American Translators Association (ATA) both have a translation examination similar to the Finnish one, but for all translation professionals who want to use the appellation 'certified translator' (ATA, 2018; CTTIC, 2018). Both assessment systems are error-based. The CTTIC assessment system has just the basic two categories of accuracy and fluency (labelled 'translation errors' and 'errors of expression'). Translation errors are failures to render the meaning of the source text, and errors of expression are errors of the target language, including violation of syntax, grammar, vocabulary, spelling and typographical rules (CTTIC, 2005). In contrast, the assessment system of the ATA translation examination has 23 different error types listed alphabetically from addition (A) to word form (WF). For the complete list, see Appendix 2.

The ATA list differs from the three other error-based systems described above in that it does not contain the accuracy/fluency distinction. Of course, making this distinction is not compulsory, but the distinction can, in fact, be seen in the descriptions of some of the ATA categories: for example, the descriptions related to diacritical marks, faux ami, grammar, spelling and syntax note that if there is a change in the meaning in connection to this type of error, the error should be marked as more serious or classified otherwise. A change of meaning can be considered as an accuracy error, as it can only be spotted by comparing the source and the target texts (see Table 10.1). By comparison, instructions for the assessors in the Finnish Authorized Translator's Examination include a rule-of-thumb similar to Lommel *et al.* (2015b: Section 1.2) to distinguish accuracy errors from fluency errors, mentioning that if there is a change of meaning, the error should be classified as an accuracy error (EDUFI, 2017: 9).

The three translator certification systems use error points to define the severity of the error, and if the sum of the points exceeds a maximum level, the candidate fails. The MQM classification, as it is a framework for building a suitable combination of issues to be taken into account in the assessment, also provides two different ways of scoring a translation: an error-counting method with severity weights and a formula for calculating the sum of error points (Lommel *et al.*, 2015a: Section 8), as well as holistic metrics, consisting of evaluating an issue either by ranking or on a scale (Lommel *et al.*, 2015a: Section 9.4).

An approach different from the traditional error-based assessment systems described above is offered by Marais (2013). He proposes a criterion-based solution to the prevailing disagreement over translation assessment among both translation scholars as well as between academia and the practitioners, although pointing out that a unified assessment instrument may be 'neither possible nor desirable' (Marais, 2013: 13–14). Marais' (2013) Assessment Instrument for Translator Education is a check-list of six main categories with two or three subcategories:

(1) the overall translation purpose
(2) culture and target audience
(3) issues of text (text type, subject field; cohesion, style of writing and register)
(4) technical aspects (visual appearance, spelling and punctuation, formal layout, consistency, readability)
(5) issues of content (accuracy and relevance of the information)
(6) issues of language (idiomatic language, syntax, terminology) (Marais, 2013: 19–20, 22).

The instrument is designed with translator education in mind and is based on functionalist translation theories (Marais, 2013). According to the functionalist thinking, all categories are assessed in terms of the translation's aim or purpose (described in the translation specification) (Marais, 2013: 22). Accuracy as a criterion is mentioned under (5), fluency is not, but issues related to fluency in the error-based assessment systems appear under (3), (4) and (6). Also, some of the MQM issues listed under fluency could be seen as violations of the translation's aim or purpose.

A similar approach using a translation check-list, also stemming from functionalist thinking, is presented by Suojanen *et al.* (2015). They introduce the User-Centered approach to translating, which means combining the ideas of the functionalist-theoretical approach with methods from usability studies, developed in engineering sciences to evaluate the usability and user-friendliness of devices and products. Their methods are designed for use by practitioners as well as in translator education and thus provide practical tools for implementing the functionalist translation theories. Suojanen *et al.* (2015) propose several different methods to be used in the different phases of the translation production process; one such method is a heuristic check-list, a tool for evaluating a translation at a point where it has been completed but not yet delivered to the customer. This is an already updated version of the original list (Suojanen *et al.*, 2015: 90), the update based on the use of the list in practice in translator education (Suojanen & Tuominen, 2015: 279):

(1) match between translation and specification
(2) match between translation and users
(3) match between translation and real world
(4) match between translation and genre
(5) consistency
(6) legibility and readability
(7) satisfaction
(8) match between source and target texts (Suojanen & Tuominen, 2015: 279; my translation based on Suojanen *et al.*, 2015: 90).

In contrast to Marais (2013), the issues are to be assessed in relation to the user of the translation, not the specification, and the specification appears as an item of its own. Fluency does not appear as a criterion in this list either, but the list contains the items (5) consistency, defined as the translation being 'consistent in terms of style, terminology, phraseology and register', (6) legibility and readability and (2) match between translation and users, where it is necessary that the 'textual choices reflect the information needs of the user' (Suojanen *et al.*, 2015: 90). Accuracy is present in (3) match between translation and real world (to check that the information is correct) and (8) match between source and target texts.

In Marais' Assessment Instrument, the issues in the list of categories are assessed both for the product (the translation) and the process. The instrument is used to assess to what extent the competencies mentioned have been acquired. Points are given for each section, and in order to pass, a student needs to score at least 70% of the points in each section. As the instrument is designed for use in translator education, for assessing the performance of students at the end of the course, such a threshold is needed. The heuristic check-list by Suojanen *et al.* (2015), in contrast, is used to improve the translation, and if shortcomings in the issues listed are found, they should be fixed. The problems may also be classified according to their severity. Suojanen *et al.* (2015: 80) propose a rating scale, taken from Nielsen (1995), ranging from 0 to 4, where 0 is not a problem, 1 is a cosmetic problem and 4 is a catastrophic problem that imperatively needs to be fixed.

As we can see from the comparison of the systems described above, they differentiate issues related to the target text and target language expression in slightly different ways. There seems to be a general agreement in Translation Studies on these two basic aspects of a translation, accuracy as relating to the (correspondence of) content between the source and the target texts, and fluency as relating to the linguistic and textual aspects. In practice, the ways of assessing these and the ways of granulating assessment criteria differ. Whereas the MQM system lists 39 possible categories with subcategories for fluency, the Finnish Authorized Translator's Examination system is content to group these under two headings, and the Canadian CTTIC only one. However, the error-based systems can be considered to be consistent with the MQM, which recommends that translation quality assessment grids 'contain at least the issue types Accuracy and Fluency if no other more granular types are included' (Lommel *et al.*, 2015a: Section 5.2).

## Conclusion

This chapter has presented an overview of how the concept of fluency is used in Translation Studies. In translating written texts, fluency is mainly used in connection with the assessment of translations, and together with accuracy (or its synonym adequacy). These two concepts form the core of what is being assessed: both the linguistic output and the content (viewed in relation to the source text). Fluency is related to the perceived fluency, which from the Translation Studies viewpoint also should be at the core, as the audience is an essential element in translating.

In the error-based translation assessment systems, fluency is, actually, defined through disfluency: the categories are examples of issues that can be disfluent in a text. In language learning, the focus has shifted away from this kind of negative assessment, where the person assessing 'only' notices what is missing in the language learner's output, and emphasis is now put on criterion-based assessment that stresses the elements that the learner is able to use or where they are good. In contrast, the variety of the error-based systems in use both in translation examinations and in the translation industry (see O'Brien, 2012) suggests that looking at what is missing is considered a usable and accurate method for improving the product to be delivered to the customer. This is, perhaps, due to the fact that the purposes in the assessment of language learning and professional translation differ: in the latter, the goal is to ensure that the output complies with the specification and has the required quality, and the object of assessment is a product, not a person's abilities. This becomes even clearer when assessing and correcting MT output, where the translation has been produced by a machine and no feelings can be hurt by 'criticising' the translation. Another aspect where the assessment of fluency differs in translating and in language use in general is the existence of a source text. The translator needs to render the source text meaning according to the terms mentioned in the specification, but the language user does not have a similar, concrete, predefined message that they need to convey. This is perhaps also why accuracy and fluency are seen as separate issues in connection with translating: there is a need to assess the correspondence of the source text to the target text, and accuracy and its synonym adequacy are the terms chosen to express this correspondence.

Although fluency can be considered a basic concept in Translation Studies as well as in the practice of professional translating, used especially when describing and assessing the quality of target texts, it does not always appear as such in the error classifications or assessment criteria used in assessing translations. The comparison of assessment grids in this chapter shows that fluency classifications can include items that range from textual cohesion to technicalities such as character encoding (for example, the MQM classification), or they can just include one item (for example, the CTTIC classification). However, the fluency of the target language expression remains an essential element for assessing translations. The assessment of language skills has shifted away from the traditional error-scoring of the language user's mistakes and begun to take into account the communicative situation. Perhaps the L2 assessment theories and practices could benefit from a glance into the functionalist theories of translation, and the assessment of written texts could seek to apply some of the methods of User-Centered Translation, such as a version of the heuristic check-list, as presented in Suojanen *et al*. (2015). Vice versa, the fluency assessment in Translation Studies might benefit from the more fine-grained conceptualisation of fluency used in language learning.

## References

AIIC (International Association of Conference Interpreters) (2018) A practical guide for applicants. https://aiic.net/page/199/ [accessed 30 September 2018].
Angelelli, C.V. (2009) Using a rubric to assess translation ability. Defining the construct. In C.V. Angelelli and H.E. Jacobson (eds) *Testing and Assessment in Translation and*

*Interpreting Studies. A call for dialogue between research and practice* (pp. 13–47). Amsterdam: John Benjamins.

ATA (2017) American Translators Association: Explanation of Error Categories, Version 2017. https://www.atanet.org/certification/aboutexams_error.php [accessed 27 August 2018].

ATA (2018) American Translators Association: A Guide to the ATA Certification Program. http://www.atanet.org/certification/aboutcert_overview.php [accessed 27 August 2018].

Banerjee, S. and Lavie, A. (2005) METEOR: An automatic metric for MT evaluation with improved correlation with human judgments. *Proceedings of the ACL Workshop on Intrinsic and Extrinsic Evaluation Measures for Machine Translation and/or Summarization*, Ann Arbor, June 2005, 65–72.

Bojar, O., Federmann, C., Haddow, B., Koehn, P., Post M. and Specia, L. (2016a) Ten years of WMT evaluation campaigns: lessons learnt. In G. Rehm, A. Burchardt *et al.* (eds) *Proceedings of the LREC 2016 Workshop 'Translation Evaluation – From Fragmented Tools and Data Sets to an Integrated Ecosystem'* (pp. 27–34).

Bojar, O., Chatterjee. R., Federmann, C., Graham, Y., Haddow, B., Huck, M., Jimeno Yepes, A., Koehn, P., Logacheva, V., Monz, C., Negri, M., Névéol, A., Neves, M., Popel, M., Post, M., Rubino, R., Scarton, C., Specia, L., Turchi, M., Verspoor, K. and Zampieri, M. (2016b) Findings of the 2016 Conference on Machine Translation (WMT16). In *Proceedings of the First Conference on Machine Translation, Volume 2: Shared Task Papers*, Berlin, Germany, August 11–12, 2016. Association for Computational Linguistics, 131–198.

Brunette, L. (2000) Towards a Terminology for Translation Quality Assessment. *The Translator* 6 (2), 169–182.

Colina, S. (2011) Evaluation/Assessment. In Y. Gambier and L. van Doorslaer (eds) *Handbook of Translation Studies, Volume 2* (2011) (pp. 43–48). [limited access]

CTTIC (2005) Canadian Translators, Terminologists and Interpreters Council: CTTIC Standard Certification Translation Examination Marker's Guide. Revised March 2005. http://www.cttic.org/examDocs/guide.markersE.pdf [accessed 27 August 2018].

CTTIC (2018) Canadian Translators, Terminologists and Interpreters Council: Certification. http://www.cttic.org/certification.asp [accessed 27 August 2018].

EDUFI (2017) Käsikirja 2017. Auktorisoidun kääntäjän tutkinto. Toimintaohjeet tutkintotehtävien arvioijalle [Handbook 2017. Authorised Translator's Examination. Instructions for Assessors of Translation Assignments]. Helsinki: Opetushallitus.

EDUFI (2019) Auktorisoidun kääntäjän tutkinto [The Authorized Translator's Examination]. Web page on the site of the Finnish National Agency for Education. https://www.oph.fi/fi/palvelut/auktorisoidun-kaantajan-tutkinto [accessed 19 September 2019].

Göpferich S., Jakobsen A.L. and Mees I.M. (eds) (2008) *Looking at Eyes: Eye-tracking Studies of Reading and Translation Processing*. Copenhagen Studies in Language Series 36. Copenhagen: Samfundslitteratur.

Göpferich S., Jakobsen A.L. and Mees I.M. (eds) (2009) *Behind the Mind: Methods, Models and Results in Translation process Research*. Copenhagen Studies in Language Series 37. Copenhagen: Samfundslitteratur.

Hale, S.B., Garcia, I., Hlavac, J., Kim, M., Lai, M., Turner, B. and Slatyer, H. (2012) Improvements to NAATI testing: Development of a conceptual overview for a new model for NAATI standards, testing and assessment. The National Accreditation Authority for Translators and Interpreters (NAATI). https://researchbank.rmit.edu.au/view/rmit:44221 [accessed 28 August 2018].

Han, I. (2018) Machine Translation Evaluation Resources and Methods: A Survey. Han, Aaron Li-Feng and Derek Fai Wong (2016). In: arXiv preprint arXiv:1605.04515.

Hattie, J.A. and Brown, G.T.L. (2010) Assessment and evaluation. In C. Rubie-Davies (ed.) *Educational Psychology: Concepts, Research and Challenges* (pp. 102–117). New York: Routledge.

Housen, A., Kuiken, F. and Vedder, I. (eds) (2012) *Dimensions of L2 Performance and Proficiency: Complexity, Accuracy and Fluency in SLA*. Amsterdam: John Benjamins.

Jääskeläinen, R. and Tirkkonen-Condit, S. (eds) (2000) *Tapping and Mapping the Processes of Translation and Interpreting*. Amsterdam: John Benjamins.

Kivilehto, M. and Salmi, L. (2017) Assessing assessment: The Authorized Translator's Examination in Finland. In G. Koby and I. Lacruz (eds) *Linguistica Antverpiensia, New Series – Themes in Translation Studies* 16, 57–70.

Koby, G.S. and Champe, G.G. (2013) Welcome to the Real World: Professional-Level Translator Certification. *The International Journal for Translation & Interpreting Research* 5 (1), 156–173.

Koby, G.S., Fields, P., Hague, D., Lommel, A. and Melby, A. (2014) Defining translation quality. *Revista Tradumatica* 12, 413–420.

Koehn, P. (2010) *Statistical Machine Translation*. Cambridge: Cambridge University Press.

Koskinen, K. and Paloposki, O. (2016) Retranslation. In Y. Gambier and L. van Doorslaer (eds) *Handbook of Translation Studies, Volume 1* (2010) (pp. 294–298). Current revision [online]: 2016. [limited access]

Krings, H.P. (1987) The use of introspective data in translation. In C. Faerch and G. Kasper (eds) *Introspection in Second Language Research* (pp. 159–176). Clevedon: Multilingual Matters.

Lennon, P. (1990) Investigating fluency in EFL: A quantitative approach. *Language Learning* 40, 387–417.

Lommel, A., Burchardt, A. and Uszkoreit, H. (2015a) Multidimensional Quality Metrics (MQM) Definition. http://www.qt21.eu/mqm-definition/definition-2015-12-30.html [accessed 27 August 2018].

Lommel, A., Burchardt, A., Görög, A., Uszkoreit, H. and Melby, A. (2015b) Multidimensional Quality Metrics (MQM) Issue Types. http://www.qt21.eu/mqm-definition/issues-list-2015-12-30.html [accessed 27 August 2018].

Lörscher, W. (1986) Linguistic aspects of translation process: towards an analysis of translation performance. In J. House and S. Blum-Kulka (eds) *Interlingual and Intercultural Communication. Discourse and Cognition in Translation and Second Language Acquisition Studies* (pp. 27–292). Tübingen: Gunter Narr Verlag.

Marais, K. (2013) Constructive alignment in translator education: Reconsidering assessment for both industry and academy. *Translation & Interpreting* 5 (1), 13–31.

Mariana, V., Cox, T. and Melby, A. (2015) The Multidimensional Quality Metrics (MQM) Framework: A new framework for translation quality assessment. *Journal of Specialised Translation* 23, 137–161.

Mauranen, A. and Kujamäki, P. (eds) (2004) *Translation Universals: Do They Exist?* Amsterdam: John Benjamins.

Mees, I., Göpferich, S. and Alves, F. (eds) (2011) *New Approaches in Translation Process Research*. Copenhagen Studies in Language Series 39. Copenhagen: Samfundslitteratur.

Melby. A., Fields, P., Hague, D., Koby, G.S. and Lommel, A. (2014) Defining the landscape of translation. *Revista Tradumatica* 12, 392–403.

Munday, J. (2016) Translation studies. In Y. Gambier and L. van Doorslaer (eds) *Handbook of Translation Studies*, vol. 1 (2010) (pp. 419–428). Current revision [online]: 2016. [limited access]

Nielsen, J. (1995) Severity ratings for usability problems. https://www.nngroup.com/articles/how-to-rate-the-severity-of-usability-problems/ [accessed 2 November 2018].

Nord, C. (2016) Functionalist approaches. In Y. Gambier and L. van Doorslaer (eds) *Handbook of Translation Studies*, vol. 1 (2010) (pp. 120–128). Current revision [online]: 2016. [limited access]

O'Brien, S. (2012) Towards a dynamic quality evaluation model for translation. *Journal of Specialised Translation* 17, 55–77.

Pradas Macías, E.M. (2015) Fluency. In F. Pöcchacker (ed.) *Routledge Encyclopedia of Interpreting Studies* (pp. 221–222). Florence: Taylor and Francis.
Pym, A., Grin, F., Sfreddo, C. and Chan, A.L.J. (2012) *The Status of the Translation Profession in the European Union*. Studies on Translation and Multilingualism, DGT/2011/TST. Brussels: European Commission. https://publications.europa.eu/en/publication-detail/-/publication/4e126174-ea20-4338-a349-ea4a73e0d850/language-en [consulted 27 August 2018].
Pöchhacker, F. (2011) Interpreting studies. In Y. Gambier and L. van Doorslaer (eds) *Handbook of Translation Studies*, vol. 1 (2010) (pp. 158–172). Current revision [online]: 2011. [limited access]
Salmi, L. and Kivilehto, M. (2018) 'User-oriented assessment': revising assessment criteria for the authorised translators' examination in Finland. Paper presented at the Transius Conference, University of Geneva, 18 to 20 June, 2018.
Segalowitz, N. (2010) *Cognitive Bases of Second Language Fluency*. New York: Routledge.
Snover, M., Dorr, B., Schwartz, R. and Micciulla, L. (2006) A study of translation edit rate with targeted human annotation. Paper presented at Proceedings of Association for Machine Translation in the Americas. http://mtarchive.info/AMTA-2006-Snover.pdf [consulted 28 August 2018]
Suojanen, T., Koskinen, K. and Tuominen, T. (2015) *User-Centered Translation*. New York: Routledge.
Suojanen, T. and Tuominen, T. (2015) Käännösten käytettävyyden heuristinen arviointi. [Heuristic evaluation of translation usability] In D. Rellstab and N. Siponkoski (eds) *Rajojen dynamiikkaa. VAKKI-symposiumi XXXV 12.–13.2.2015.* (pp. 270–280). VAKKI Publications 4. Vaasa.
Tavakoli, P. and Hunter, A.-M. (2018) Is fluency being 'neglected' in the classroom? Teacher understanding of fluency and related classroom practices. *Language Teaching Research* 22 (3), 330–349.
Tirkkonen-Condit, S. (2004) Unique items – over- or under-represented in translated language? In A. Mauranen and P. Kujamäki (eds) *Translation Universals: Do They Exist?* (pp. 177–184). Amsterdam: John Benjamins.
Toury, G. (2012) *Descriptive Translation Studies – and beyond* (rev. 2nd edn). Amsterdam: John Benjamins.
trans-k (2018) Glossary of Translation and Interpreting Terms. http://www.trans-k.co.uk/glossary.html [accessed 30 September 2018].
Translator/Interpreter Handbook (2014) Kansas Office of the Governor. https://www.ksde.org/LinkClick.aspx?fileticket=nMvB0a-owr8%3D&tabid=647&portalid=0&mid=1746 [accessed 30 September 2018].
Turner, B., Lai, M. and Huang, N. (2010) Error deduction and descriptors – a comparison of two methods of translation test assessment. *Translation & Interpreting. The International Journal for Translation & Interpreting Research* 2 (1), 11–23.

## Appendix 1: List of issues grouped under Fluency in the MQM Framework (Lommel et al., 2015b: Section 1.1.4)

- Ambiguity
  - Unclear reference
- Character encoding
- Coherence
- Cohesion
- Corpus conformance
- Duplication

- Grammar
  - Function words
  - Word form
    - Agreement
    - Part of speech
    - Tense/mood/aspect
  - Word order
- Grammatical register
- Inconsistency
  - Inconsistent abbreviations
  - Images vs text
  - Inconsistent link/cross-reference
  - Inconsistent with external reference
- Index/TOC
  - Index/TOC format
  - Missing/incorrect TOC item
  - Page references
- Link/cross-reference
  - Document-external link
  - Document-internal link
- Nonallowed characters
- Offensive
- Pattern problem
- Sorting
- Spelling
  - Capitalisation
  - Diacritics
- Typography
  - Punctuation
  - Unpaired quote marks or brackets
  - Whitespace
- Unintelligible

## Appendix 2: The error types used in assessing the ATA translation examination (ATA, 2017)

- Addition
- Ambiguity
- Capitalisation
- Cohesion ('a text is hard to follow because of inconsistent use of terminology, misuse of pronouns, inappropriate conjunctions, or other structural errors')
- Diacritical marks / Accents
- Faithfulness ('the target text does not respect the meaning of the source text as much as possible')

- Faux ami
- Grammar ('lack of agreement between subject and verb, incorrect verb tenses or verb forms, and incorrect declension of nouns, pronouns, or adjectives')
- Illegibility
- Indecision ('the candidate gives more than one option for a given translation unit')
- Literalness ('a translation that follows the source text word for word results in awkward, unidiomatic, or incorrect renditions')
- Mistranslation
- Misunderstanding
- Omission
- Punctuation ('the conventions of the target language regarding punctuation are not followed, including those governing the use of quotation marks, commas, semicolons, and colons. Incorrect or unclear paragraphing is also counted as a punctuation error.')
- Spelling / Character
- Syntax ('the arrangement of words or other elements of a sentence does not conform to the syntactic rules of the target language')
- Terminology
- Text Type ('some component of the translation fails to meet specifications')
  - Register
  - Style
- Unfinished
- Usage ('conventions of wording in the target language are not followed')
- Word form / Part of speech
- Other errors

# 11 The Effects of Songs on L2 Proficiency and Spoken Fluency: A Pedagogical Perspective

Leena Maria Heikkola and Jenni Alisaari

## Introduction

A growing number of studies indicate that music benefits learning (see e.g. Engh, 2013). Singing in particular is seen as an effective way to teach a second language, and as singing can have a positive effect on the recall of words, it may also benefit the development of spoken fluency (Koponen & Riggenbach, 2000). Moreover, rhythmic presentation of linguistic material (Purnell-Webb & Speelman, 2008) and rhythmic reciting have been shown to be beneficial for language learning (Heikkola & Alisaari, 2017). However, classroom studies on the topic are lacking.

In this chapter, we present our study on how three teaching techniques, namely singing, listening to songs and reciting song lyrics, affect the development of spoken fluency and proficiency. First, we introduce the multifaceted concept of fluency. Second, we present previous research on the effects of music and songs on language learning in particular. Third, we introduce the methodology of the present study, and finally, we present the results of the study and discuss their implications for second language teaching.

## Background

### Fluency in second language speaking

Fluency in second language (L2) speech is often understood as smooth and speedy delivery of speech without pauses, repetitions and repairs (Lennon, 1990). Segalowitz (2010) divides L2 fluency into three categories: (1) cognitive fluency (the ability to translate thoughts into speech),

(2) utterance fluency (the ability to produce speech without hesitations, repetitions, and repairs) and (3) perceived fluency (the inference listeners make about speaker's ability to produce speech). Recently, Götz (2013) has suggested a thorough framework for spoken fluency including measuring various aspects of fluency. Götz (2013: 2) lists three different aspects regarding productive spoken fluency: (1) temporal variables (e.g. length of runs, pause ratios, speech rate), (2) the use of formulaic language and (3) certain performance phenomena (e.g. self-repairs, hesitation phenomena, the use of discourse markers). In her framework, Götz also includes perceptive fluency, which refers to other global variables (e.g. accuracy, idiomaticity, intonation, accent, use of pragmatic features, lexical diversity, sentence structure). Segalowitz' (2010) utterance fluency overlaps with Götz' (2013) productive fluency, and perceived fluency (Segalowitz, 2010) is similar to Götz' (2013) perceptive fluency.

Traditionally, research on fluency in second language acquisition (SLA) has focused on temporal fluency, such as speech–pause relationships and disfluency markers (Lennon, 1990), which supports the 'fluency equals automaticity' approach (cf. Koponen & Riggenbach, 2000). Fluency can thus be seen as an impression that speech planning and speech production are functioning easily and efficiently (Lennon, 1990), reflecting the control speakers have over their L2 knowledge (Wolfe-Quintero *et al.*, 1998).

In this chapter, we focus on the spoken fluency of the speaker, and we understand fluency in the 'narrow' sense (Lennon, 1990). We investigate productive fluency using a temporal measure (see Götz, 2013). We also include a measure for overall oral productivity. We measure temporal fluency as speech rate (words/min), because it has been shown to correlate well with perceived spoken fluency (Kormos & Dénes, 2004), and it is often used to measure speed fluency (Tavakoli & Skehan, 2005). In addition, we measure oral productivity as the total number of words. The measure has been used as an indicator of written fluency (Wolfe-Quintero *et al.*, 1998), and including this measure in the study enables us to compare the results of this study to our previous results on written fluency (Alisaari & Heikkola, 2016).

## Music and language learning

There are a growing number of studies on the positive effects of music and songs on L2 learning (for a review, see Engh, 2013). Some studies show that melody and rhythm together result in the greatest benefits to language learning, and that singing is the most efficient learning technique for verbatim recall of sentences (Ludke *et al.*, 2014) and for developing written fluency in a L2 (Alisaari & Heikkola, 2016). There is also evidence for the benefits of melody combined with language for the recall of words (e.g. Sammler *et al.*, 2010). Other studies, however, have shown that it is rhythm that helps language learning the most when language materials are presented musically (see e.g. Purnell-Webb & Speelman, 2008).

L2 learning can be enhanced by many techniques, including songs and music, as it is an active, conscious, psychological and social process (Van Lier, 2000). Comprehensible input and available affordances are crucial for language learning (Van Lier, 2000) but active language production is also needed (Swain, 2000). When learners sing or recite songs, both affordances and production are present, especially if the understanding of the lyrics is supported by visual cues (Alisaari, 2016). Fluent speaking skills are essential for fluent communication. Since singing can improve the recall of linguistic elements (e.g. Ludke *et al.*, 2014), it can be hypothesised that singing may help to develop the spoken fluency of language learners. The positive effect of singing on L2 learning can be seen especially in learning new words, since melody combined with words helps learners to memorise words more effectively than mere linguistic input (Legg, 2009; Ludke *et al.*, 2014; Sammler *et al.*, 2010; Thaut *et al.*, 2005). Thus, it can be assumed that singing can increase spoken fluency, since the increase in linguistic features in L2 knowledge (see Wolfe-Quintero *et al.*, 1998) can be thought to make speech production easier (Lennon, 1990).

Even though there is evidence for the benefits of using songs for L2 learning, there are only a few studies on how songs can be used in the classroom to increase fluency and oral productivity. In the present study, we investigate how three teaching techniques (singing, listening to songs and reciting song lyrics rhythmically) affect spoken fluency and proficiency in Finnish second language learners. The reason for investigating all the three teaching techniques is that we can differentiate the potential effects of melody and rhythm versus rhythm only, as well as produced melody and rhythm versus perceived melody and rhythm. Also, by including all three techniques we will be able to compare the results of this study to our previous studies on written fluency. As there are no previous classroom studies on the links between rhythmically produced language and L2 learning, it is interesting to include this in the investigation to find out whether it may have similar positive links to L2 learning as singing (see earlier studies e.g. Engh, 2013).

### Research questions

In this study, we investigate how three teaching techniques (singing, listening to songs and reciting song lyrics) are linked to the development of proficiency and spoken fluency. This will be done by answering the following two research questions:

(1) Do the proficiency levels of the students change during intensive courses in Finnish language and culture?
(2) Is there a relationship between the three teaching techniques (singing, listening to songs and reciting song lyrics) and the development of spoken fluency and oral productivity?

## Methodology

### Participants

The participants were students in two 4-week intensive courses in Finnish language and culture, organised by a Finnish university in cooperation with the Center for International Mobility (CIMO, for more information, see cimo.fi). CIMO and the local course organisers preselected the participants ($n = 67$) for courses I (beginner level) and IIA (intermediate level). The participants on the beginner level course were mainly at language proficiency level A1–A2, according to the *Common European Framework of Reference for Languages* (CEFR) (Council of Europe, 2001), and had studied Finnish for 0.5 to 1 year. The participants in the intermediate level course were at language proficiency level A2–B1, and had studied Finnish for 1 to 2 years. The participants were university students mainly from Europe and North America. The most common native languages of the participants were German, Russian and Spanish as well as other Indo-European languages. All participants ($n = 67$) were between 18 and 33 years of age and had given their written consent to participate in the study.

The authors of the study re-evaluated the proficiency levels, initially evaluated by the students' Finnish teachers at their home universities, according to the CEFR. The evaluations were made based on the oral stories told in the pretest for the current study. The inter-rater reliability was over 97%. The students' oral language proficiency level varied from A1.1 to B2.2 (see Table 11.1). The 61 participants who completed both the spoken pretest and posttest are included in the analysis.

**Table 11.1** Course participants' proficiency levels in different groups at the beginning of the course

| Groups | Proficiency level | | | | | | | | |
|---|---|---|---|---|---|---|---|---|---|
| | A1.1 (n) | A1.2 (n) | A1.3 (n) | A2.1 (n) | A2.2 (n) | B1.1 (n) | B1.2 (n) | B2.1 (n) | B2.2 (n) |
| Singing group I ($n = 10$) | 2 | 3 | 3 | 2 | 0 | 0 | 0 | 0 | 0 |
| Listening group I ($n = 9$) | 0 | 1 | 1 | 3 | 4 | 0 | 0 | 0 | 0 |
| Reciting group I ($n = 8$) | 0 | 0 | 1 | 2 | 5 | 0 | 0 | 0 | 0 |
| Singing group IIA ($n = 11$) | 0 | 1 | 3 | 6 | 1 | 0 | 0 | 0 | 0 |
| Listening group IIA ($n = 11$) | 0 | 2 | 2 | 0 | 3 | 2 | 2 | 0 | 0 |
| Reciting group IIA ($n = 12$) | 0 | 0 | 0 | 0 | 4 | 4 | 3 | 1 | 0 |
| Total ($n = 61$) | 2 | 7 | 10 | 13 | 17 | 6 | 5 | 1 | 0 |

In the present study, we studied the effects of three different teaching techniques on spoken fluency: singing, listening to songs and reciting song lyrics. Based on the results of a placement test given by the local organisers on the first day of the courses, the students were divided into three groups within a course, comprising six groups in total. The teaching techniques were randomly assigned to the groups in the following way: singing was assigned to the weakest group, listening to songs to the middle group and reciting song lyrics to the strongest group for both courses I and IIA. Although the differences in the L2 proficiency levels within a course level were not great (see Table 11.1), the group division into the six groups by the course organisers was not ideal for the purposes of this study. This was taken into consideration in the analysis by using the L2 proficiency level as a covariate, in order to examine the possible effect of L2 proficiency on spoken fluency and oral productivity.

## Teaching techniques

The intensive Finnish language and culture courses consisted of 80 hours of teaching. The instruction was organised as workshops in interaction, vocabulary and grammar and reading comprehension. All the students ($n = 61$) participated in the seven study-related teaching sessions (singing, listening or reciting). These sessions lasted for 15 minutes each, in total 105 minutes, and they were evenly spaced out during the course (see Table 11.2). The singing groups learned Finnish by singing, the listening groups by listening to the same songs and the reciting groups by reciting the lyrics of the same songs rhythmically. The same songs were used in all groups, only the teaching technique differed. Altogether 18 songs (11 Finnish children's songs and seven pop songs) were used in the teaching sessions. The children's songs were selected because of their easier melodies and lyrics, as this has been shown to benefit language learning (Racette & Peretz, 2007). The pop songs were chosen to retain the interest of the participants and to introduce current Finnish music and culture to the participants. Both the children's songs and pop songs had similar vocabulary and structures, in order to fit the changing daily themes of the course, which included, but were not limited to, food, nature and culture.

Table 11.2 Schedule for the singing, listening and reciting sessions, and the pretest and posttest related to the study

|  | Monday | Tuesday | Wednesday | Thursday | Friday |
| --- | --- | --- | --- | --- | --- |
| Week 1 | Students arrive in Finland | Placement test Pretest (study) |  | Session 1 | Session 2 |
| Week 2 | Session 3 | Session 4 | Session 5 |  |  |
| Week 3 |  |  | Session 6 | Session 7 |  |
| Week 4 |  | Posttest (study) | Students leave Finland |  |  |

The children's songs were sung, listened to or recited during two or more separate teaching sessions. Some of the children's songs (8 of 11) were combined with gestures and movement or play. This was done because embodiment has been shown to enhance learning and the recall of the lyrics (see e.g. Coyle & Gómez Garcia, 2014). All the song lyrics were given to the participants on handouts that included visual cues to facilitate understanding. The meanings of the lyrics were discussed in all the groups.

In the research-related teaching sessions, the singing groups and the reciting groups differed from each other only in that the singing groups used melody in addition to rhythm. The listening groups differed the most from the other groups, as their role was the most passive, while the other groups were encouraged to actively produce Finnish in their teaching sessions. Apart from the study-related teaching sessions taught within the 80 hours of teaching, the courses were the same for all the participants within the same course level.

## Procedure

The data for the present study were collected in a pretest administered on the second day of the course and a posttest administered on the second-to-last day of the course. In the pretest and the posttest, the participants were asked to orally tell two stories in the target language, based on two comic strips depicting everyday events. The comic strips were designed for language teaching and learning by Schubi (1990). The participants did not have any time restrictions on telling the stories.

Similar narrative monologues based on picture story sequences have previously been widely used in L2 fluency research (see e.g. Lennon, 1990). Such narratives enable a more systematic comparison of the told stories; moreover, narratives are a frequently occurring form of informal spoken language and are usually deemed an ecologically valid way to study spoken fluency. In order to exclude possible story-specific problems for the subjects, the two stories used in the pretest and posttest were identical, as differences in a task may have an effect on performance (Thelen & Corbetta, 2002: 61).

The elicited stories were transcribed, their length in minutes was recorded and the total number of words in the story was calculated (for absolute values presented individually for each participant, see Appendix). In order to automatically calculate the number of words in the produced stories, all the non-linguistic information (e.g. coughing, sneezing) and the hesitation sounds (e.g. *um*), were removed from the transcriptions. In addition, the restart(s) of the same one word were counted as one word, for instance, *lei-lei-leipää* (bread). These restarts and repairs were included in the transcription, since these can be a part of fluency (repair fluency, Skehan, 2009). These will be used in our future studies of speech fluency in L2 learners of Finnish.

## Analysis

In the present study, we investigated which teaching technique (singing, listening or reciting) would be the most effective when it comes to the development of spoken fluency and overall L2 proficiency in the stories told by the participants. The students also had other support for learning, namely song lyrics explained in pictures printed on handouts, and gestures in the singing and reciting groups. First, we investigated fluency as the speech rate (words per minute). Second, we analysed overall oral productivity as the number of words produced in the oral stories. In addition, we investigated whether language proficiency levels improved during the course.

To investigate the development of the fluency of the participants' oral stories, we carried out a repeated measures ANCOVA, using a 4-step proficiency scale from A1 to B2 as per CEFR as a covariate, in order to find out whether there was an interaction between the development of fluency, defined as the speech rate of the oral narratives, development of oral productivity, defined as the number of words, and the different teaching techniques (singing, listening or reciting). The covariate is usually assumed to be a linear variable, which the language proficiency scale is not. However, we also did the analysis by using the L2 proficiency level as one of the factors in repeated measures ANOVAs, and the results are similar to the ones reported in this chapter. In order to investigate the change in language proficiency, we also carried out a repeated measures ANOVA on the pretest and posttest language proficiency levels.

## Results

In this section, we will present the results of the study. First, we present the results of the change in L2 proficiency from the beginning to the end of the courses. Then, we discuss the results for the development of spoken fluency measured as speech rate and oral productivity measured in the total number of words in the three teaching groups (singing, listening to songs and reciting song lyrics). We will first present the results for the whole participant group ($n = 61$), and then for the beginner (I) and intermediate (IIA) level courses separately.

### The development of L2 proficiency

In order to answer the first research question, we evaluated the proficiency levels of the participants at the beginning and the end of the course using the CEFR. In order to minimise possible biases, the authors were not aware of whether the narratives were produced in the pretest or posttest when assessing the proficiency levels. The proficiency levels were assessed on a four-step scale (1 = A1, 2 = A2, 3 = B1, 4 = B2).

All the participants were on L2 proficiency levels A1–B2. The singing group was, on average, at proficiency level A1 at the beginning of the course (M = 1.4, SD = 0.5), and closer to level A2 by the end of the course (M = 1.6, SD = 0.5). At the group level, the listening group started a little below level A2 (M = 1.9, SD = 0.7), and passed level A2 toward the end of the course (M = 2.2, SD = 0.5). The reciting group started a little above level A2 (M = 2.4, SD = 0.8), and almost reached level B1 at the end of the course (M = 2.7, SD = 0.9), on average.

A repeated measures ANOVA test revealed that L2 proficiency improved during the course ($F_{1,58}$ = 11.227; $p$ = 0.001; *partial eta²* = 0.162) (see Figure 11.1). The proficiency level is given on the Y-axis, and the line depicts the development of proficiency level from the pretest to the posttest. For all three groups, proficiency level thus improved significantly during the course. The three groups also differed significantly from each other in in the development of proficiency levels from the pretest to posttest ($F_{2,58}$ = 16.530; $p$ < 0.001; *partial eta²* = 0.363). In pairwise comparisons, singing group's proficiency was lower than the reciting group's ($p$ < 0.001), and lower than the listening group's proficiency ($p$ = 0.02). The listening group's proficiency was lower than the reciting group's proficiency ($p$ = 0.02). Thus, the reciting group's proficiency was the highest, the listening group's the second highest, and the singing group's the lowest. There was no interaction between the group and the proficiency level, meaning that the change in the proficiency levels was not linked to a specific group. Thus, the three teaching techniques did not affect the language proficiency of the participants in different ways.

When examining the two courses separately, in the beginner course, the singing group was, on average, a little over level A1 at the beginning (M = 1.2, SD = 0.4), and clearly over level A1 at the end of the course (M = 1.3, SD = 0.5). The listening group were almost at level A2 (M = 1.8, SD = 0.4), and made their way to level A2 by the end of the course (M = 2.0, SD = 0.0). The reciting group started a little below level A2

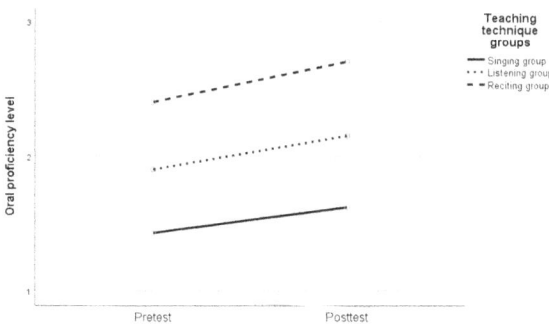

**Figure 11.1** Change of L2 proficiency from pretest to posttest in the three groups (singing, listening and reciting) using the four-step scale (1 = A1, 2 = A2, 3 = B1, 4 = B2)

(M = 1.9, SD = 0.4), and ended up at level A2 by the end of the course (M = 2.0, SD = 0.5).

In the intermediate course, the singing group was a little above level A1 (M = 1.6, SD = 0.5), and as a group, almost reached level A2 by the end of the course (M = 1.9, SD = 0.3). The listening group started at level A2 (M = 2.0, SD = 0.9), and by the end of the course, the group was above level A2 (M = 2.3, SD = 0.7), on average. The reciting group was well above proficiency level A2 (M = 2.8, SD = 0.6) at the beginning of the course, and reached level B1 by the end of the course (M = 3.2, SD = 0.7). Thus, L2 proficiency improved during the course for all groups on both the beginner and the intermediate courses.

Based on repeated measures ANOVAs on the separate courses, the proficiency level improved significantly only for course IIA ($F_{1,31}$ = 9.594; $p$ = 0.004; *partial eta²* = 0.236). The groups differed in their proficiency levels from each other on both course I ($F_{2,24}$ = 14.874; $p$ < 0.001; *partial eta²* = 0.553) and course IIA ($F_{2,31}$ = 13.312; $p$ < 0.001; *partial eta²* = 0.462). In pairwise comparisons for the beginner course, the singing group's proficiency was significantly lower than the listening group's ($p$ < 0.001) and the reciting group's proficiency ($p$ < 0.001). The listening group's proficiency and the reciting group's proficiency did not differ significantly. Overall, the reciting group improved their proficiency level the most. For the intermediate course, the singing group's proficiency was lower than the reciting group's ($p$ < 0.001), and the listening group's proficiency was lower than the reciting group's ($p$ = 0.005). The proficiency levels did not differ significantly between the singing and listening groups. Also in course IIA, the reciting group improved the most. The interactions between the proficiency level and group were not significant for either course. The results are similar for the beginner and intermediate courses, as for the whole group together. The reciting group's proficiency level was the highest and also improved the most.

## The development of spoken fluency and oral productivity in the three teaching technique groups

To answer our second research question, we examined spoken fluency in the narratives told orally by the participants as speech rate (words per minute) and oral productivity as the total number of words. We will present the results from repeated measures ANCOVA tests for the development (i.e. change from the beginning to the end of the courses) in fluency in the three different groups (singing, listening to music and reciting song lyrics). The initial L2 proficiency levels for the courses (four-step scale) were included in the analysis as a covariate.

First, we examined the development of oral productivity during the course as the total number of produced words in the oral narratives (see Figure 11.2). Based on the mean values, the number of words increased the most in the reciting group (pretest: M = 163, SD = 56; posttest: M = 174, SD = 72), followed by the singing group (pretest: M = 109, SD = 39; posttest: M = 112, SD = 38), and it decreased in the listening group (pretest: M = 133, SD = 41; posttest: M = 123, SD = 30). In the repeated measures ANCOVA with the proficiency level as a covariate, proficiency levels improved during the course ($F_{1,57} = 31.590; p < 0.001; partial\ eta^2 = 0.357$). The groups did not differ statistically significantly from each other in their produced number of words, however, nor did the change in the total number of words change significantly from the pretest to the posttest. Also, there were no interactions between the total number of words and proficiency level, nor between the total number of words and the group, which means that these variables were not linked. Thus, due to the effects of proficiency level differences between the three groups, even though the development of the total number of words from the pretest to the posttest is positive for the reciting and singing groups, and negative for the listening group, the difference between the three groups was not significant.

Next, we investigated whether there were differences between the beginner and intermediate courses in the total number of words produced in the pretest and posttest, in order to see whether beginner-level or more advanced-level students benefited more from the three teaching techniques (singing, listening to songs and reciting song lyrics). First, for the beginner course, the total number of words increased only in the reciting group (pretest: M = 148, SD = 36; posttest: M = 157, SD = 68). Surprisingly, the total number of words decreased in the singing group (pretest: M = 95, SD = 32; posttest: M = 82, SD = 27) and in the listening group (pretest: M = 136, SD = 41; posttest: M = 120, SD = 24). For course IIA, the total number of words increased the most in the singing group (pretest: M = 122, SD = 41; posttest: M = 139, SD = 23), followed by the reciting group (pretest: M = 174, SD = 18; posttest: M = 186, SD = 75). In the

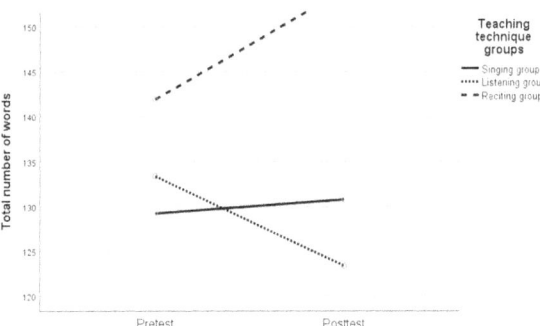

**Figure 11.2** Change of oral productivity measured as the total number of words from pretest to posttest in the three groups (singing, listening and reciting). Covariates appearing in the model are evaluated at the following values: L2 proficiency level (four-step scale) = 1.90

listening group, however, the total number of words decreased (pretest: M = 131, SD = 44; posttest: M = 126, SD = 36).

By measuring the total number of words in the narratives, a tendency for a difference could be seen between the groups in the beginner course ($F_{1,23} = 2.854$; $p = 0.078$; $partial\ eta^2 = 0.199$). The reciting group increased the number of total words more than the listening group. The groups in the intermediate course did not differ from each other significantly. The total number of words from the beginning to the end of the course did not change significantly for either course. The L2 proficiency level between subjects differed significantly from the beginning to the end of the course, but only for the intermediate course ($F_{1,30} = 20.633$; $p < 0.001$; $partial\ eta^2 = 0.408$). There were no interactions for either course.

The results can be interpreted in the way that for the whole group, differences in proficiency levels explain the differences in the number of produced words and the development from the pretest to posttest. However, looking at the two courses separately, the groups in the beginner course tend to differ in the number of produced words: the reciting group increases their total number of words towards the posttest, but the singing and the listening groups produce fewer words at the posttest. Interestingly, for the beginner course, proficiency levels do not explain these differences between the groups. Thus, it seems that reciting song lyrics can have affected the production of this group.

Second, we examined the development of spoken fluency as speech rate (words per minute) (see Figure 11.3). It increased the most in the reciting group (pretest: M = 34, SD = 17; posttest: M = 40, SD = 17), the second most in the listening group (pretest: M = 28, SD = 13; posttest: M = 33, SD = 10), and the least in the singing group (pretest: M = 22, SD = 9; posttest: M = 26, SD = 11) In the repeated measures ANCOVA

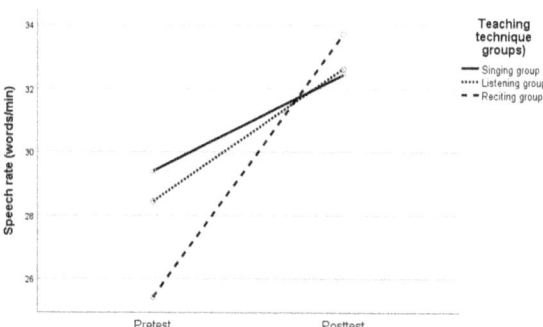

**Figure 11.3** Change of spoken fluency measured as the speech rate (words per minute) from pretest to posttest in the three groups (singing, listening, and reciting). Covariates appearing in the model are evaluated at the following values: L2 proficiency level (four-step scale) = 1.90

with the 4-step proficiency scale as a covariate, the speech rate became faster during the course ($F_{1,57} = 12.368$; $p = 0.001$; *partial eta²* $= 0.178$), and the proficiency level improved ($F_{1,57} = 72.897$; $p < 0.001$; *partial eta²* $= 0.561$). However, there were no differences between the groups. There was a significant interaction between speech rate and the proficiency level ($F_{1,57} = 4.700$; $p = 0.034$; *partial eta²* $= 0.076$), meaning that the higher the proficiency level was, the faster the speech rate became. Thus, the results point to the fact that proficiency, not the teaching technique, explains the improvement of fluency. On the other hand, all teaching techniques seem to facilitate speech fluency.

The examination of the two courses separately showed that fluency was improved in all the groups for both the beginner and the intermediate courses. For the beginner course, speech rate increased the most in the listening group (pretest: M = 23, SD = 6; posttest: M = 29, SD = 7), followed by the singing group (pretest: M = 15, SD = 5; posttest: M = 19, SD = 8), and the least in the reciting group (pretest: M = 21, SD = 4; posttest: M = 24, SD = 6). For the intermediate course, the increase was on average the greatest in the reciting group (pretest: M = 43, SD = 17; posttest: M = 51, SD = 13), the second greatest in the singing group (pretest: M = 27, SD = 9; posttest: M = 33, SD = 9), and the smallest in the listening group (pretest: M = 33, SD = 16; posttest: M = 35, SD = 12).

For the beginner course, language proficiency improved during the course ($F_{1,23} = 6.828$; $p = 0.016$; *partial eta²* $= 0.229$). There was no significant difference between the groups. However, in pairwise comparisons, there was a tendency toward a difference between the singing and listening groups ($p = 0.070$), the listening group improving more. Moreover, for the intermediate course, speech rate increased significantly ($F_{1,30} = 15.714$; $p < 0.001$; *partial eta²* $= 0.344$). In addition, language proficiency improved significantly ($F_{1,30} = 32.242$; $p < 0.001$; *partial eta²* $= 0.518$). There was also a significant interaction between speech rate and the proficiency level ($F_{1,30} = 9.655$; $p = 0.004$; *partial eta²* $= 0.243$), meaning that the higher the proficiency level, the more the speech rate increased toward the end of the course. There was also a significant interaction between speech rate and the group ($F_{2,30} = 4.032$; $p = 0.028$; *partial eta²* $= 0.212$), that is, the groups improved their speech rate in different ways. In pairwise comparisons, however, no differences between the three groups were found.

Fluency measured as speech rate (words per minute) seems to increase during the course when looking at the whole group together. However, there are no significant differences between the three teaching technique groups, and instead, proficiency level explains the increase in fluency. In the beginner course, all groups improve their fluency, although not significantly. Yet there is a tendency towards the listening group improving their fluency more than the singing group. In the intermediate course, speech rate increased from the pretest to the posttest, and this increase is linked to both proficiency level and group. As for the whole group, the increase in speech rate in the intermediate course was explained mostly by proficiency level.

## Discussion

L2 proficiency improved significantly for all three teaching groups (singing, listening and reciting). The proficiency level was the highest in the reciting group throughout the course, the second highest in the listening group and the lowest in the singing group. These results reflect the non-ideal differences in the proficiency levels of the groups at the beginning of the course, with the reciting group being the most advanced group, the listening group the second most-advanced and the singing group the least advanced group. When looking at the development of the proficiency levels in the beginner and intermediate courses separately, the proficiency level improved significantly only for the intermediate course. However, there were significant differences between the groups for both courses. For both courses, the reciting groups' proficiency levels were the highest in the beginning of the course, and also improved the most. As this could affect the results of the development of spoken fluency and oral productivity, we included proficiency level as a covariate in our further analysis.

Overall oral productivity was investigated as the total number of words. Only the proficiency level had a significant effect on the development of the number of words produced. In other words, the more proficient the learners were, the more words they produced towards the end of the course. Therefore, even though the total number of words increased in the reciting and singing groups, but decreased in the listening group, there were no significant differences between the groups due to the effect of proficiency level, which was used as a covariate in the analysis. These results contradict our previous results that singing improves written fluency the most compared to the other techniques (Alisaari & Heikkola, 2016), even when L2 proficiency level was taken into account. As there are no previous studies on the effects of rhythmic production on L2 learning, we cannot compare the results to previous research directly. However, it has been shown that songs, poems and chants can improve L2 pronunciation and increase spoken fluency (Lems, 2005; Morley, 1991). Also, according to the results of our previous study on L2 pronunciation, there are indications that rhythmic production can have a positive impact on L2 spoken production (Heikkola & Alisaari, 2017).

Next, we looked at the total number of words for the beginner and intermediate courses separately. For the beginner course, there was a tendency for a difference between the groups, but there was no significant change in the total number of words. For the intermediate course, the proficiency level increased significantly toward the end of the course, but the total number of words did not. The results point to the fact that proficiency explains the possible differences between the groups in the number of produced words for the intermediate group. However, looking at the beginner course, the reciting group seems to increase the total number of words produced during the course more than the other two groups. As this difference cannot be explained by a change in proficiency level, this may point to the fact that spoken production has automatised the most in this group (Koponen & Riggenbach, 2000), which may be taken as preliminary evidence for reciting being an effective teaching technique for improving oral productivity.

We also examined spoken fluency as the change in speech rate (words per minute) (see Tavakoli & Skehan, 2005) from the pretest to the posttest. Speech rate became significantly faster toward the posttest. Also, there was a significant interaction between speech rate and the proficiency level, meaning that the more proficient the speakers were, the faster they spoke. However, the fact that the reciting group improved their speech rate the most could be explained by previous studies indicating that reciting and rhythm is a beneficial teaching technique because of its influence on the recall of linguistic chunks (Purnell-Webb & Speelman, 2008). It has been shown that rhythm and rhythmic movement can improve recall (Holme, 2009), which is important for automatising language. Further, reciting enables the learner to practise production, which is important for learning (Swain, 2000).

Investigating the development of fluency as the change in speech rate from the pretest to the posttest for the beginner and intermediate courses separately, fluency improved during the course, and there was a tendency towards a difference between the groups in the beginner course. It seems that the listening group improved more than the singing group. These results are different from our results on the development of written fluency (Alisaari & Heikkola, 2016), where singing increased written fluency the most. However, writing and speaking are very different processes, and thus, they are not directly comparable. However, Ludke *et al.* (2014) have found that singing is more beneficial for language production than rhythm. Further research is needed for investigating the possible reasons for these contradictory findings.

For the intermediate course, both speech rate and L2 proficiency increased during the course, and these were linked; the more proficient the participants were, the faster they spoke. There was also a significant interaction between these; the better the L2 proficiency, the faster the language production. As for the oral productivity measured as the total number of words, these results contradict earlier research claiming that L2 learners in the beginner phase develop the total number of written words produced the fastest (Alisaari & Heikkola, 2016).

As in all classroom studies, there are limitations. As the division of participants into the teaching technique groups was less than ideal, we had to take this into consideration in the analysis. Using covariate analysis naturally decreases the possibilities of finding statistically significant results, which was also the case in this study. In future studies, if possible, the intervention groups should be formed more randomly, minimising possible effects on the variables under investigation.

The results of this study point to proficiency being an important factor in the development of oral productivity measured by the total number of words, and spoken fluency measured by speech rate (words per minute). For the whole group together, as well as for the beginner and intermediate courses separately, the total number of words and speech rate increase the most in the most proficient speakers. Thus, the differences in proficiency levels between the groups may mask the differences in spoken fluency and oral productivity between the teaching technique groups investigated in this chapter. In the future, the groups under investigation should be more ideally distributed regarding their proficiency level at the beginning of the intervention.

## Conclusion

The results of this study point to the fact that L2 proficiency level is tightly linked to the development of oral productivity measured as the total number of words produced, and spoken fluency measured as speech rate. Based on previous results, unexpectedly, the total number of words and speech rate increased the most in the reciting group that had the highest proficiency level at the end of the intervention. For both these measures, proficiency level was linked to the observed development. Tentatively, especially for the more advanced course, it seems that also reciting as a teaching technique may have been beneficial for learning. This is in line with our previous research that shows reciting to be beneficial for learning pronunciation in L2 Finnish (Heikkola & Alisaari, 2017). By reciting Finnish song lyrics rhythmically, speaking Finnish becomes more automatised (Koponen & Riggenbach, 2000), and thus fluency also increases.

This chapter has presented one of the first intervention studies looking at L2 learners of Finnish where different types of teaching techniques related to songs were investigated. Classroom research is a valuable way to study which methods work best in the language classroom. The results of this study point to reciting song lyrics rhythmically being a good way to promote both proficiency and spoken fluency. The main contribution of this study is that all the three methods can be used in the language classroom. However, according to our previous research, language teachers use all the techniques discussed in this study quite little, and reciting song lyrics or poems hardly at all (Alisaari & Heikkola, 2017). Thus, based on the results of this study, we encourage language teachers to use these techniques in the language classroom.

## References

Alisaari, J. (2016) *Songs and Poems in the Second Language Classroom: The Hidden Potential of Singing for Developing Writing Fluency*. Publications of the University of Turku, B 426. Turku: University of Turku.

Alisaari, J. and Heikkola, L.M. (2016) Increasing fluency in L2 writing with singing. *Studies in Second Language Learning and Teaching* 2, 271–292.

Alisaari, J. and Heikkola, L.M. (2017) Songs and poems in the language classroom: Teachers' beliefs and practices. *Teacher and Teacher Education* 63, 231–242.

Council of Europe (2001) *Common European Framework of Reference for Languages: Learning, Teaching, Assessment*. Cambridge: Cambridge University Press. Retrieved from https://rm.coe.int/1680459f97.

Coyle, Y. and Gómez Garcia, R. (2014) Using songs to enhance L2 vocabulary acquisition in preschool children. *Teaching English to Young Learners* 68 (3), 276–285.

Engh, D. (2013) Why use music in English language learning? A survey of the literature. *English Language Teaching* 6 (2), 113–127.

Götz, S. (2013) *Fluency in Native and Nonnative English Speech*. Amsterdam: John Benjamins.

Heikkola, L.M. and Alisaari, J. (2017) Laulun sanoja lausumalla taitavaksi ääntäjäksi? [Reciting song lyrics leads into good pronunciation skills?] In M. Kuronen, P. Lintunen and T. Nieminen (eds) *Näkökulmia toisen kielen puheeseen – Insights into Second Language Speech*. AFinLA-e: Soveltavan kielitieteen tutkimuksia 10. Jyväskylä: Finnish Association of Applied Linguistics AFinLA, 18–44.

Holme, R. (2009) *Cognitive Linguistics and Language Teaching*. Basingstoke: Palgrave Macmillan.

Koponen, M. and Riggenbach, H. (2000) Overview: Varying perspectives on fluency. In H. Riggenbach (ed.) *Perspectives on Fluency* (pp. 5–25). Ann Arbor, MI: University of Michigan Press.

Kormos, J. and Dénes, M. (2004) Exploring measures and perceptions of fluency in the speech of second language learners. *System* 32, 145–164.

Legg, R. (2009) Using music to accelerate language learning: An experimental study. *Research in Education* 82 (1), 1–12.

Lems, K. (2005) Music works: Music for adult English language learners. *New Directions for Adult and Continuing Education* 107, 13–21.

Lennon, P. (1990) Investigating fluency in EFL: A quantitative approach. *Language Learning* 40, 387–417.

Ludke, K.M., Ferreira, F. and Overy, K. (2014) Singing can facilitate foreign language learning. *Memory and Cognition* 42 (1), 41–52.

Morley, J. (1991) The pronunciation component in teaching English to speakers of other languages. *TESOL Quarterly* 25 (3), 481–520.

Purnell-Webb, P. and Speelman, C. (2008) Effects of music on memory for text. *Perceptual and Motor Skills* 106, 958–962.

Racette, A. and Peretz, I. (2007) Learning lyrics: To sing or not to sing? *Memory and Cognition* 35, 242–253.

Sammler, D., Baird, A., Valabrègue, R., Clément, S., Dupont, S., Belin, P. and Samson, S. (2010) The relationship of lyrics and tunes in the processing of unfamiliar songs: An fMRI adaptation study. *Journal of Neuroscience* 30 (10), 3357–3578.

Schubi (1990) *Und dann?* Bildergeschichten. Schaffhausen: SCHUBI Lernmedien AG.

Segalowitz, N. (2010) *Cognitive Bases of Second Language Fluency*. New York: Routledge.

Skehan, P. (2009) Modelling second language performance: Integrating complexity, accuracy, fluency, and lexis. *Applied Linguistics* 30, 510–532.

Swain, M. (2000) The output hypothesis and beyond: Mediating acquisition through collaborative dialogue. In J.P. Lantolf (ed.) *Sociocultural Theory and Second Language Learning* (pp. 97–114). Oxford: Oxford University Press.

Tavakoli, P. and Skehan, P. (2005) Strategic planning, task structure, and performance testing. In R. Ellis (ed.) *Planning and Task Performance in Second Language* (pp. 239–273). Amsterdam: John Benjamins.

Thaut, M.H., Peterson, D.A. and McIntosh, G.C. (2005) Temporal entrainment of cognitive functions: Musical mnemonics induce brain plasticity and oscillatory synchrony in neural networks underlying memory. *Annals of the New York Academy of Science* 1060, 243–254.

Thelen, E. and Corbetta, D. (2002) Microdevelopment and dynamic systems: Applications to infant motor development. *Microdevelopment: Transition Processes in Development and Learning* 7, 59–79.

Van Lier, L. (2000) From input to affordance: Social-interactive from an ecological perspective. In J. Lantolf (ed.) *Sociocultural Theory and Second Language Learning* (pp. 245–260). Oxford: Oxford University Press.

Wolfe-Quintero, K., Inagaki, S. and Kim, H.-Y. (1998) *Second Language Development in Writing: Measures of Fluency, Accuracy, and Complexity*. Honolulu: University of Hawaii Press.

## Appendix: Results per participant

The number of words, the length of the narratives in seconds, and the speech rate in the pretest and posttest for individual participants and the loss/gain in number of words, length, speech rate, as well as percentages.

| Participant code | Number of words | | | | Length of narrative (s) | | | | Speech rate (words/min) | | | |
|---|---|---|---|---|---|---|---|---|---|---|---|---|
| | | | Gain/loss from pretest to posttest | | | | Gain/loss from pretest to posttest | | | | Gain/loss from pretest to posttest | |
| | Pretest | Posttest | Words | Percentage | Pretest | Posttest | Lenght | Percentage | Pretest | Posttest | Speech rate | Percentage |
| IL1 | 72 | 79 | 7.00 | 1.10 | 205 | 259 | −54.00 | 1.26 | 21.07 | 18.30 | −2.77 | 0.87 |
| IL2 | 78 | 137 | 59.00 | 1.76 | 351 | 238 | −113.00 | 0.68 | 13.33 | 34.54 | 21.20 | 2.59 |
| IL3 | 102 | 84 | −18.00 | 0.82 | 387 | 200 | −187.00 | 0.52 | 15.81 | 25.20 | 9.39 | 1.59 |
| IL4 | 173 | 97 | −76.00 | 0.56 | 446 | 269 | −177.00 | 0.60 | 23.27 | 21.64 | −1.64 | 0.93 |
| IL5 | 97 | 74 | −23.00 | 0.76 | 333 | 208 | −125.00 | 0.62 | 17.48 | 21.35 | 3.87 | 1.22 |
| IL6 | 99 | 67 | −32.00 | 0.68 | 307 | 197 | −110.00 | 0.64 | 19.35 | 20.41 | 1.06 | 1.05 |
| IL7 | 92 | 54 | −38.00 | 0.59 | 564 | 254 | −310.00 | 0.45 | 9.79 | 12.76 | 2.97 | 1.30 |
| IL9 | 49 | 66 | 17.00 | 1.35 | 359 | 597 | 238.00 | 1.66 | 8.19 | 6.63 | −1.56 | 0.81 |
| IL11 | 106 | 109 | 3.00 | 1.03 | 596 | 407 | −189.00 | 0.68 | 10.67 | 16.07 | 5.40 | 1.51 |
| IL12 | 81 | 50 | −31.00 | 0.62 | 375 | 312 | −63.00 | 0.83 | 12.96 | 9.62 | −3.34 | 0.74 |
| IK1 | 136 | 116 | −20.00 | 0.85 | 399 | 285 | −114.00 | 0.71 | 20.45 | 24.42 | 3.97 | 1.19 |
| IK2 | 191 | 155 | −36.00 | 0.81 | 401 | 250 | −151.00 | 0.62 | 28.58 | 37.20 | 8.62 | 1.30 |
| IK3 | 190 | 116 | −74.00 | 0.61 | 337 | 170 | −167.00 | 0.50 | 33.83 | 40.94 | 7.11 | 1.21 |
| IK4 | 113 | 102 | −11.00 | 0.90 | 339 | 301 | −38.00 | 0.89 | 20.00 | 20.33 | 0.33 | 1.02 |
| IK6 | 138 | 112 | −26.00 | 0.81 | 409 | 196 | −213.00 | 0.48 | 20.24 | 34.29 | 14.04 | 1.69 |
| IK7 | 168 | 164 | −4.00 | 0.98 | 543 | 407 | −136.00 | 0.75 | 18.56 | 24.18 | 5.61 | 1.30 |
| IK8 | 123 | 103 | −20.00 | 0.84 | 275 | 192 | −83.00 | 0.70 | 26.84 | 32.19 | 5.35 | 1.20 |
| IK9 | 78 | 93 | 15.00 | 1.19 | 254 | 239 | −15.00 | 0.94 | 18.43 | 23.35 | 4.92 | 1.27 |
| IK10 | 90 | 122 | 32.00 | 1.36 | 356 | 270 | −86.00 | 0.76 | 15.17 | 27.11 | 11.94 | 1.79 |

(Continued)

| Participant code | Number of words | | | | Length of narrative (s) | | | | Speech rate (words/min) | | | |
|---|---|---|---|---|---|---|---|---|---|---|---|---|
| | | | Gain/loss from pretest to posttest | | | | Gain/loss from pretest to posttest | | | | Gain/loss from pretest to posttest | |
| | Pretest | Posttest | Words | Percentage | Pretest | Posttest | Lenght | Percentage | Pretest | Posttest | Speech rate | Percentage |
| IR2 | 155 | 151 | −4.00 | 0.97 | 393 | 263 | −130.00 | 0.67 | 23.66 | 34.45 | 10.78 | 1.46 |
| IR3 | 121 | 151 | 30.00 | 1.25 | 388 | 361 | −27.00 | 0.93 | 18.71 | 25.10 | 6.39 | 1.34 |
| IR4 | 159 | 118 | −41.00 | 0.74 | 458 | 275 | −183.00 | 0.60 | 20.83 | 25.75 | 4.92 | 1.24 |
| IR5 | 173 | 136 | −37.00 | 0.79 | 520 | 425 | −95.00 | 0.82 | 19.96 | 19.20 | −0.76 | 0.96 |
| IR6 | 75 | 85 | 10.00 | 1.13 | 393 | 364 | −29.00 | 0.93 | 11.45 | 14.01 | 2.56 | 1.22 |
| IR7 | 194 | 311 | 117.00 | 1.60 | 497 | 719 | 222.00 | 1.45 | 23.42 | 25.95 | 2.53 | 1.11 |
| IR10 | 159 | 175 | 16.00 | 1.10 | 364 | 407 | 43.00 | 1.12 | 26.21 | 25.80 | −0.41 | 0.98 |
| IR11 | 147 | 125 | −22.00 | 0.85 | 444 | 329 | −115.00 | 0.74 | 19.86 | 22.80 | 2.93 | 1.15 |
| IIL1 | 186 | 148 | −38.00 | 0.80 | 327 | 300 | −27.00 | 0.92 | 34.13 | 29.60 | −4.53 | 0.87 |
| IIL2 | 125 | 155 | 30.00 | 1.24 | 332 | 347 | 15.00 | 1.05 | 22.59 | 26.80 | 4.21 | 1.19 |
| IIL3 | 202 | 143 | −59.00 | 0.71 | 254 | 232 | −22.00 | 0.91 | 47.72 | 36.98 | −10.73 | 0.78 |
| IIL4 | 80 | 125 | 45.00 | 1.56 | 203 | 272 | 69.00 | 1.34 | 23.65 | 27.57 | 3.93 | 1.17 |
| IIL5 | 112 | 179 | 67.00 | 1.60 | 254 | 213 | −41.00 | 0.84 | 26.46 | 50.42 | 23.97 | 1.91 |
| IIL6 | 81 | 119 | 38.00 | 1.47 | 296 | 308 | 12.00 | 1.04 | 16.42 | 23.18 | 6.76 | 1.41 |
| IIL7 | 80 | 95 | 15.00 | 1.19 | 193 | 160 | −33.00 | 0.83 | 24.87 | 35.63 | 10.75 | 1.43 |
| IIL9 | 93 | 163 | 70.00 | 1.75 | 227 | 342 | 115.00 | 1.51 | 24.58 | 28.60 | 4.01 | 1.16 |
| IIL10 | 129 | 132 | 3.00 | 1.02 | 224 | 169 | −55.00 | 0.75 | 34.55 | 46.86 | 12.31 | 1.36 |
| IIL11 | 139 | 131 | −8.00 | 0.94 | 328 | 246 | −82.00 | 0.75 | 25.43 | 31.95 | 6.52 | 1.26 |
| IIL12 | 110 | 142 | 32.00 | 1.29 | 328 | 282 | −46.00 | 0.86 | 20.12 | 30.21 | 10.09 | 1.50 |
| IIK1 | 168 | 155 | −13.00 | 0.92 | 214 | 202 | −12.00 | 0.94 | 47.10 | 46.04 | −1.06 | 0.98 |

| | | | | | | | | | | | | |
|---|---|---|---|---|---|---|---|---|---|---|---|---|
| IIK2 | 90 | 90 | 90 | 0.00 | 1.00 | 226 | 240 | 14.00 | 1.06 | 23.89 | 22.50 | -1.39 | 0.94 |
| IIK3 | 186 | 141 | -45.00 | 0.76 | 176 | 194 | 18.00 | 1.10 | 63.41 | 43.61 | -19.80 | 0.69 |
| IIK4 | 83 | 92 | 9.00 | 1.11 | 220 | 163 | -57.00 | 0.74 | 22.64 | 33.87 | 11.23 | 1.50 |
| IIK5 | 123 | 134 | 11.00 | 1.09 | 197 | 210 | 13.00 | 1.07 | 37.46 | 38.29 | 0.82 | 1.02 |
| IIK6 | 180 | 139 | -41.00 | 0.77 | 216 | 157 | -59.00 | 0.73 | 50.00 | 53.12 | 3.12 | 1.06 |
| IIK7 | 86 | 112 | 26.00 | 1.30 | 340 | 287 | -53.00 | 0.84 | 15.18 | 23.41 | 8.24 | 1.54 |
| IIK8 | 82 | 70 | -12.00 | 0.85 | 275 | 294 | 19.00 | 1.07 | 17.89 | 14.29 | -3.61 | 0.80 |
| IIK10 | 109 | 100 | -9.00 | 0.92 | 390 | 210 | -180.00 | 0.54 | 16.77 | 28.57 | 11.80 | 1.70 |
| IIK11 | 185 | 179 | -6.00 | 0.97 | 326 | 268 | -58.00 | 0.82 | 34.05 | 40.07 | 6.03 | 1.18 |
| IIK12 | 147 | 171 | 24.00 | 1.16 | 233 | 230 | -3.00 | 0.99 | 37.85 | 44.61 | 6.75 | 1.18 |
| IIR1 | 144 | 193 | 49.00 | 1.34 | 253 | 220 | -33.00 | 0.87 | 34.15 | 52.64 | 18.49 | 1.54 |
| IIR2 | 151 | 108 | -43.00 | 0.72 | 258 | 133 | -125.00 | 0.52 | 35.12 | 48.72 | 13.61 | 1.39 |
| IIR3 | 129 | 146 | 17.00 | 1.13 | 277 | 221 | -56.00 | 0.80 | 27.94 | 39.64 | 11.70 | 1.42 |
| IIR4 | 167 | 169 | 2.00 | 1.01 | 383 | 298 | -85.00 | 0.78 | 26.16 | 34.03 | 7.86 | 1.30 |
| IIR5 | 210 | 187 | -23.00 | 0.89 | 220 | 162 | -58.00 | 0.74 | 57.27 | 69.26 | 11.99 | 1.21 |
| IIR6 | 149 | 169 | 20.00 | 1.13 | 213 | 203 | -10.00 | 0.95 | 41.97 | 49.95 | 7.98 | 1.19 |
| IIR7 | 150 | 149 | -1.00 | 0.99 | 290 | 210 | -80.00 | 0.72 | 31.03 | 42.57 | 11.54 | 1.37 |
| IIR8 | 349 | 405 | 56.00 | 1.16 | 264 | 503 | 239.00 | 1.91 | 79.32 | 48.31 | -31.01 | 0.61 |
| IIR9 | 244 | 227 | -17.00 | 0.93 | 215 | 169 | -46.00 | 0.79 | 68.09 | 80.59 | 12.50 | 1.18 |
| IIR10 | 109 | 152 | 43.00 | 1.39 | 213 | 171 | -42.00 | 0.80 | 30.70 | 53.33 | 22.63 | 1.74 |
| IIR11 | 134 | 176 | 42.00 | 1.31 | 210 | 251 | 41.00 | 1.20 | 38.29 | 42.07 | 3.79 | 1.10 |
| IIR12 | 148 | 147 | -1.00 | 0.99 | 224 | 185 | -39.00 | 0.83 | 39.64 | 47.68 | 8.03 | 1.20 |

Note: I = course I; II = Course IIA; s = singing teaching method; L = listening teaching method; R = reciting teaching method.

# 12 Synthesising Approaches to Second Language Fluency: Implications and Future Directions

Pekka Lintunen, Maarit Mutta and Pauliina Peltonen

## Introduction

The chapters in this volume have offered various perspectives into fluency in second language (L2) learning and use, encompassing both what has traditionally been referred to as second language acquisition and foreign language learning. The emphasis has mainly been on the narrow sense of fluency, following Lennon's (1990) terminology, and the most influential framework as the basis of the chapters has been Segalowitz' (2010) three dimensions of fluency: cognitive, utterance and perceived fluency. In addition, L2 proficiency has been discussed from the perspective of speaking, writing, listening and reading. After the two introductory chapters, the other chapters in this volume have focused on processing and cognitive fluency (Chapters 3–5), fluent productions in L2 learning and use (Chapters 6–8) and the assessment and development of fluency (Chapters 9–11). In this concluding chapter, we will draw together the main themes of this book and the contributions of individual chapters to illustrate the current understanding of fluency.

In this chapter, we will revisit the theme of the book, fluency in L2 learning and use, while discussing two continua: learning-use and fluency-disfluency. First, we will illustrate the continuum between learning and use by addressing fluency from the user's perspective with reference to the *Common European Framework of Reference (CEFR) for Languages* (Council of Europe, 2001). Fluency is present in the CEFR both implicitly in the descriptions of competent language use and explicitly as a specific assessment criterion. The CEFR contains elements of both narrow and broad senses of fluency and demonstrates that the division between the two senses is not always clear-cut. This is linked to our discussion of the second continuum, which relates to L2 fluency and disfluency: they cannot be considered opposites but rather as natural overlapping phases in the dynamic processes of producing spoken or written language or receiving oral or aural language input. Fluency is context-dependent and associated with interspeaker and intraspeaker variation. It should also be acknowledged that native speakers can vary in their first language (L1) fluency (e.g. Fillmore, 1979; Lennon, 1990). After our discussion of the two continua, we will discuss the theoretical implications of this book and the gaps that still remain in our knowledge about L2 fluency. We will conclude the chapter with the pedagogical implications for L2 learners, teachers and assessors.

## Revisiting Fluency in L2 Learning and Use

### The user perspective in the CEFR

Language learning and use can be viewed as a continuum; in the *Common European Framework of Reference for Languages* (Council of Europe, 2018a), learners are considered language users. We begin our discussion by commenting on this continuum, followed by an overview of the CEFR's conceptualisation of fluency. We demonstrate the implicit aspects of fluency in the CEFR by linking the descriptions of proficient language use to Segalowitz' (2010) three senses of fluency. In our discussion, we also show that the CEFR contains apparent elements of both narrow and broad senses of fluency, as defined by Lennon (1990).

Language learning is frequently regarded as occurring in formal education (Council of Europe, 2001: 139), whereas in out-of-school environments learners become users. However, the distinction between these two categories is not sharply defined; therefore, the term language user is often applied when speaking of adult L2 users to emphasise the fact that they have achieved a command of the target language that makes them proficient users in some domains and should not be considered inferior to native speakers. Often, questions of identity are central: when the learner's overall L2 proficiency increases, they gradually start using the language in contexts that are not related to learning in formal contexts alone. In other words, users can operate in their L2 in their daily activities and may no longer identify as learners of that language. To put it simply, we can talk about L2 language users whenever these people use the L2 language for communication.

In the CEFR, the language user competences are defined according to descriptor scales related to different communicative language competences: linguistic, sociolinguistic and pragmatic (Council of Europe, 2018a: 130). The CEFR calls Lennon's broad sense 'a holistic way' to understand fluency, and it is associated with appropriate contents in the context and talking at length. Interestingly, a narrower understanding of fluency is located under pragmatic competence and related explicitly only to spoken language, including fluency in interactive situations. In this sense, 'talking at length implies a lack of distraction through breaks and long pauses in the flow of speech' (Council of Europe, 2018a: 139). That is, the main emphasis here is on maintaining the flow of speech and avoiding pauses or other hesitations. However, fluency is implicitly included in other competences as well and clearly linked, for instance, with the prosodic features of phonological control under linguistic competences. The mastery level C2 language user, that is, a proficient user on the CEFR scale, can, for instance:

- formulate thoughts precisely with no signs of having to restrict what s/he wants to say (reflecting cognitive and utterance fluency);
- understand at ease any kind of spoken language and follow complex interactions, (reflecting cognitive fluency);
- understand all forms of written language, scan quickly a variety of texts and identify relevant information (reflecting cognitive fluency);
- write clear, smoothly flowing, complex well-structured texts in an effective and appropriate style which help the reader to find significant points (reflecting cognitive, utterance and perceived fluency);
- produce clear, smoothly flowing well-structured speech with an effective logical structure which helps the recipient to notice and remember significant points, and converse comfortably and appropriately, unhampered by any linguistic limitations in conducting a full social and personal life (reflecting cognitive, utterance and perceived fluency). (Council of Europe, 2001, ch. 4–5; 2017: 217; Segalowitz' fluency categories added by the authors)

These examples of the CEFR C2 level illustrate the ultimate level of broad (or holistic) fluency observable in the language users' comprehension and production perceived by interlocutors. Naturally, the C2 level is an idealistic proficiency level, which does not even describe all speakers in their L1 (see e.g. Huhta *et al.* in this volume). Nonetheless, this CEFR description also provides the ultimate learning objectives when learners, stage by stage, become more fluent users of the L2.

More specifically, the CEFR also includes a narrower (or 'traditional' as described in the CEFR) description under spoken fluency. The framework has even been adapted to sign language via the project 'Signed language for professional purposes (PRO-Sign)' (Council of Europe, 2018b; see also Leeson *et al.*, 2016). The description of signed fluency (given in written and signed forms) is identical to the framework's description of narrow fluency under pragmatic competence (Council of Europe, 2018a: 144):

> C2: Can express him/herself at length with a natural, effortless, unhesitatingly flow. Pauses only to reflect on precisely the right words to express his/her thoughts or to find an appropriate example or explanation.

The features mentioned in the description can be regarded as features of utterance fluency in Segalowitz' terminology. Effortless expression can refer to automatic lexical access reflecting cognitive fluency. That said, while researchers have been interested in potential typological differences in L2 fluency and called for more research with different target languages, describing fluency in sign language is a novelty which has been studied only to a limited (but see e.g. Degand *et al.*, 2019). Fluency is a natural part of expression in sign language, but the fluency features have to be operationalised differently from the spoken mode. Sign language fluency has to be approached from a multimodal perspective, which should in general be explored further in future fluency studies. Human interaction is multimodal, and interaction is the key function of language use in the CEFR.

The above-mentioned CEFR scale descriptors have a practical and pedagogical purpose in education and assessment. Moreover, the CEFR proficiency levels can be used for professional purposes when, for instance, documenting one's competence in various L2s. While not using specific L2 fluency research terminology, the descriptors allude to fluency in the narrow sense (i.e. an aspect of oral competence) or performance in the (very) broad sense (i.e. as general L2 proficiency). The CEFR descriptions are good general overviews of L2 proficiency; however, L2 users and teachers often need more detailed and in-depth descriptions of fluency to improve L2 skills. Moreover, in research rigorous measures are needed to describe different aspects of fluency.

## The fluency-disfluency continuum

All language use, including L1 use, contains many disfluency features, such as long pauses and other hesitations. These features can be caused by psycholinguistic or sociolinguistic variables, such as the anxiety level experienced by the speaker (Eysenck *et al.*, 2007), uneven power relations between interlocutors (Nogami, 2013; Norton & Toohey, 2011) or dialectal variation (Jacewicz *et al.*, 2010). However, this is not always acknowledged in L2 teaching and learning; instead, in L2 studies, disfluency features have been considered deficit features of non-native speech, and learners have often been compared to idealised native speakers. Moreover, clinical disfluencies, such as stuttering (see e.g. Howell & van Borsel, 2011), are not included as variables in most L2 fluency studies, but rather often used as a criterion to exclude research participants to make groups homogeneous in nature.

Following some recent studies (see e.g. Degand *et al.*, 2019), we also challenge the traditional fluency-disfluency dichotomy: the so-called disfluency features can in some contexts even facilitate communication and make it more fluent. While disfluency is often understood as the opposite of fluency, these concepts should not be approached as polar opposites, or as Fulcher (2015: 60) describes, a 'janus-faced' construct. Fluency is context-dependent and to some extent also an idiosyncratic feature: it seems to be influenced, for example, by the personality of the speaker (Dewaele & Furnham, 2000) or the task at hand (e.g. Tavakoli & Skehan,

2005). For instance, some speakers by nature have a slower speech rate or are prone to hesitate more when they speak. Recent studies have shown that the natural tendencies of L1 fluency can influence L2 fluency (e.g. De Jong et al., 2015; Huensch & Tracy-Ventura, 2017; Peltonen, 2018); consequently, learners' L2 performance should not only be compared to native speaker control groups (or more advanced L2 users sharing the same L1) but also to their own L1 performance to establish the learners' individual fluency profile in spoken or written language production. The context-dependent nature of fluency also poses challenges regarding its measurement; for instance, measures used in L2 monologue contexts should be adapted for dialogue contexts (e.g. Tavakoli, 2016). Particularly in the dialogue setting, various disfluencies may have other communicative functions, such as holding the floor during one's turn with the help of filled pauses or repetitions (e.g. Clark & Wasow, 1998; Pallotti, 2005; Peltonen, 2017). From a L2 learner's perspective, it is beneficial to learn to use, for instance, filled pauses and repetitions strategically to enhance fluent dialogue. Therefore, these features should not be automatically and categorically avoided or discouraged in L2 teaching and learning but their functions could be addressed explicitly. These dialogue settings need more emphasis in teaching and future research.

Considering the interspeaker and intraspeaker variation in both L1 and L2 fluency, different speaking, writing, and language use situations can be placed on a continuum from more fluent to more disfluent uses of language. For the sake of communication, the final language product should be fluent enough for the communicative situation in question. Optimal fluency varies: for instance, dialogues among L2 speakers may allow a slower pace than dialogues among L1 speakers. On the other hand, a maximally rapid speech rate does not mean maximal fluency or comprehensibility from the perspective of the interlocutor (e.g. Munro & Derwing, 2001); that is, seemingly good utterance fluency does not always translate as optimal perceived fluency and guarantee successful communication, as for instance shown by studies in the English as a lingua franca (ELF) framework (e.g. Deterding, 2013; Hynninen in this volume). Similarly to optimal speech rate, which depends on the context, it should also be noted that features of speech associated with disfluency, such as silent pauses, are natural features in spoken language and serve various functions. A pause, in itself, is thus not a sign of disfluency; speakers use pauses to breathe, plan, or to emphasise certain parts of the utterance. When measuring fluency, distinguishing natural articulatory pauses (e.g. breathing) from other pauses indicating disfluency is particularly important; the minimum length for a silent pause (shorter pauses being considered micropauses) is often set at 0.25 seconds (e.g. De Jong, 2016; for fluency and pause lengths in writing, see Mutta in this volume).

Contributions from other fields not traditionally linked to L2 speech fluency research can also shed light on the fluency-disfluency continuum by providing explanations for disfluencies. Cognitive fluency, in particular, can be studied with psycholinguistic methods to elucidate how an individual's working memory functions in different situations. The capacity limitations of the working memory become evident when the automatic processing is affected, for instance, due to a lack of linguistic resources (Just & Carpenter, 1992). Consequently, inaccuracies (i.e. disfluencies) in linguistic production appear and the speech rate slows. Fluency and disfluency are thus counterparts that show a balanced interplay between automatic and controlled processes (see Olkkonen & Mutta in this volume). Moreover, fluency research can benefit from studying the mechanisms behind disfluencies. For instance, dyslexia studies have demonstrated connections between reading or writing difficulties and cognitive deficits in the phonological and orthographic systems (e.g. Wengelin & Arfé, 2018). Spoken and written language are intertwined in the learners' minds, and inaccuracies in one mode can be explained by using the form of the word from another mode (see Anckar & Veivo in this volume; see also Veivo, 2017; Veivo *et al.*, 2018). Disfluent language use, such as slower spoken or written production, can thus be the result of phonetic and orthographic competitors, from any language known by the user, slowing the process.

We have highlighted that fluent and disfluent language use form a continuum between two extremes, and disfluency features are common in everyday language use. In addition, we have illustrated how the different conceptualisations of fluency (cognitive, utterance and perceived fluency) underlie the notion of a fluent language user in the CEFR. As the proficiency descriptions in the CEFR also show, the proportion of disfluencies is reduced when learners become more advanced, but even on the highest level, the language that users produce may include some disfluencies. In a similar manner, receptive language use may at times be disfluent due to, for instance, fatigue or context-induced anxiety that temporarily prevents the language user from performing optimally. Optimal language use in receptive skills usually refers to rapid, automatic and therefore fluent behaviour. In productive skills, as we have argued, optimal performance may more often contain, for instance, strategically used features that are traditionally considered disfluencies.

## Implications for Researchers and Practitioners

### Fluidity of production and factors affecting fluency

As a whole, the individual contributions in this book have offered various approaches to L2 fluency. Many under-researched areas have been mapped to advance fluency research to be able to form a more comprehensive picture of the multifaceted phenomenon. That said, one prevailing challenge for all fluency research is terminological haziness. The lack of uniform terminology makes comparing results across studies difficult and is a potential source for misunderstandings if L2 researchers, teachers, assessors and learners understand some key concepts differently. Widely used frameworks, such as Segalowitz' three dimensions and Lennon's two senses of fluency are valuable and helpful when conducting research, disseminating research results or describing what L2 fluency contains for any interested party, but they may not be familiar for, for instance, in-service teachers. Furthermore, the narrow, broad and very broad senses of fluency (Tavakoli & Hunter, 2018) are often mixed when fluency is discussed.

A potential source of confusion and an explanation for the mixed use of the term are the fairly general definitions of fluency provided in dictionaries. For instance, on Princeton University's WordNet, the word *fluency* refers to 'powerful and effective language', 'skilfulness in speaking or writing' and 'the quality of being facile in speech and writing'. In addition, in everyday language use, fluency is mostly used to describe general language proficiency. In other words, definitions often describe fluency in the broad or very broad sense and refer to general proficiency and ease (and mostly referring to productive language skills alone). Additionally, learners' intuition may direct their understanding towards the broad sense of the word (see Lintunen & Peltonen in this volume), which may also be more familiar for teachers (see also Tavakoli & Hunter, 2018).

For the purposes of the general public, adopting terminology that draws a clearer distinction between the different senses of fluency could be considered. Using a near-synonym for the narrow sense of fluency while reserving the term fluency for the broad or very broad sense of fluency could be one solution. An obvious candidate is *fluidity*. The word *fluid* refers to something that is 'smooth and unconstrained in movement' and 'capable of flowing'. Fluidity can be understood as the property of something flowing smoothly, for instance, the fluidity of movement when speaking or writing (or signing). In this sense, we could talk about the fluid delivery of language describing smoothly produced language. The word has been used, for instance, when studying stuttering, which involves problems in the fluidity of words, syllables and sounds (e.g. Ardila *et al.*, 1994; for more on stuttering and fluency, see e.g. Penttilä *et al.*, 2019), or when describing fluid movements in sign language (e.g. Wilbur, 1980), but often not in the field of L2 fluency research. Nonetheless, the narrow sense of fluency refers to the speed, smoothness and effortlessness of speech or the writing process and can be examined in terms of temporal elements, which could also be understood as contributing to the degree of fluidity. As *fluency* is easily associated with L2 speaking or writing proficiency, to enhance learners' and the general public's understanding of the two senses of fluency, *fluidity* could be considered as a term that refers to narrowly defined temporal elements in the speech and writing process.

An example would be that a lower-level learner can produce fluid stretches of speech or writing with certain fixed expressions, such as

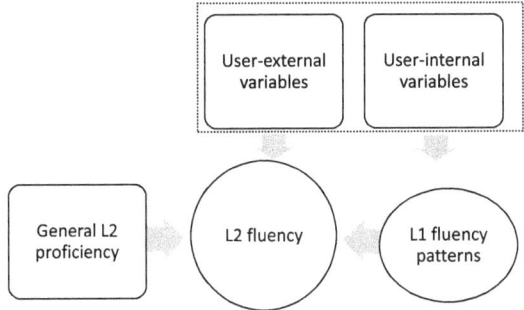

**Figure 12.1** Factors affecting L2 fluency

formulaic sequences, without being widely proficient or fluent in the broad sense. Moreover, a proficient L2 user may sometimes be less fluid, but this may be caused by context-dependent variables and not be an index of their proficiency at large. As these examples demonstrate, fluency as a term could thus be reserved for the broad sense, referring to the more general proficiency including receptive skills, as it is currently used in everyday language, while fluidity could be used in L2 fluency research contexts to capture the narrow sense of fluency, in both written and spoken productions.

Following from the previous terminological discussion, we illustrate in Figure 12.1 our conception of factors affecting L2 fluency in the narrow sense. The abstract, linguistic level of L2 proficiency, also known as L2 fluency in its broadest sense, is realised when producing language in the spoken or written mode. The manner in which fluency emerges in a given situation may depend on a number of factors. In addition to the general proficiency level, which is an individual feature for all L2 users, the language that is produced (in L1 or L2) is affected by other variables. These variables include context-dependent variables, which could be user-external (e.g. formality of the situation, power relations, goal of interaction) or user-internal variables (e.g. personality, affective variables, fine motor skills). Some user-internal variables are more trait-like (i.e. relatively permanent attributes, such as personality, fine motor skills), whereas others are more state-like (i.e. more context dependent, such as affective variables), although the distinction between trait-like and state-like variables is not clear-cut. Moreover, L2 fluency patterns are affected by L1 fluency patterns, which are, for their part, also influenced by the same user-internal and user-external variables. As a whole, L2 fluency is to a large extent context-dependent and heavily dynamic in two ways: L2 fluency develops as the general proficiency level improves and at any level it varies according to intralearner variables.

In a sense, this model applies to fluency in all language skills. Cognitive fluency underlies all four skills (reading, writing, speaking and listening) and can therefore also be seen as directly linked to general L2 proficiency.

Psycholinguistic experiments, tapping into cognitive fluency (see e.g. Olkkonen, 2017), can also be used to examine fluency in any productive or receptive language skill. Productive skills have been emphasised in fluency research, but the variables affecting fluency in receptive skills are the same. The difference between productive and receptive fluency is that fine-motor skills, a user-internal variable, are required while speaking or writing (e.g. fluid articulation and manual dexterity) but not when listening or reading in the same way. Receptive fluency assumes the active role of auditive or visual processes (receptive listening or reading fluency, while acknowledging that, for instance, visually impaired users reading tactile Braille writing need also fine-motor skills). In future, receptive skills, reading and listening, should be more widely studied from a fluency perspective.

## Future directions for L2 fluency research

In addition to pointing to the need to clarify fluency-related terminology, this volume has introduced aspects that should be further explored in future L2 fluency research. Importantly, the empirical and review chapters of this book have provided starting points for studying fluency in contexts that have rarely employed the concept, including sign language studies and ELF studies. Sign language offers a novel environment for fluency studies (e.g. Kanto & Haapanen, this volume), and considering the fluidity of signers' expressions can help us to understand multimodal communication better in general. Moreover, the multimodal nature of interaction should be examined more from a fluency perspective: the role of gestures as fluency-enhancing devices offers new insights into fluency in native and non-native interaction (see also Peltonen in this volume). The chapters of this book have also provided implications for L2 assessment: as the role of fluency in assessment criteria, whether spoken L2 performance or the quality of written translations, seems to vary (see e.g. Salmi in this volume), the usability and transparency of rating criteria could be improved by integrating findings from recent fluency studies into assessing grids and unifying practices across the field.

In line with the recent developments in the field of second language acquisition and considering that the objective of L2 learning is to become a multilingual user of several languages, learners' language repertoires should also be taken into account in fluency research. For instance, multilingual users' fluency in different languages and different subskills could be compared. Translanguaging, when multilingual language users use their entire linguistic repertoire to communicate (Creese & Blackledge, 2010), could be examined from a fluency perspective. For instance, moving from a monolingual to bi- and multilingual modes could be a fluency-enhancing change in certain contexts. Interactional fluency may be at its highest level when all interlocutors use all the linguistic resources they have. In addition, a multilingual group could be even more fluent in interaction than a monolingual one (see ELF studies; e.g. Hynninen in this volume), but this has seldom been studied from a fluency perspective.

As discussed, this book has provided various perspectives into fluency in L2 learning and use. The chapters have also looked into topics that have not often been approached from a fluency perspective. In addition to the novel avenues for L2 fluency research identified above, before concluding this section we will summarise other future directions for fluency research. An interesting perspective for such research would be to look into the links between receptive and productive fluency:

- How are different language skills linked when it comes to fluency?
- Does one subskill develop before the other subskills?
- Does fluency transfer from one subskill to the other?

Moreover, individual L2 users have different fluency profiles, which are partly linked to their L1 fluency profile (e.g. De Jong *et al.*, 2015; Huensch & Tracy-Ventura, 2017; Peltonen, 2018). This can be seen, for instance, in the tendency for L1 speech rate to affect L2 (or any subsequent additional language) speech rate. It would be interesting to compare L2 fluency profiles between L2s, within modalities, spoken and written language, or even across modalities:

- How are learners' fluency profiles linked between additional languages?
- In which way are L2 users' reading and writing fluency linked?
- How are listening and speaking fluency linked?
- How do, for instance, multilingual users' pronunciation skills affect their listening fluency?

Links between different language skills have been revealed (e.g. Wengelin & Arfé, 2018; Veivo, 2017; Veivo *et al.*, 2018), but studies have seldom been conducted from a fluency perspective. When approached crossmodally, one could be interested, for instance, in the link between the writing and speaking fluency of the same individuals: how do aspects of fluency requiring fine motor skills during written or oral production correlate? To answer this question, neurolinguistic crossmodal research on brain plasticity could open new directions for fluency research. For fine motor skills in particular, sufficient practice is vital. Before the production of certain sounds, syllables and words in the continuous flow of spoken language is automatised, fluent and fluid, it needs to be sufficiently practised and repeated. In a similar manner, producing written language has to be practised before it can be fluid and fluent, be it writing by hand or typing on keyboard (e.g. Olive, 2014). Interesting questions to consider could be:

- How is writing fluency affected when the writing system, keyboard, keypad or device (e.g. computer vs mobile phone) change?

- How could digital writing fluency be described and / or assessed?

Additional new openings in fluency research relate to the following questions:

- How does fluency in human-computer interaction manifest itself? Are human-computer interactions fluency-enhancing or fluency-reducing contexts?
- What is the role of multimodal features as fluency-enhancing devices in interaction?
- What kinds of implications does knowledge of sign language fluency have for L2 fluency research?
- What is the role of multilingual resources, for instance code-switching, as fluency-enhancing features for L2 users in all language skills or in interaction?
- What is the role of affective features in L2 fluency development?
- Which (un)conscious strategies do L2 learners use when their try to make their production more fluent?
- How do power relations and /or the formality of language used influence fluency in interaction?

Examining and expanding fluency research in these directions will benefit L2 learners and teachers as well as L2 assessment professionals by offering vital information on the nature of L2 fluency.

### Pedagogical and practical implications

As practice seems to be a mandatory condition for fluency development, L2 fluency is also an aspect that can be learnt and taught. Practice is needed for developing fluency in all language skills. Moreover, as there are essential 'environmental ingredients' that facilitate optimal L2 learning in general (Ortega, 2009: 79), there are also optimal conditions for L2 users to produce L2 output or receive L2 input fluently, enabling them to perform at the level their general L2 proficiency allows without context-dependent variables negatively affecting the process. These optimal conditions include, for instance, a familiar and interesting topic, a friendly atmosphere between the interlocutors and no time pressure or fear of a negative evaluation due to a test situation, all of which could potentially lower the anxiety levels experienced (Eysenck *et al.*, 2007). Naturally, individuals also vary with respect to the situations they find optimal or anxiety-provoking.

In formal language teaching, addressing fluency, its importance and features explicitly is essential. Learners, especially at more advanced levels, should become aware of the different aspects of fluency and learn to distinguish the broad and narrow senses, or as we have suggested, fluency in general and fluidity of production. Realising how fluent L2 speech is linked to the intelligibility and pleasantness of one's performance (e.g. Lee *et al.*, 2019) helps to motivate learners to focus on fluency-related features in speech and develop their skills. Moreover, learners can be asked to consider how they could use certain features traditionally understood as disfluency features, or multimodal features to enhance fluency in interaction and hold the floor while speaking.

As mentioned previously, from the pedagogical perspective, sufficient practice and repetition is needed for fluency development. For instance, the 4/3/2 activities have been found beneficial for fluency development (Nation, 1989): in this technique, the learner first tells a story (or discusses a topic) in four minutes, then in three and finally in two minutes. When the same story is repeated, the learner gradually produces more fluent speech. Furthermore, the use of formulaic sequences has been found to be a good strategy to improve one's fluency. These chunks are stored as wholes and can therefore be accessed as single units (Myles & Cordier, 2017). When learners are able to produce commonly occurring prefabricated chunks, their speech rate is not affected by pauses caused by lexical retrieval within the chunk (Guz, 2014). In a similar manner, other familiar lexical items or collocations ('lexical teddy bears' as Hasselgren (1994) puts it) have the potential to enhance fluency when produced without intraphrasal pauses (on the effect of repeating song lyrics on the development of spoken fluency, see Heikkola & Alisaari, this volume). The use of formulaic sequences in spoken language is an indicator of cognitive fluency and increases utterance (as measured, for instance, by the mean length of run) and perceived fluency. Similarly, formulaic sequences can also facilitate the writing process and improve the quality of the written product. Commonly used formulaic sequences seem to improve fluency not only productively but also receptively: when the sequence is known, understanding it becomes faster, too. The language user can, for instance, deduce the missing parts if some words were inaudible or incorrectly pronounced (or spelt). This naturally presupposes that the expressions are common enough. In the ELF framework, for instance, native speakers' frequent use of idiomatic expressions has been found to hinder the flow of communication when they are unfamiliar to all interlocutors and might even be a source of misunderstandings (Prodromou, 2008). Nevertheless, common prefabricated chunks have a clear potential for increasing fluency, and mastering them benefits the learner substantially.

The observation that native speakers' use of their L1 is not always optimal for L2 interlocutors, as it may sometimes be too fast or include rare idiomatic expressions, is related to the current trend that native speakers are no longer automatically considered perfect role models for L2 learners. This is also the case for L2 fluency, as native speakers have been found to vary in their fluency. This is also a motivation to understand disfluency features as a natural characteristic of language use, especially when the contextual variables are not optimal (e.g. a demanding task under time pressure in an exam can cause disfluencies in both L1 and L2 production). In L2 fluency studies, native speaker control groups are not always necessary. In fact, it would be often more important to compare a L2 user's fluency in any subskill to their L1 fluency in the same subskill. In teaching, recordings of L1 and L2 speech samples can be used to raise the learners' awareness of their individual speaking styles: by listening to and comparing their own L1 and L2 speech, learners may identify, for instance, idiosyncratic fillers they use in both languages. Comparing L1 and L2 speech can help to reveal their own personal characteristics as well as provide more information for the L2 researcher, teacher and assessor on how close the user's L2 performance is to their L1 performance and what aspects could be improved to reach the same fluency level as they have in their L1. On the other hand, when learners notice how much and under which conditions native speakers produce or receive language disfluently (or how much their own L1 use has features of disfluency), they learn that language use is not always perfectly fluent and that this is not the ultimate goal in L2 learning. As realising this might lower their anxiety levels in L2 use, it is important to raise awareness of these factors in L2 instruction.

To sum up, some pedagogical suggestions for teachers and educators include:

- encourage the use of formulaic sequences;
- use teaching methods that incorporate several subskills;
- incorporate non-linguistic support (e.g. music and rhythm) in teaching to facilitate spoken fluency in particular
- encourage learners to practise fluent language use in all four language skills;
- raise awareness of fluency in the broad and narrow sense;
- discuss the main mechanisms contributing to fluent language use, and the contextual (user-external and user-internal) variables that affect it;
- discuss examples of target language use that have characteristics of disfluent language use, but can function as strategic means contributing to successful communication;
- ask learners how they feel about their native language fluency in different language skills and how this could be reflected in their L2 use;
- help learners to identify similarities between their L1 and L2 productions;
- encourage learners to use their entire linguistic repertoire to improve fluent language use.

We have argued that L2 interaction and language use is often multilingual and multimodal in nature. To encourage learners to communicate more fluently, teachers can introduce multilingual and multimodal strategies that can be used to overcome communicative challenges due to, for instance, limited language capacity. This is an aspect of L2 use that should be taken into account in future fluency research as well as language assessment. Fluency is an aspect of L2 use that can be practised and developed, therefore meriting greater attention from learners and teachers. What this book has emphasised above all is the prevailing and central role of fluency in L2 learning and use.

## References

Ardila, A., Bateman, J., Niño, C., Pulido, E., Rivera, D. and Vanegas, C. (1994) An epidemiologic study of stuttering. *Journal of Communication Disorders* 27, 37–48.

Clark, H.H. and Wasow, T. (1998) Repeating words in spontaneous speech. *Cognitive Psychology* 37, 201–242.

Council of Europe (2001) *Common European Framework of Reference for Languages. Learning, Teaching, Assessment.* Cambridge: Cambridge University Press. Retrieved from https://rm.coe.int/1680459f97.

Council of Europe (2018a) *Common European Framework of Reference for Languages. Learning, Teaching, Assessment. Companion Volume with New Descriptors.* Council of Europe. Retrieved from https://rm.coe.int/cefr-companion-volume-with-new-descriptors-2018/1680787989.

Council of Europe (2018b) *Sign languages and the Common European Framework of Reference for Languages: Descriptors and Approaches to Assessment.* Available: https://www.ecml.at/ECML-Programme/Programme2012-2015/ProSign/PRO-Sign-referencelevels/tabid/1844/Default.aspx.

Creese, A. and Blackledge, A. (2010) Translanguaging in the bilingual classroom: A pedagogy for learning and teaching? *The Modern Language Journal* 94 (1), 103–115.

De Jong, N.H. (2016) Fluency in second language assessment. In D. Tsagari and J. Banerjee (eds) *Handbook of Second Language Assessment* (pp. 203–218). Berlin: De Gruyter Mouton.

De Jong, N.H., Groenhout, R., Schoonen, R. and Hulstijn, J.H. (2015) Second language fluency: Speaking style or proficiency? Correcting measures of second language fluency for first language behavior. *Applied Psycholinguistics* 36, 223–243.

Degand, L., Gilquin, G., Meurant, L. and Simon, A.C. (eds) (2019) *Fluency and Disfluency across Languages and Language Varieties.* Louvain-la-neuve: Presses Universitaires de Louvain.

Deterding, D. (2013) *Misunderstandings in English as a Lingua Franca. An Analysis of ELF Interactions in South-East Asia.* Berlin: De Gruyter Mouton.

Dewaele, J.-M. and Furnham, A. (2000) Personality and speech production: A pilot study of second language learners. *Personality and Individual Differences* 28, 355–365.

Eysenck, M.W., Derakshan, N., Santos, R. and Calvo, M.G. (2007) Anxiety and cognitive performance: Attentional control theory. *Emotion* 7, 336–353.

Fillmore, C.J. (1979) On fluency. In C.J. Fillmore, D. Kempler and W.S.-Y. Wang (eds) *Individual Differences in Language Ability and Language Behavior* (pp. 85–102). New York: Academic Press.

Fulcher, G. (2015) *Re-examining Language Testing: A Philosophical and Social Inquiry.* London: Routledge.

Guz, E. (2014) Formulaic sequences as fluency devices in the oral production of native speakers of Polish. *Research in Language* 12 (2), 113–129.

Hasselgren, A. (1994) Lexical teddy bears and advanced learners: A study into the ways Norwegian students cope with English vocabulary. *International Journal of Applied Linguistics* 4 (2), 237–258.

Howell, P. and van Borsel, J. (eds) (2011) *Multilingual Aspects of Fluency Disorders.* Bristol: Multilingual Matters.

Huensch, A. and Tracy-Ventura, N. (2017) Understanding second language fluency behavior: The effects of individual differences in first language fluency, cross-linguistic differences, and proficiency over time. *Applied Psycholinguistics* 38, 755–785.

Jacewicz, E., Fox, R.A. and Wei, L. (2010) Between-speaker and within-speaker variation in speech tempo of American English. *Journal of the Acoustical Society of America* 128, 839–850.

Just, M.A. and Carpenter, P.A. (1992) A capacity theory of comprehension: Individual differences in working memory. *Psychological Review* 99, 122–149.

Lee, J., Kim D.J. and Park H. (2019) Native listeners' evaluations of pleasantness, foreign accent, comprehensibility, and fluency in the speech of accented talkers. In J. Levis, C. Nagle and E. Todey (eds) *Proceedings of the 10th Pronunciation in Second Language Learning and Teaching Conference* (pp. 168–178). Ames, IA: Iowa State University.

Leeson, L., van den Bogaerde, B., Ratmann, C. and Haug, T. (2016) *Sign Languages and the Common European Framework of Reference for Language*. Strasbourg: Council of Europe Publishing.

Lennon, P. (1990) Investigating fluency in EFL: A quantitative approach. *Language Learning* 40, 387–417.

Munro, M. and Derwing, T. (2001) Modeling perceptions of the accentedness and comprehensibility of L2 speech: The role of speaking rate. *Studies in Second Language Acquisition* 23, 451–468.

Myles, F. and Cordier, C. (2017) Formulaic sequence (FS) cannot be an umbrella term in SLA: Focusing on psycholinguistic FSs and their identification. *Studies in Second Language Acquisition* 39, 3–28.

Nation, P. (1989) Improving speaking fluency. *System* 17 (3), 377–384.

Nogami, Y. (2103) Negotiation of second language identities in shifting power relations: Voices of Japanese L2 English users. *Hiroshima Journal of International Studies* 19, 81–100.

Norton, B. and Toohey, K. (2011) Identity, language learning, and social change. *Language Teaching* 44, 412–446.

Olive, T. (2014) Toward a parallel and cascading model of the writing system: A review of research on writing processes coordination. *Journal of Writing Research* 6 (2), 173–194.

Olkkonen, S. (2017) *Second and Foreign Language Fluency from Cognitive Perspective: Inefficiency and Control of Attention in Lexical Access*. Jyväskylä Studies in Humanities 314. Jyväskylä: University of Jyväskylä.

Ortega, L. (2009) *Understanding Second Language Acquisition*. London: Hodder Education.

Pallotti, G. (2005) Variations situationnelles dans la construction des énoncés en L2: Le cas des autorépétitions [Situated variations in constructing L2 sentences: the case of self-repetition]. *Acquisition et Interaction en Langue Étrangère* 22, 102–130.

Peltonen, P. (2017) L2 fluency in spoken interaction: A case study on the use of other-repetitions and collaborative completions. In M. Kuronen, P. Lintunen and T. Nieminen (eds) *Näkökulmia toisen kielen puheeseen – Insights into Second Language Speech*. AFinLA-e: Soveltavan kielitieteen tutkimuksia 10. Jyväskylä: Finnish Association of Applied Linguistics AFinLA, 118–138.

Peltonen, P. (2018) Exploring connections between first and second language fluency: A mixed methods approach. *The Modern Language Journal* 102, 676–692.

Penttilä, N., Korpijaakko-Huuhka, A.M. and Kent, R.D. (2019) Disfluency clusters in speakers with and without neurogenic stuttering following traumatic brain injury. *Journal of Fluency Disorders* 59, 33–51.

Prodromou, L. (2008) *English as a Lingua Franca: A Corpus Based Analysis*. London: Continuum.

Segalowitz, N. (2010) *Cognitive Bases of Second Language Fluency*. New York: Routledge.

Tavakoli, P. (2016) Fluency in monologic and dialogic task performance: Challenges in defining and measuring L2 fluency. *International Review of Applied Linguistics in Language Teaching* 54 (2), 133–150.

Tavakoli, P. and Hunter, A.-M. (2018) Is fluency being 'neglected' in the classroom? Teacher understanding of fluency and related classroom practices. *Language Teaching Research* 22 (3), 330–349.

Tavakoli, P. and Skehan, P. (2005) Strategic planning, task structure, and performance testing. In R. Ellis (ed.) *Planning and Task Performance in a Second Language* (pp. 239–273). Amsterdam: John Benjamins.

Veivo, O. (2017) *Orthographe et reconnaissance des mots parlés chez les apprenants tardifs de L2*. [Orthography and spoken-word recognition in late L2 learners]. Turku: University of Turku.

Veivo, O., Porretta, V., Hyönä, J. and Järvikivi, J. (2018) Spoken second language words activate native language orthographic information in late second language learners. *Applied Psycholinguistics* 39 (5), 1011–1032.

Wengelin, Å. and Arfé, B. (2018) The complementary relationships between reading and writing in children with and without writing difficulties. In B. Miller, P. McCardle and V. Connelly (eds) *Writing Development in Struggling Learners: Understanding the Needs of Writers Across the Lifecourse*. Leiden: Brill.

Wilbur, R.B. (1980) The linguistic description of American Sign Language. In H. Lane and J. Grosjean (eds) *Recent Perspectives on American Sign Language* (pp. 7–31). New Jersey: Lawrence Erlbaum Associates.

# Index

accommodation 23, 25, 27, 85–86, 88
accuracy (*see also* inaccuracy) 5–6, 8, 10, 12, 17–18, 21, 23–26, 35–36, 39, 41, 44, 51–53, 57–58, 65, 67, 68, 73–75, 112, 132, 142, 146–147, 149–150, 152–160, 167
articulation rate 5, 116–117, 133
assessment 1–2, 5–6, 9, 11–12, 16–19, 31, 34, 42, 57–59, 91–92, 106–107, 126, 129–143, 146–147, 149–160, 186, 189, 194, 196, 199
  automatic 133, 139, 141, 153, 154–155
automatic(ity) 3–4, 10, 22, 24, 29, 34, 36–39, 43–44, 51, 53, 55, 57–58, 64, 68, 76, 87, 133, 139–141, 153, 167, 191

bilingual(ism) (*see also* multilingual) 4, 38, 42, 77, 98, 149, 151, 153
bottom-up 50, 53–58

Common European Framework of Reference for Languages (CEFR) 5, 7, 57, 67–68, 74–75, 90–92, 114, 134–135, 137, 169, 172, 186–189, 191

disfluency/disfluent 1, 5–6, 11–12, 23, 26–27, 29, 34, 36, 38, 39, 41, 44, 73, 77, 83, 85–87, 92, 97–98, 100, 102–104, 106, 114, 117, 120, 140, 159, 167, 186–187, 189–191, 197–198

efficiency/efficient(ly) (*see also* inefficiency) 3–4, 10, 19, 35–36, 39–40, 44, 54–56, 83, 85, 96, 102–103, 106, 123, 136, 167

effortless(ness) xi, 5, 10–11, 16–17, 18–19, 22, 41, 44–45, 49, 51, 53–54, 57, 59, 63–64, 71, 73, 81, 96, 104, 112, 137, 140, 188, 192
English as a lingua franca (ELF) 2, 3, 10–11, 81–92, 190, 194–195, 197
error(-free) 8, 10, 21, 26–27, 37–39, 42–43, 64–65, 68, 77, 102, 104, 142, 152–160, 164–165
evaluation 10, 58–60, 63, 67–68, 73–76, 83, 132, 150–151, 153–154, 156, 169, 198

first language (L1) (*see also* native language) 6, 8,10, 13, 19, 37–44, 48–53, 59, 64–65, 81, 84, 86, 89–91, 97–98, 101, 114, 125, 137, 142, 148, 187–190, 193, 195, 197–198
flow xi, 10–11, 20, 50–51, 54–55, 67–68, 70–71, 75–77, 112–113, 122, 126, 135–137, 188, 192, 195, 197
fluency
  breakdown 3–6, 85, 87–89, 112, 131, 133–134
  broad 3, 5, 7, 11, 17–22, 25–27, 29–31, 64–65, 96, 104, 106, 111–113, 126, 131, 134, 143, 148, 150, 186–189, 192–193, 196, 198
  cognitive 3–5, 7–10, 18, 23–24, 34–45, 59, 63–64, 71, 73, 76–77, 83–85, 89, 112, 146, 166, 186, 188, 191, 193, 194, 197
  dimension(s) 3, 5–6, 8, 12, 16, 18, 26, 59, 83, 89, 91, 112, 129, 132, 138–139, 142, 186, 192

framework 2–3, 5, 7–9, 11–12, 17–18, 23, 26, 34, 39, 41, 44–45, 56, 58–59, 63, 77, 104, 106, 112–113, 125, 134–135, 146, 149, 155, 163, 167, 186, 188, 196
higher-order 3–5, 17, 21, 27, 30, 148
in first/native language (L1) 27–28, 49, 142, 187, 190, 193, 195, 198
individual 45, 57, 82–83, 86–92, 112, 121, 142, 190, 193, 195–196, 198
interactional 10–11, 13, 22, 82–83, 85–92, 111–126, 194
lower-order 3–5, 17, 23, 26, 150
measures 4–7, 10–11, 17–18, 35–37, 39–41, 44, 58, 64, 68, 75–77, 85, 99, 102, 112, 116–117, 129, 133, 136, 139, 141, 167, 172, 176–177, 180, 190, 197
narrow 3, 5–6, 17–19, 31, 111–112, 134, 138, 142–143, 147, 150, 167, 186–189, 192–193, 196, 198
perceived 3–4, 6, 7–10, 12, 18–19, 25, 27, 34–35, 59, 63–64, 73, 77, 82–83, 88–90, 92, 100–101, 106, 126, 146, 150, 154, 159, 167, 186, 188, 190–191, 197
rating of 6, 11, 18, 126, 129–130, 132–134, 138–139, 142
repair 3–6, 17, 35, 45, 83, 85, 87, 89, 91, 103, 112, 131, 133, 139, 167, 171
speed 3–6, 35, 51–53, 55–57, 65, 76, 83, 85, 87–89, 91, 100, 102, 112, 131, 133–136, 139, 142, 167
utterance 3–6, 8–10, 18, 21–22, 24, 27, 34–35, 37–39, 44, 59, 63–64, 77, 83, 85–89, 101–103, 112, 146, 150, 167, 186, 188, 190–191, 197
fluidity 64, 96, 102, 139, 191–194, 196
formulaic language/sequence 6, 54, 83–84, 167, 193, 197–198

gesture 11, 26, 111–126, 171–172, 194

inaccuracy (*see also* accuracy) 9–10, 28, 34, 39–45, 48, 191
inefficiency (*see also* efficiency) 41–43, 45, 48, 104

interaction 2, 7, 10–11, 13, 22, 31, 38, 40, 50, 57, 59, 81–92, 111–113, 115–117, 119–126, 131, 133, 135, 142, 170, 172–177, 179, 188–189, 193–198

lexical access 4, 8, 10, 27, 34, 39–41, 44, 64, 101, 188
listening 1–2, 4, 7–8, 10, 12, 16–17, 22, 30, 49–60, 166, 168–178, 185–186, 193–195, 198

mean length of run/burst 6, 77, 133–134, 197
multilingual(ism) (*see also* bilingual) 66, 76–77, 90, 134, 194–196, 198
multimodal 11, 111–113, 123, 125–126, 189, 194, 196–198
music 12, 166–168, 170, 174, 198

native language (*see also* first language) 27–28, 103, 169
native signer 99–100, 103
native speaker 2, 19–21, 24, 26–28, 63, 81, 84, 89–90, 98, 137, 139, 141, 187, 189–190, 197–198
non-verbal 11, 23, 26, 111–115, 117–120, 122, 123–126

pause 5–6, 19, 23–24, 26, 43, 63–75, 77–78, 86–90, 92, 102–103, 112, 116–118, 120–122, 128, 133–138, 140–142, 150, 166–167, 188–190, 197
  silent 5–6, 85, 90, 102–103, 118, 120–122, 133, 135, 136, 142, 190
  filled 5, 86, 92, 102–103, 112–114, 118, 120, 122–123, 125, 128, 133, 142, 190
processing 1, 3–4, 8–10, 18, 21–23, 31, 34–36, 38, 40–41, 44–45, 50–57, 59–60, 63–64, 66, 71–72, 83–87, 89, 97–98, 101–102, 104, 114, 118, 125, 186, 191
productive skills (*see also* speaking, writing) 7, 9, 12, 17, 22–23, 30–31, 51, 191–192, 194–195

proficiency
   language 3, 26, 29–31, 38, 54, 57, 64, 106, 173, 177, 192
   level of 12, 30, 40–41, 54–55, 57, 76, 101, 114–115, 138, 168–170, 172–180, 188–189, 193
   oral 5, 7, 16–18, 21, 23, 34, 112, 126, 130, 132–133, 141
profile 10, 41, 45, 63–66, 72, 75–77, 190, 195
pronunciation 6, 19, 21, 23–24, 26, 29, 31, 41–43, 45, 48, 85, 132, 135–139, 141, 178, 180, 195

rating scale 11, 129–130, 134, 138–139, 141–142, 159
reading 1–2, 4, 7–8, 10, 12, 16–17, 21–22, 30, 36–37, 39–45, 51, 53, 57, 65, 139–140, 151, 170, 186, 191, 193–195
receptive skills (*see also* listening, reading) 2, 7, 9, 12, 17, 21–23, 30–31, 51, 191, 193–194, 195
repetition 6, 11, 36, 38, 45, 48, 55, 77, 85–87, 92, 103, 111–113, 115, 123, 125, 131, 133, 135–137, 140–142, 166–167, 190, 197

sign language 2, 11, 96–107, 188–189, 192, 194, 196
speaking 3–4, 7–8, 16, 18–19, 21–22, 25, 30, 40, 45, 51, 53, 56, 59, 84, 86, 125, 130, 132–133, 138–140, 142, 148, 150, 166, 168, 179–180, 186, 190, 192–195, 197–198

speech rate 5–6, 17, 40, 57, 85, 87–88, 112, 126, 132, 141, 150, 167, 172, 174, 176–180, 182–184, 190–191, 195, 197
speed 3–7, 17, 19, 36, 39–41, 43, 51–53, 55–58, 65, 68, 70–71, 76, 83, 85, 87–89, 91, 99–100, 102–103, 112, 131–139, 142, 167, 192
stalling mechanism 11, 111–115, 118, 123, 125
strategy/strategic 4, 7, 23, 26, 39, 43, 45, 50–51, 53–59, 76, 92, 103, 106–107, 112–114, 190–191, 196–198
   communication 11, 24, 26, 111–126

teaching xi, 1, 9, 11–12, 16–17, 20, 31, 56, 59, 101, 131, 166, 168, 170–175, 177–180, 189–190, 196, 198
testing (*see* assessment)
top-down 50, 52, 54–58
translation 2, 11–12, 146–154, 156–160, 164–165

vocabulary 7, 19, 23–24, 26–27, 30, 35, 42, 54–55, 105, 114, 132, 157, 170

word recognition 36, 40–41, 44, 52
working memory 4, 9, 35–37, 64, 68, 191
writing 1–2, 4, 7–8, 10, 16–18, 21–22, 30, 36, 40, 42, 43, 45, 51, 63–77, 148, 157, 179, 186, 190–197

For Product Safety Concerns and Information please contact our EU Authorised Representative:

Easy Access System Europe

Mustamäe tee 50

10621 Tallinn

Estonia

gpsr.requests@easproject.com